DESIGNS FOR LIVING: A COMPARATIVE APPROACH TO NORMALISATION FOR THE NEW MILLENNIUM

For Mark

Designs for Living: A Comparative Approach to Normalisation for the New Millennium

STEVEN CARNABY

Ashgate

Aldershot • Brookfield USA • Singapore • Sydney

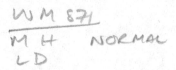

© Steven Carnaby 1999

Published by
Ashgate Publishing Ltd
Gower House
Croft Road
Aldershot
Hants GU11 3HR
England

Ashgate Publishing Company
Old Post Road
Brookfield
Vermont 05036
USA

Ashgate website: http://www.ashgate.com

British Library Cataloguing in Publication Data
Carnaby, Steven
    Designs for living : a comparative approach to
    normalisation for the new millennium
    1.Learning disabled - Services for - Great Britain
    2.Learning disabled - Services for - Italy 3.Learning
    disabled - Rehabilitation - Great Britain 4.Learning
    disabled - Rehabilitation - Italy
    I.Title
    362.2'0425'0941

Library of Congress Catalog Card Number: 99-73636

ISBN 1 84014 831 4

Printed in Great Britain

Contents

Acknowledgements

I would like to give special thanks to all the service users in London and Milan, their families and support staff who kindly agreed to talk to me about their services and allowed me to gain a sense of their daily lives.

My thanks to Sally Sainsbury at the London School of Economics for her unfaltering support, encouragement and inspiration throughout the time I have been working on this project.

In addition, this study would not have been possible without support and advice from the following people: Laura Barnes, Jill Bradshaw, Hilary Brown, Salvatore Cassaro, Giovanna Cassaro, Elio Ferraro, Caroline Mitchell and David Stewart.

Trish Barton deserves my gratitude for her patience and dedication while typing this manuscript.

Introduction

Services for people with learning disabilities in Britain are generally founded upon the principles of normalisation (Ward 1992), described by Wolfensberger (1972) as the

> utilisation of means which are as culturally normative as possible, in order to establish and/or maintain personal behaviours and characteristics which are as culturally normative as possible.

More recently, the approach has been implemented using the Five Service Accomplishments as set out by O'Brien (1985). This reformulation of Wolfensberger's ideas stipulates that people with learning disabilities should be present in their local communities and be supported in making choices about their lives, as well as being afforded respect and the opportunities for developing competence and participation in everyday life.

While it is acknowledged that normalisation has been responsible for a revolution in terms of the way that society approaches people with learning disabilities (Ward 1992), particularly in terms of deinstitutionalisation, there has been increasing criticism during the 1990's for its tendency to advocate a white, male, middle class set of values (e.g. Baxter *et al* 1990) and devalue relationships between people with disabilities (e.g. Szivos 1992;1993), as well as overlook the difficulties faced by people with profound and multiple disabilities (Smith 1994).

The hegemony of normalisation

From the time of the Jay Report (1979), normalisation has gained ever widening support to the point where, for the last decade at least, it appears to have achieved a position of hegemony. The unchallenged prevalence of the normalisation approach in British learning disability services has led to great difficulties in terms of allowing alternative views of supporting disability to be considered, or even their existence realised. Developing a critique is fraught with obstacles, the central issues being that research purporting to explore the significance and impact of the O'Brien's Five Service Accomplishments (op cit.), and therefore normalisation, is likely to assess *outcomes in services*, rather than develop a coherent criticism of the principles themselves. For example, studies interested in quality of life

1

issues will monitor the number of relationships service users have with non-disabled others (e.g. Ralph & Usher 1995), or the frequency of opportunities available for forming such relationships (Kennedy, Horner & Newton 1990). Such approaches fail to question the assumption, according to the principles of normalisation, that relationships with non-disabled people are more valuable than those formed with disabled peers. Quality of life is measured by the range of opportunities offered for integrating with the local community, without considering whether self esteem and the security needed (Szivos 1992) - by *everybody* but particularly vulnerable people (Townsend 1962) - might result from support best obtained in the first instance from peers and perhaps involved members of the family or similar significant others.

A shift in the methodological framework

This book tries to address many of the issues outlined above by using a comparative approach to studying the impact of normalisation. Previous research which purports to consider the quality of life of people with learning disabilities can only really be said to have 'tinkered' around the edges of the methodological problem. It is essential that the effects of implementing ideology are carefully scrutinised. Ironically, while choice is a key concept in service delivery and a rhetorical benchmark of good practice, the lack of choice offered to service providers with regard to ideological thinking and models of care has led to a stifling situation where managers and direct support staff alike are often at a loss to think creatively about service design. Normalisation - more commonly referred to in the 1990's as 'ordinary living' - has come to mean everything that is acceptable about learning disability services. The concern here is that those providing support have stopped questioning the foundations upon which their work is built, always working in the name of normalisation without being critical and aware of its effect.

Why now, why Italy?

The new millennium seems as good a time as any for thinking seriously about how normalisation can be modernised in ways which maintain its relevance as a framework for those supporting people with disabilities - and indeed any other group of vulnerable people who use support services. The recommendations and ideas for taking normalisation into the 21st century are derived from an exploratory, qualitative study which aims to highlight important issues and outcomes in the London services described by comparing them with similar provision in Milan, Italy. The choice of Italy as a partner nation was made for a number of reasons: initial contacts with professional bodies and agencies led to a conducive working atmosphere accepting of research, while other work studying mental health services has proved important in developing greater understanding of how similar services operate in another culture - as well as arguably providing important insight into the Italian way of life (e.g. Ramon 1981; Donnelly 1992).

However, as the main objective of the comparative study is to directly analyse practices and ideology in Britain by contrasting findings in services with a partner nation, there are two key reasons for choosing Italy:

- both Britain and Italy have used legislation to close institutions for people with learning disabilities, while

- deinstitutionalisation in Italy has not utilised the normalisation approach to achieve this task, providing a sharp contrast to the process operating in Britain.

This enables the research to neatly 'step outside' the normalisation framework in order to assess more vividly the impact of ordinary living on the lives of individual people with learning disabilities.

Italy also provides an important contrast in that the thinking and perspective which influenced deinstitutionalisation was in many ways the culmination of a process which had been evolving throughout the country's psychiatric services. The framework adopted in Lombardia, the region relevant to the services studied here, can be seen as part of a developing approach to vulnerable people which can be traced back to before the *Risorgimento* of 1861. It is seen here as the rich mixture of Italian cultural life - through which strong historical traditions permeate - and the energetic debate which resulted from the profound organisational and regional changes experienced during and after reunification.

The focus is not to decide which local authority provides the 'better' or more appropriate services, as systematic analysis is not the objective of the study. Rather, the comparative approach can underline key areas of interest which are more difficult to reveal using a conventional, intra-national research paradigm.

There are three foci for the study:

- **How is service policy organised?**
Each of the participating authorities has established organisational structures - individual service plans - within the specific frameworks

set out by legislation. In each case, these structures act as a central plank and can help explain differences between the two approaches, enabling scrutiny of the ways in which ideology can be translated into practice. In the London service, which stresses the importance of participation in its mission statement, 21 users and their keyworkers were interviewed to hear about their experiences and understanding of the process, while 16 service users were observed taking part in their own planning meetings. In contrast, the Milanese individual planning process is not focused on involving service users in decision making: while the assessment which takes place aims to study the person's needs in relation to the family environment, neither service users nor relatives are invited to planning meetings. It is thus the documentation which is studied here, along with the relationship between the individual planning process mission statement and the operational policy for the service it supports.

- **How is service policy implemented and what are the outcomes for service users?**

Understanding the thinking behind the design and planning of services and gaining a sense of how individuals are involved in that planning leads to a need to look at service outcomes. The two approaches taken to service design lead to two sets of experiences: the case study presented here involves 7 men in Milan and 5 in London, all of whom have lived in the community for about a year at the time of writing. The study asks them about their new lifestyles, and talks to staff who support the men (6 staff in Milan and 5 in London) to find out about their perception of the support worker role and approach. Data collection takes the form of individual interviews which look at a wide selection of issues about the residents' lifestyles, and participant observation, which samples the relationship between residents, and between residents and staff.

- **How do service providers equip staff to implement service policy?**

The case study reveals certain issues about the relationships between policy and practice, and the background to these relationships from the personnel point of view is explored by looking more closely at infrastructure, specifically at the framework used for training staff in the two services. This contributes to the discussion about the implementation of service policy, illustrating the ways in which the principles of each approach inform staff practice. The comparison is made between the legislated professional course established in the Milanese services, and the training opportunities and requirements for support staff working in London.

These three main areas form the book's structure and organisation. Chapter One discusses the 'problem of normalisation', exploring further the evidence for hegemony, the circularity currently prevalent in research and the stale ideological environments within which professionals find themselves working. The extent of this effect is illustrated in Chapter Two, which outlines the historical path that Lombardia in Northern Italy has taken towards deinstitutionalisation and describes the present geography of service provision.

Chapter Three introduces the research methods adopted in the study, and considers the risks of an experimental approach, placing the paradigm described here within the wider context of 'quality of life' research. The main body of data collected, the case study of residential services, forms Chapter Four, with time spent detailing the findings from semi-structured interviews and participant observation. With daily life thus sampled and reflected upon, the tool with which staff implement underpinning ideology in services is considered: individual planning is the main conduit through which concepts such as 'choice' and 'individuality' are filtered, and Chapter Five is a comparison between the ways the London and Milanese services operationalise the individual planning process. This provides material which helps toward a better understanding of why normalisation as an approach can be immensely difficult to realise.

One of the important impressions retained from both the residential services case study and the comparison of individual planning processes, is confirmation of the feelings of many working in services: training is central to the provision of effective support. In addition, evidence is presented in Chapter Six to suggest that it is the *nature* of support and its philosophical foundation which needs careful attention. This then leads to the formulation of 'lessons learned' in Chapter Seven culminating in recommendations for development of practice and approach in Chapter Eight.

1 Arriving at Normalisation: An Historical Perspective on Learning Disability Services, Legislation and Research

Normalisation can be understood as a reaction to a particular set of policy developments which advocated an institutional approach to supporting people with learning disabilities. Given the unquestioned support for normalisation, it is important to understand what it was a reaction *to*.

This chapter provides a brief historical context, which aims to describe the ways in which these policy developments moved away from one end of a continuum, segregation, towards the other extreme - community integration. An emphasis on the relatively rapid *rate* of this change is noted here; the comparisons made with the Milanese services in this study attempt to highlight the difficulties which have arguably arisen as a result.

Terminology: A history of labels

The term "people with learning disabilities" is current in a long list of labels given to the group of people once referred to as "mentally handicapped". While the labels have changed, society has continually found it difficult to identify specific criteria for inclusion under the particular term in vogue. Ryan & Thomas (1980) suggest that the labels themselves form the history: dated terms such as "fool" or "idiot" have now passed into ordinary language, notably as terms of abuse. At the beginning of this century, the phrases "mentally deficient" and "mentally retarded" were coined, and in the 1950's, sociologists and health workers adopted the term "subnormal". Labelling or diagnosis is usually based upon what much research has shown to be unreliable - the person's I.Q. or Intelligence Quotient. People with learning disabilities have always been marginalised by society, and the extent of this marginalisation has varied according to the contemporary economic, political and social climates. An attempt will be made here to outline the important stages and developments both in the attitudes of society and in legislation. This will be followed by a review of research trends in the field of learning disability.

The beginnings of reform

Provision for the education and care of idiots [sic] began in the early 19th century, although it is not until the writings of Seguin (1846) that any logical process of development can be traced. The first schools and asylums concentrated on providing education rather than considering aetiology, and were concerned with making improvements in the condition of idiocy. Seguin spoke of an untapped potential, suggesting that an 'idiot' is "one of us in mankind but shut up in an imperfect envelope." In contrast, there were also comparisons with animals, and even the pro-education lobby aimed to "[remove] the mark of the brute from the forehead of the idiot" (Shuttleworth 1895). This justification for reform in the treatment of people with learning disabilities in terms of making them more socially acceptable still underlies reform in the field today (e.g. Emerson 1992).

The nature of asylums

Early asylums in the 1850's offered many occupations for residents, including leisure. Good health, nutrition and exercise were encouraged:

> Idiots require more room, air, warmth and light to improve their weak and sluggish natures. (Seguin 1846)

Advocates of asylums also saw value in their social nature, as many people with learning disabilities had previously lived in isolation. Educational techniques were developed, and were quite sophisticated, often using elements still considered important in realising an individual's potential - for example, imitation, repetition and reward. Educationalists felt that they were making significant progress, helping people to recover their humanity while encouraging society to view people with learning disabilities as being part of the human race.

However, this was to change, and most significantly. Asylums became overcrowded, individually taking an average of 400 residents in 1864 and over 2000 by 1914. As a consequence, people with learning disabilities were housed in workhouses and asylums for the insane, as well as institutions specifically designed for their "improvement".

The apparent increase in the number of people with learning disabilities could have simply been due to the fact that authorities became more efficient at making referrals, but it is equally likely that their numbers included the mentally ill - a population which increased dramatically at this time. The educationalists had also overestimated the number of people who would return to their communities - asylums were never meant to provide care for life, but families were often impossible to trace to resettle residents, or were unwilling to take their relatives back.

Overcrowding may well have been one factor, but Ryan & Thomas (1980) go on to suggest that standards of care in the asylums also fell because of a shift in philosophy by the educationalists. Teachers began to control rather than support their charges, and what had been established as a social learning process became a denial of privacy and a denial of the individual. At the same time, management of the asylums was increasingly taken over by medical professionals, who were predominantly interested in descriptions and classifications of people with learning disabilities.

The impact of industrial society

This picture is incomplete: all of the above needs to be viewed within the important changes that were occurring in social life at this time. Ryan & Thomas (1980) argue that schools and asylums for idiots were not created as a result of the humanitarian movement alone, neither did they arise from the "spirit" of the French Revolution; these considerations are important, but must be seen within the framework of change in the lives of ordinary people.

Family life experienced overwhelming change due to the industrial reorganisation of labour during the second half of the 19th century. The virtual "social collapse" (Ryan & Thomas (op cit.)) which led to an increase in the number of institutions, signifying a major shift in social attitudes; dependent and "difficult" people began to be supported by public provision, rather than the family or local community. Public workhouses were used for those who were unable to support themselves economically, and thus idiots lived side by side with the insane, criminals, the sick and the able-bodied unemployed. Segregation among these groups began with the building of specialist asylums and the creation of professions to work within them.

The Industrial Revolution had a major effect on all those depending on others for support, be it social or economic. Women and children were now employed in factory-based work, while the overcrowding in cities, heavy demands of labour and the general chaos of working life resulted in great misery for people with disabilities. Factory work was fast, stressful and very disciplined, and did not take into account the slower worker or appreciate any individualised skills which people had acquired in the effort to integrate with the ordinary community.

A person staying at home to care for a relative with learning disabilities meant the loss of a valuable wage. Dependent people were therefore locked up, left alone or were forced to live on the streets. While asylums had existed before industrialisation, the end of the 19th century saw an increasing reliance on and justification for such provision. Trends in societal attitudes, together with a quickening in the demand for efficient labour, had circuitous influences on each other.

Educationalists had been intent on the reformation and education of idiots, but looked at teaching as a benefit in isolation. The harsh realities of social life - making it difficult for *anyone* to survive, let alone a person with learning disabilities - were overlooked, but the ideas behind the education movement took precedence over the context in which people were living or had been living. The responsibility for the system's failure was therefore placed upon those being "reformed" - they were idiots, and therefore useless after all.

It did not take much for this realisation to become vindictive, with idiocy being seen as a social threat. Interest grew in hereditary causes, with the blame placed squarely on the shoulders of parents indulging in any of the social ills of the day - drunkenness, masturbation, inter-marriage, for example. Medical textbooks provided descriptions of idiots and even compared them to non-European people - supposedly more primitive. The obvious example of this is that of Langdon Down, who compared one group of idiots with the Mongolian race, claiming that facial characteristics are similar. The "animal" nature of idiots was greatly emphasised and exaggerated by the Victorians - concordant with the repressive nature of society at the time - and by 1896, pressure groups appeared, eager to segregate "mental defectives" from the rest of society for life (e.g. National Society for the Care and Control of the Feeble Minded). Supported and inspired by the middle class Eugenics movement - which warned of the deprecating effect that "mental defectives" would have on society - these pressure groups campaigned to repress sexuality and reproduction among people with learning disabilities, taking a similar approach to that used with the poor in general.

Developments in legislation

The 1910 general election saw a campaign by the National Association for the Care and Control of the Feeble Minded, which was concerned with "discouraging parenthood in feeble-minded and other degenerate types", and separate, segregated institutions. This came to fruition with the 1913 Mental Deficiency Act, which set up a separate service providing compulsory certification for those admitted to institutions as mentally defective, thus excluding them from the welfare and education systems. Compulsory sterilisation, which had been the objective of the eugenics movement, had been avoided.

Implementation of the Act was not immediate: in 1929, the Wood Committee along with the 1930 Board of Control Report stated once again the "undesirability of allowing defectives to marry", and spoke of the heredity threat that this group posed to society. Eugenics theory was obviously still prevalent and influential, supporting moves to adhere more strongly to the 1913 Act's recommendations.

Between 1918 and 1931, the number of places in institutions tripled, and by 1939 had reached 32,000. Furthermore, there remained a paucity of services outside the asylums, despite an increase in the number of guardianship and supervision orders. Community services received little, if any, investment.

Developing the welfare state: The impact of the post-war period

The post war period played an essential part in the development of both the social security scheme and the National Health Service. According to Glennerster (1995), the former initially acquired widespread support after 1945, with this support soon waning due to the failure of these plans being realised. The NHS however, "..soon established itself as one of the most popular of the institutions created at this time (p43)", despite the post-war Labour government's radical plans for expanding coverage to the entire population at first being met with disapproval. The NHS aimed to allow access to free care for all those who needed it. Although this goal proved to be over-ambitious, the degree of success achieved surpassed any of the scheme's predecessors or any other service developed during this period.

In a sense, these strategies were a reflection of the public's expectations. Universal health care had been promised since the First World War, and it would seem that the atmosphere created as a result of second world war atrocities accelerated this feeling. At this point, for example, services for the elderly and for people with disabilities were still provided under the Poor Law of 1834, and politicians were only too aware of the need for combating increasing post-war disillusionment with a more extensive Welfare State. Glennerster (1995:69) cogently summarises this key period in British social policy:

> ...all these services were creatures of their age, the age of belief in the virtues of central planning and monopoly provision...The social services they [Labour politicians] created were in the image of the other economic institutions of the time ...this made it possible to allocate resources more fairly to different parts of the country, to equalise opportunities of access...

Drawing parallels with the work of Durbin (1949), which looked at the fate of the nationalised industries, Glennerster (1995) comments that the social services were also to "fall into the hands of the providers and not the consumers". It is interesting to place this observation alongside the current drive by researchers, academics and service providers to place consumers or service users at the centre of debate about the efficacy and purpose of personal social services.

Post-war legislation and learning disability

With the development of scientific knowledge after World War II, people with learning disabilities began to be viewed in more clinical and/or behavioural terms, still ignoring their social or personal experiences. The "social threat" attitude - which had been taken to its horrific, violent extremes under Hitler's fascism - moved towards a view that people with learning disabilities are useless and sick. This is illustrated by the 1959 Mental Health Act, which divides people into the "psychopathic" and the "subnormal", albeit within a medical framework. People were admitted to hospitals for what were considered 'health' reasons. The mentally handicapped became patients, with medical rather than educational treatment taking precedence. This "medicalisation" of the mentally handicapped is also shown by the incorporation of the asylums into the NHS at this time.

Reforming services: The 1959 Mental Health Act and beyond

Moves towards reforming services for people with learning disabilities began with the 1954-57 Royal Commission, which led to the 1959 Mental Health Act. This recommended that the concept of voluntary or informal in-patient status should be introduced for the majority of people with "mental disorders", and suggested that services could be provided in the community. There are also feelings that the medical profession, unable to find "cures", lost interest in people with learning disabilities (Ryan & Thomas op cit.).

    This trend towards community-based provision was given impetus with the disclosure of a series of scandals, outlining allegations of abuse in several of the mental handicap hospitals. Investigations led to the 1971 White Paper "Better Services for the Mentally Handicapped"; although not possessing the full force of legislation, it stands as an important watershed and part of a movement towards humanitarian policy for people with learning disabilities. Among other things, it set targets for local authority provision on a 20 year time scale. In 1979, the eponymous Jay Report ("Report of the Committee of Enquiry into Mental Handicap Nursing and Care") set out to review nursing practice and training, but ultimately achieved much more, outlining a model of community care based on the concepts of ordinary living. Work by researchers such as Wolfensberger on normalisation (e.g. 1972), suggesting that an ordinary life for those living in institutions is desirable, was very influential (see later discussion on the principles, implications and implementation of normalisation). The concept of 'ordinary living' has a longer history in Britain - the 1948 Children Act, for example, argues that all children should be given the opportunity to experience a normal home life.

The 1971 White Paper was reviewed in 1980 (DHSS Mental Handicap: Progress, Problems and Priorities). This report observed some improvements in terms of provision, but recommended substantial development of local services. Such development was the aim of the 1983 launch of the All Wales Mental Handicap strategy, which was of immense importance in terms of ideas about people with learning disabilities attaining any sense of identity within society. The project outlined three main aims:

(a) People with learning disabilities have a right to a normal lifestyle in the community, residing in ordinary housing if they wish.
(b) They have the right to be treated as individuals, as opposed to homogeneous members of a client group.
(c) People with learning disabilities should have free and ready access to a full range of professional services.

Strategies for achieving these goals were lucid: to provide an organisational model of development; to establish a timescale of 10 years; to complete regular evaluation of service provision; to confirm specific grants to be obtained from the Welsh Office.

This clear and forward-thinking approach appeared to inspire further pragmatic reform, as well as helping to shape the views of influential figures:

> There is no reason to believe that local authorities, given the staff and the finance, could not provide an adequate service for mentally handicapped people, nor that they would not. (From the 1985 House of Commons Select Committee on Social Services report: "Community Care: With Special Reference to Adult Mentally Ill and Mental Handicapped People").

Collins (1992) suggests that while such ideological rhetoric is heartening for those professionals and supporters campaigning for the empowerment of people with learning disabilities, it is by no means a logical transition from this ideology to practice. In real terms, community care appears to suggest a change in responsibility: people were once the responsibility of the N.H.S., and legislation now requires them to be the responsibility of local authorities. This brings with it many potential areas of concern, the most obstructive one being that of finance. According to Collins, a study of ten areas of England suggested that Social Services managers agree that people with learning disabilities are the responsibility of local authorities, but are unable to finance such a position. Money used by Health Authorities for social care as well as health care needs to be "ring-fenced" - that is, targeted for transfer to the relevant local authority -

but it appears that this is a very complicated and bureaucratic process, mainly due to the perceived major differences between Health and Social Services. Both have very different approaches to organisation, management and general practice, and staff tend to have different sets of expectations. Increasing acceptance of the social care model, implicit in Community Care policy, has diminished the extent of N.H.S. provision for people with learning disabilities, with the 1990 N.H.S. and Community Care Act actively encouraging Health and Local Authorities to communicate effectively with each other.

Obstacles to community care - lack of clarity and understanding about its form and objective; financial limitations; infra-structural barriers to inter-agency communication and collaboration - are noted by a number of investigative committees, namely the Audit Commission 1986, the Griffiths Report 1988, the Audit Commission 1989 and the Social Services Committee 1990.

What is Community Care?: Developments in definition, interpretation and legislation

The concept of 'community care' has been widely used over the past 30 years, and it might be useful at this point to revisit some of the most widely held definitions and interpretations.

The campaigning organisation Values Into Action (formerly Campaign for the Mentally Handicapped) has created a clear outline of what it believes community care needs to be:

> Community Care must not be dominated by institutional structures, whether physical, managerial or administrative. People, whatever their degree of need, should be enabled to live in their own homes as owner or tenant; these homes should be indistinguishable from the homes of other members of the population, and adequate support services should be provided as part the overall social and community services of the neighbourhood.

In other words, people with learning difficulties should be treated as ordinary citizens, and should receive support services which do not segregate or alienate them from the rest of society...community care means the use of community services and facilities by, with and for the community at large.

This provides one idea as to what, perhaps, people with learning disabilities deserve to receive if they are to be recognised as "regular" members of society, but there is still a need to unpack some of the terminology.

Some definitions

Bulmer (1987) takes the words "community" and "care" in isolation in order to trace their development into contemporary policy. Taking "community" first: Bulmer suggests that the majority of definitions are positive in tone:

> From the outset, the issue is clouded because "community" carries with it an aura, a sense of goodness. For it is a normative as well as an analytic and descriptive concept. It refers to society as it is but also to social elements which are valued either in the past, the present or prospectively, whether or not they exist (p.26).

This is supported by Goodwin (1985) who describes the word as used in phrases such as "moral community" or "community of principle" which themselves seem to conjure up images of mutual respect and a sense of common responsibility. This concept is powerful, because when used in the context of social care, it immediately suggests that "community" involvement is positive and desirable. There are also elements of the definition which can be traced to the model family:

> [The archetype of the community] both historically and symbolically, is the family, and in almost every type of genuine community, the nomenclature of the family is prominent. (Nisbet 1966 p48).

Other approaches to definition have slightly different emphases: the Barclay Report (1982), which set out to study the role of social workers, defined 'community' as "a network or networks of informal relationships between people connected with each other by kinship, common interests, geographical proximity, friendship, occupation or the giving and receiving of services - or various combinations of these" (p199). Sociologists, however, use 'community' to imply a group of people who live in a specific geographical area, whereas the term could also refer to a group sharing an identity or interest, although not existing in geographical proximity to each other - for example, 'the Asian community' (Wilmott 1984).

Underpinning these more contemporary perspectives, Weber (1947) argues that communality is "based on a subjective feeling of the parties, whether affectual or traditional, that they belong together...The type case is most conveniently illustrated by the family" (p137). Despite these concise and illuminating postulations, all of which appear to have value and relevance and seem able to coexist in terms of a generic definition, the situation is perhaps best overviewed by Halsey (1974) who claims that:

> All attempts to give this concept a precise empirical meaning have

failed and certainly in complex societies there is no total social system, that is a social network in which the whole of one's life may be passed, which is also a local territorial unit (p130).

Bulmer (1987) helpfully points to an escape from this tangle of philosophical debate by suggesting that the term "community" has merely to be described effectively in the context in which it is to be used, in order for it to have any valuable meaning. He continues by saying that:

> The two elements that are central to a definition of community in the context of social care are the focus upon local social relations within a geographical area and the sense of belonging which is also entailed in the concept (p29).

This is in support of Willmott (1984), who outlines three major tenets of a community: a significant degree of interaction between people in a particular locus or geographical area; a similarly obvious extent of shared interests and values; thirdly, an ability for the members of the community to identify and feel bonded with that community.

What is 'care'?

Defining 'care' is not quite as complicated and potentially entangling as defining 'community'. Parker (1981) draws a distinction between 'concern' - being aware and having sympathy, perhaps empathy, for a person or group of people - and the actual contract of working with or looking after people with a specified dependence. Bulmer (1987) refers to this latter distinction as 'tending', which might involve psychological or emotional support, as well as the more stereotypical personal care comprising of washing and feeding. There is also some debate as to the difference between paid and unpaid carers, or formal and informal care. Bulmer believes that for the unpaid carer, it is far more difficult to be emotionally detached from the person being cared for, and not only because the relationship is often of an intimate nature from the outset (e.g. mother/daughter) - but even the paid carer has some degree of emotional involvement (Weber 1947). Studies have looked at the preferred nature of care - formal or informal. West *et al* (1984) found evidence to suggest that:

> There is in general much less preference for care by the community than care in the community; the public are unwilling to place the major burden of care on informal carers which in practice means the family and women in particular. They are especially unwilling to allocate the major responsibility for care to close kin; the children or siblings of dependent persons (p294).

The Seebohm Report and beyond

Defining the two words 'community' and 'care' in this way provides some foundation to help explain why the term 'community care' has become something of a problematic term, perhaps to an alarming degree with relation to social policy for people with learning disabilities. The 1968 Report of the Committee on Local Authority and Allied Services, now the eponymous Seebohm Report, looked at how social services departments tackled contemporary problems. The conclusion was that the current situation was the result of social conditions, and that clients receiving social services were involved in:

> a network of relationships, in social situations. The family and community are seen as the contexts in which problems arise and in which most of them have to be resolved or contained (p44).

The Report goes on to discuss a broader approach to social problems, which by its very nature would help to resolve not only those individual difficulties, but go some way in contributing to the health of the community. Those familiar with the early work of Townsend (1962) are able to see the foundations upon which the Report is built - a definition of community that relies on an understanding of networks and mutual social relationships. This had significant implications: in areas where there was a lack of any positive concept of 'community', social services would be required to encourage its foundation and development, thereby effectively stemming social problems such as child abuse and mental illness. This perhaps suggests that social services departments were given a new identity as a proactive component within a supportive, community-wide network, as opposed to an agency working in isolation.

This sounds pragmatic and prescriptive, but it did not allow for the changes which local communities have undergone since the Seebohm Committee reported in 1968. It has failed to predict the extent to which the advantaged - who enjoy, by the very nature of that term, choice and opportunity - seek activity, stimulation, employment and leisure *beyond* their immediate communities. In contrast, the disadvantaged, taken here to include those with learning disabilities, have in the main no such comparable choices. Hence, achieving integration in most communities as the Seebohm Report recommended is now highly unlikely to any satisfactory extent. Advantaged members of society entering a new community already possess a strong sense of self-worth and value, an identity; people with learning disabilities throughout their existence have usually carried the marginalising burden of the 'problem' label (Clarke 1982). It needs to be acknowledged here, however, that while this is valid for the majority of people living their lives in institutions, those fortunate to have lived with their families might experience this to a lesser extent, while enjoying all the advantages that family environments can bring.

Noting the inadequacies of its predecessor, the Barclay Report (1982) attempted to avoid such precise recommendations, the result being that its content tends to have no clear meaning (Bulmer 1987). The Report purports to focus on the locality, but includes in its discussion many types of interpersonal relationships and networks usually included in that context. To some extent, the Report recognises its own shortcomings:

> The idea of community is both intangible and paradoxical. It is intangible because it has not yet been satisfactorily defined in the setting of an industrial society, and paradoxical because historically it has inspired some of the most paternalistic philosophies and some of the most liberal ones (p241-2).

It is hoped that present and future research involving people with learning disabilities moving to, or already living in, "the community", can help in assessing the extent to which the paradox continues, particularly with regard to the tension between individuals being empowered to make choices whilst functioning within the collective.

Research trends in learning disability: From survival of the fittest to survival in the community

Having traced the approach to learning disability taken by society and services, the extent to which parallels exist in the history of research can be established. Placing research within an historical context may enhance both its meaning and potential importance: the following represents an attempt at summarising prominent trends and movements, illuminating the developments in ideas from the time of Darwin and his "On the Origin of Species" (1859) to contemporary approaches to community care which are, or may be, of importance to learning disability.

The 19th century is an important place to begin looking at learning disability research literature. In 1859, Darwin argued that during the process of evolution, the 'fittest' become ascendant in the struggle for survival, passing on their characteristics to the progeny. This biological theory was adopted by writers such as Galton (1869) and applied to social matters - the 'threat of the unfit' became one of the major justifications for the incarceration of those people perceived as posing a threat to society:

> ...the wisest policy is that which results in retarding the average age of marriage among the weak, and in hastening it among the vigorous

classes, whereas unhappily for us, the influence of various social agencies has been strongly and banefully exerted in precisely the opposite direction...its effect would be such as to cause the race of the prudent to fall, after a few centuries, into an almost incredible inferiority of numbers to that of the imprudent...[it would] bring utter ruin upon the breed of any country. It may seem monstrous that the weak should be crowded out by the strong, but it is still more monstrous that the races best fitted to play on the stage of life, should be crowded by the incompetent, the ailing and the desponding (Galton 1869 p352-6).

Views such as that held by Galton gained credence at the beginning of the 20th century for two main reasons. Firstly, the advent of compulsory education exposed wide differences in academic competence. Secondly, the permeation of eugenics theory, a simplistic approach to understanding genetic inheritance, developed a belief that higher levels of reproduction among the 'least fit' would result in national degeneracy.

Supportive studies were unsophisticated in design: Goddard (1912) researched the Kallikak family, aiming to show that intelligence and social fitness are straightforwardly inherited. In the study, Goddard describes two groups of children, all fathered by a Martin Kallikak - those born to a 'feeble-minded woman' were considered 'social parasites', while those born to a 'woman of good stock' became 'virtuous citizens'. Goddard's evidence is not only incomplete and anecdotal, one can see that the factors of hereditary and environment are confounded.

This concentration on heredity can be linked with the practices of segregation and sterilisation of people with learning disabilities and other groups then considered to be 'feeble-minded'. A etiological studies became prevalent, but with correlates often mistaken for causes - tuberculosis and alcoholism were both considered to be causes of mental retardation.

Other approaches to research include that of Langdon Down (1866), who proposed a theory of 'atavistic regression' to explain the origins of some clinical conditions. Elsewhere, work began on trying to 'improve' mental retardation; towards the end of the 19th century, studies looked at 'mental measurement' (see Clarke & Clarke 1991) - an example is Binet's study of intelligence assessment, which "combined deep humanism with scientific objectivity".

Research on the problems raised by mental retardation was affected by two important and sometimes overlapping social trends at the beginning of the 20th Century - the development of a liberal concern towards disadvantaged groups, and the campaign of the eugenics movement, which reflected concern about the mental health and future of the human race. Institutions were seen as a solution by the eugenicists and, later, advocates of the medical model, with some becoming centres for research - Stoke Park Hospital being one example.

The implementation of legislation in the field of learning disability enabled the collection of information on prevalence, cause and treatment, leading to a fashion for epidemiological studies between the 1920's and 1940's, which were very influential. Penrose (1938) produced the Colchester Survey, which drew distinctions between severe and mild impairment, and recorded prevalence. The study indicated strong correlations with age, with an emphasised decrease in post-school age subjects.

In the post-war period, Clarke & Clarke (1991) note three important developments:

1. Optimism and humanism - there was an increased awareness of disadvantaged groups in society. A general interest in the field of learning disability led to moves towards seeking preventive and remedial measures.

2. Increasing trust in scientific methodology.

3. The emergence of parents' pressure groups, which campaigned on their children's behalf, and ultimately influenced both legislation and practice to some degree.

The 1950's saw the beginnings of a shift away from clinical and medical approaches towards a more socio-psychological model. Sarason (1949) is credited with the first psychosocial book on learning disability, the mainly descriptive "Psychological problems in Mental Deficiency". This was followed by the work of Hilliard & Kirman (1957), which contained papers by non-medical academics, and Clarke & Clarke's (1958) "Mental Deficiency: The Changing Outlook", which was predominantly written by psychologists.

This trend continued, resulting in the establishment of three main areas of research, referred to by Clarke & Clarke (1991) as description, prevention and amelioration.

(i) Description

Research into the *description* of an individual's learning disability can serve an educational as well as a clinical function.

Between 1960 and 1980, the reliability and validity of the Intelligence Quotient (I.Q.) was questioned extensively, and much of this discourse was incorporated into descriptions of people with learning disabilities. Critics argue that I.Q. tests are out of context and do not help with the difficulties faced by service-users and their supporters in daily life, although it still has its defendants (e.g. Zigler & Hodapp 1986). I.Q. tests do seem to describe people in terms of educational achievement (or, more importantly, failure) and social competence.

For some time, social competence was used for the diagnosis of learning disability, and has been the major cue for legislative action. The measure of 'adaptive behaviour' attempts to assess these criteria objectively - for example, the Adaptive Behaviour Scale (Nihiva *et al*, revised by Bortner 1978). The scale aims to objectify various areas of social competence, including self-direction, responsibility and socialisation. An impressive body of literature reporting adaptive behaviour measures by Hawkins & Cooper (1990) notes an increasing use of adaptive behaviour measuring tools, and cogently remarks that a perfect adaptation of institutional life as recorded by one of the many behaviour scales can make no predictions as to the potential a person has for adaptation to the wider community.

(ii) Prevention

Accepting that understanding cause leads to taking action for the prevention of learning disability, some research relies heavily on correlates. High maternal age has been linked with Down's Syndrome, but as with other conditions, may be the result of an interaction between several factors rather than just one. Penrose's "The Biology of Mental Defect" (1949, updated 1954, 1963, 1972), describes developments and changes in the understanding of aetiologies. Advances in research have included that which looks at spinabifida and encephaly (e.g. Brock 1976).

The 1950's and 1960's saw many advances in preventive research, leading to a statement by the President's Committee on Mental Retardation (1972):

> "Using present knowledge and techniques from the biomedical and behavioural sciences, it is possible to reduce the occurrence of mental retardation by 50% before the end of the century."

In 1976, Clarke & Clarke argued that three-quarters of people with learning disabilities are affected to a 'mild' degree; no impact had been made on their prevalence, rendering the prediction incorrect. This was accepted by the Committee, which later agreed to confine its statement to people with more severe disabilities.

Other important developments include those in genetics, including work on tuberous sclerosis (Fryer *et al* 1987) and Down's Syndrome (St. Clair 1987). A huge project was undertaken by Wahlstrom (1990), who developed a 'gene map' linking various conditions with mental retardation, while Stern (1985) reviewed a body of work studying the biochemistry of many forms of learning disability.

(iii) Amelioration

While physical, interventionist approaches have emerged - such as surgery for hydrocephalus and dietary considerations for people with P.K.U. - most attempts at amelioration have striven to alter behaviour.

As noted earlier in this chapter, the 1913 Mental Deficiency Act legislated to protect the public from people with learning disabilities (amongst others) and from national degeneracy, resulting in widespread segregation. In terms of research, no significant changes in trend are noted during the inter-war period.

In 1948, the Social Psychiatry Research Unit at the Maudsley Hospital included Tizard and O'Connor, who were briefed to work on the social problems of mental deficiency, marking the beginning of post-war rehabilitation research. An important report by the team appeared in 1956, revealing institutional life as so deprived, that psychiatrists in the main abandoned the earlier trend of descriptive work and concentrated on techniques intended to improve conditions for the institutionalised. The key to behavioural change at this time was deemed to be an understanding of the nature and potential for learning in those with learning disabilities.

Tizard is considered the first to recognise the importance of learning studies, producing work which suggests that people with learning disabilities have a potential for learning simple tasks, responding to incentives, acquiring the skills of learning and transferring those skills to other tasks.[1] Eventually, 'real life' settings for these studies increased the validity of research (e.g. Clarke & Mermelin 1955), enabling service providers to realise how service users can perform simple industrial tasks, leading to the establishment of sheltered workshops and other sheltered schemes. While it can be said that these developments in research acknowledged the abilities of people with learning disabilities, the nature of the working environments they were assigned to only seemed to accentuate their 'differentness'.

The challenge to the clinical and medical approach to learning disability from the psychologists in the 1950's arrived with a societal shift from an emphasis on heredity to an acknowledgement of the importance of environmentalism. In the context of full employment and an expanding economy, parents began campaigning on behalf of their children with learning disabilities. The move towards viewing those with learning disabilities as 'people not patients' gained increasing impetus (Mitler 1979), eventually leading to the development of the principles of normalisation and community integration programmes (Bank-Mikkelson 1969; Nirje 1969; Gunzberg 1970; Wolfensberger 1972). The success of early psychosocial research paved the

---

[1] For a comprehensive review of the history of learning studies, see Clarke & Tizard (1983).

way for the foundation of the Hester Adrian Research Centre, which has had a major impact on service practice.

The development of psychological approaches

The more powerful techniques which aim to help the individual develop socially adaptive skills and discourage maladaptive behaviour - known as systematic behaviour modification - have origins in animal experimentation. Studies informed by Pavlov's classical conditioning (1927) and Skinner's operant conditioning (1938) were developed by the researchers at the Hester Adrian Research Centre. Kiernan (1985) suggests that such techniques can eradicate unacceptable behaviour, but often fail when trying to develop communication skills. Foxx *et al* (1986) also warns that some professionals in the field are unaware of the power of behaviour modification, as well as the skills needed to make the change in behaviour permanent.

Psychosocial research began in the 1930's, with what is now considered weak methodological foundations (Clarke & Clarke 1991). In the 1950's, a view began to emerge suggesting that levels of functioning can be enhanced with appropriate support (e.g Clarke & Clarke 1958), and by the 1960's, intervention programmes became very popular - particularly in the context of work done with children experiencing sustained changes to their environments. However, 'Head Start' programmes in the USA failed to meet expectations on the whole, although supporters maintain that quality intervention programmes can enhance educational and social status in later years.

Recent developments: quality monitoring in service provision

The last decade has witnessed a shift away from the behavioural focus towards evaluation studies looking at various types of service. Some research teams seem to be aiming to clarify the essential and/or ideal components of a community support service (Mittler & Serpell 1985). More recently still, the experiences of a range of community services have contributed towards the concept of challenging behaviour as a way of describing difficulties encountered when encouraging integration.

Research is also becoming more sensitive to the ways in which service users are involved, with ethics committees having an important role in the development of research projects. There is still concern, however, with regard to the ways in which research findings are fed back into services. Academics need to find ways of encouraging both service providers, service users and their carers not only to consent to research taking place in their services, but to help generate the research questions themselves. Ownership of the issues - or at least participation in debate - could further bridge the gaps between policy and practice which have resulted from inconsistent and unclear guidelines for the implementation of the Community Care Act as it affects the lives of people with learning disabilities and the people who support them.

The future could well provide researchers with a bounty of phenomena to tackle. Moves towards community care are still taking place: the reluctance of the general public to tolerate 'inadequately' prepared service users, coupled with a lack of resources at many levels - human and material - together indicate anything but a smooth progression towards complete integration with society. There is potential for amelioration; psychosocial research can perhaps aid this process, but only when important findings are effectively applied to ordinary practice.

Interest in the experience of community integration has meant that research has begun to move away from looking purely at the process of deinstitutionalisation itself and has begun to look at the nature of outcomes for service users. The term 'quality of life' permeates much of this work, to the extent that there is potential confusion over its definition. This warrants closer examination and will now be detailed to enable clearer understanding of the difficulties arising when discussing 'effective' services.

2 Current Research Trends: What is 'Quality of Life?'

Introduction

Research trends have connections with the contemporaneous social, economic and political climates, as the previous chapter attempts to illustrate. More recently, attention has turned to the impact of deinstitutionalisation on quality of life for service users (Parmenter 1992), and a growing body of research continues in the mission to increase our understanding of what constitutes a 'quality' lifestyle.

The development of quality of life research

The closure of institutions, the moves towards community care and the softening of discriminatory attitudes towards some disadvantaged groups in society, have together been the inspiration of research in social science and arguably the results of particular government legislation, policy and pressure. Perhaps the most obvious shift in focus has been that of moving away from concentrating solely on identifying physiological syndromes and providing staff with strategies for difficult behaviour and teaching skills - be they from a medical or more recently from a psychological platform - towards evaluations of new and existing services.

Studies which are concerned with the cost of services and those which are focused around service user experience, the two main areas of research into quality of life described below, provide a useful, contrasting introduction to this complex field.

1.   *Costing services*

Financial concerns constitute a considerable body of the quality of life research literature. Confusion over the precise cost of putting community care into practice has triggered a flurry of investigative studies. Main concerns have been possible or real underfunding, as well as the identification of potential factors responsible for projected budgets being overspent.

This approach is illustrated by Schiell *et al* (1992), who set out to examine the financial considerations of community residential facilities for adults with a learning disability. A sample of 123 such facilities provided evidence to suggest that high costs incurred were usually associated with service users with higher levels of dependency, particularly those people inhabiting small domestic scale accommodation. The authors suggest that such anxiety usually arises when people are moving from large scale to small scale accommodation, and when there are significant resource implications e.g. people presenting a challenge to the service, be it due to difficult behaviour or the severity of their disability.

Studies of financial aspects of relocation also attempt to disentangle confusion regarding the exclusion or inclusion of specific budget categories in overall estimates (Davies 1988), mainly because overall costs of a service are normally calculated by a number of different agencies, all with different accounting methods. Davies (op cit.) suggests this issue is surmountable by introducing research-based estimates which are not only comprehensive and systematic, but include all costs no matter their agency of origin.

An interesting comparison can be made between the work of Schiell *et al* and that of Knapp (1990). The former study, which looked at established residential facilities, found that the cost per capita for people with learning disabilities living in the community was approximately £16,370 per annum at that time. In contrast, Knapp, who looked at people moving from hospital to the community, found the cost to be an average £18,400 per capita, having taken rates of inflation into consideration. Shiell *et al* suggest that this difference in cost arises because people moving from institutions to less restrictive environments have a greater level of need than those already living in the community.

Implications for service managers can be divided into two main areas. The initial level of dependency of residents, staffing levels and other resources are given constraints, while matters under managerial control include the skill-mix that s/he develops, the effectiveness to which staff are deployed on a daily basis and the size, location and standard of decor of the facilities.

As well as interest concerning the relative economics of deinstitutionalisation and established services, there are also political motives behind such research. Service planners are keen to discover alternative ways of delivering the same service with fewer or more staff, in smaller or larger facilities. If an alternative situation is both desirable and attainable, one needs to ascertain the projective costs and degree of quality; in turn, if the quality is to increase or decrease, planners and resource managers need to know whether such additional expenditure or reduced expenditure can be justified.

2.   *Service user-led research*

In complete contrast to a focus on economics, other research has attempted to evaluate services in terms of how the people receiving the service are actually affected. For example, Booth *et al* (1990) devised criteria which enables services to be assessed to establish their levels of success in meeting objectives. This involved interviewing parents and carers, staff members and the service users themselves, completing checklists which made assessments as to the quality and suitability of the environment, and observing service users in terms of community participation and skill acquisition. All of the measures were taken pre-move, post-move and after a suitable follow-up period. The study was interested in what has been termed 'transition shock' (Macy 1984), which is described as a reaction to stress, the symptoms of which can include emotional, behavioural and mental health changes. Much of the data for the research were collected from people other than those actually moving home; staff and relatives provided the bulk of the material, but attempts were made to access the feelings of the movers by using happy, sad and neutral line-drawn faces, which subjects could either point to or recognise.

The researchers claim that they were "interested in two areas of investigation: the management of the moves and how subjects and their families coped with the stress and upheaval of the transition." There is also reference to quality, as the study aimed to identify 'quality of service indicators', which they suggest are related to opportunities for 'self-determination', 'personal choice' and the availability of 'specialist services' to meet particular needs. These indicators appear to have been allocated somewhat arbitrarily, with no concrete definitions being offered. One could also argue that while 'specialist services' obviously have a place for many individuals, current thinking in the learning disability field does point towards access to generic services which adapt to meet all levels of need in the attempt to achieve quality (Baldwin & Hattersley 1991).

Quality of life research : The new Shibboleth?

Services for people with learning disabilities could be said to have been given their greatest impetus in terms of working towards a user-led approach by the implementation of the principles of normalisation (see chapter 4). Usually ascribed to Wolfensberger (1972, 1975, 1980), the concept was originally defined in the context of Danish services for people with learning disabilities:

> ...to let the mentally subnormal obtain an existence as close to the normal as possible (Bank-Mikkelsen 1969).

Subsequently, Nirje (1970) interpreted this to mean that society needs to make available to people with learning disabilities, patterns and conditions of day-to-day life which resemble as far as possible the patterns and norms of mainstream society. In Britain, O'Brien & Tyne (1981) provided the following definition:

> The use of means which are valued in our society in order to develop and support personal behaviour; experiences and characteristics which are likewise valued in our society.

Unfortunately, no light is shed upon the problem of how to determine what is valued by society, or by whom this judgement is made. For professionals in the field of learning disability, the approach has led to the development of three main service objectives. Firstly, services should actually encourage and support people to acquire the skills and personal characteristics valued in our society, and provide them with opportunities for using and expressing these skills. Secondly, the service provision needs to be provided in a manner which values all people with a learning disability, regardless of the extent of that disability. Thirdly, the community should be supported in its capacity to accept people with learning disabilities and their 'differentness', thus helping to achieve effective community integration.

These principles can be applied to any other disadvantaged group of people at risk of being devalued by society, as implicit in the definition is the condition that services are to be designed to genuinely enable people to participate in the mainstream of life, allowing them to take risks, make choices and carry responsibilities. The majority of services operate in conjunction with a risk taking policy, designed to ensure that any risks that are taken are both appropriate and reasonable. In reality, principles of good practice require that resource managers recognise the importance of involving the person or persons affected by the risk at every level of the process.

The principles of ordinary living

The principles of an "ordinary life", developed by the King's Fund (1980) and detailed by Towell (1985), develop the concept of normalisation. There are seven main points:

1. People with learning disabilities have the same human value and the same human rights as other people. These values and rights apparently enjoyed by people without learning disabilities are not defined, and this notion is contentious.

2. All people with a learning disability have the right to the same opportunities in the community as people without learning disabilities, and are entitled to the support needed to enable this to happen.

3. People with learning disabilities are developing human beings, and services should assist them towards greater independence as part of an age-appropriate lifestyle.

4. They should be involved as far as possible in decisions affecting their lives.

5. Services should affirm and enhance dignity, self-respect and consider people as individuals, rather than assuming that all service users have similar needs.

6. Services need to support networks which people with learning disabilities have already established, and contribute towards their continuity.

7. Services should be local, accessible and as comprehensive as possible, and include health centres and other sources of support. The advantage of facilities being in the vicinity not only enables people with mobility difficulties to have easier access, it also provides opportunities for people to become members *of* a community, and hopefully reach a stage where they feel able to participate spontaneously, not just with the assistance of support workers.

In conclusion, the King's Fund states:

> Our goal is to see mentally handicapped people in the mainstream of life, living in ordinary housing in ordinary streets, with the same range of choices as any citizen and mixing as equals with other and mostly non-handicapped members of their own community.

These ideas have helped to form the opinion amongst professionals that "ordinary" or "normal" living implies that people with learning disabilities should be afforded a quality of life equivalent to other citizens. Two questions arise here: this can only be meaningful if the quality of life for non-disabled people is defined clearly, and secondly, the value of people with and without learning disabilities living alongside each other in the community needs to be explored and understood so that the principles of ordinary living can be placed in context.

Assessing the quality of service users' lifestyles

The King's Fund statement might appear logical, but it is in danger of becoming tokenistic unless it can be reliably observed and reported in practice. A wealth of research has attempted to do this.

Hemming *et al* (1981) looked at a policy for building new small units as an attempt at reducing overcrowding in large institutions, as implemented by the Welsh Office. The project planned to meet the needs of people with all levels of ability, similar to that described by Grunewald (1972) in Scandinavia. This pre-empted recommendations concerning the provision of local facilities for people with all levels of need as outlined in the Jay Report (1979), and its underlying aim was to improve the quality of peoples' lives.

Work of this type has at its foundation the assumption that reducing the size of a facility increases the quality of life for residents. This is contentious for many researchers: Butler & Bjaanes (1978) found that using their measures, quality of life varied amongst small units, ranging from the apparently "family-type" to those replicating the most restrictive and punitive aspects of institutionalisation. Similarly, Edgerton (1975) argues that many large institutions with open-type settings can provide more "normal"-type experiences than other facilities purporting to be exemplifying the principles of ordinary living.

Hemming *et al* (1981) suggest there are five dimensions which can be combined to outline a concept of "quality of life":

• *Size of the institution and the degree of institution-oriented practice*
Using a scale of characteristics of total institutions (Goffman 1970), one can determine whether a facility has institution-oriented or resident-oriented practices. King *et al* (1971) made a study of a range of residential facilities, and found that management practices are unrelated to size of facility. Large hospitals were considered to have the highest degree of institutional practice, followed by voluntary and then local authority hostels.

• *Beneficial staff-resident interaction*
Tizard (1975) claims that staff with autonomy and flexible routines use more 'informative' speech, speak for longer and use more complex routines compared to staff with less autonomy and more rigid routines. Whatmore *et al* (1975) suggest that non-utilisation of institution-oriented practices does not necessarily lead to beneficial staff-resident interaction. This is supported by Pratt *et al* (1976).

• *Degree of participation in culturally normal activities*
Butler & Bjaanes (1978) provide a useful framework here by characterising institutions into three types: therapeutic - with habilitative programmes, community interaction and ongoing attempts to enhance the degree of normalisation as well as residents' social competence; custodial - which provide little or nothing in terms of the philosophy of normalisation, with the low occurrence of activity often leading to retrogression; maintaining - institutions with their guidelines operating somewhere between the two other types, with people apparently remaining at the same level of competence.

• *Institutionalisation and its influence on behaviour*
Skeels (1966) provides evidence to suggest that institutionalisation retards development, while Clark *et al* (1958) suggest that any improvement in people's behaviour seen after admission to the institution is generally a result of readmission experience.

• *Measuring maladaptive behaviour*
Many instruments have been devised, one of the most popular being the A.A.M.D. Adaptive Behaviour Scale (1974).

Hemming *et al* (op cit.) took all of the above into consideration in their quality of life, but also utilised the Raynes Scale of Management Practice in order to obtain a rough indicator of the quality of care people were receiving before and after resettlement in the community. It required a small amount of observation of staff-resident interaction - a valuable, albeit time-consuming measure.

This study yielded interesting findings. While resident-oriented practices and staff-resident interaction are both found to increase after resettlement, participation in 'normal' or near-normal activity decreased for more able people. Adaptive behaviour saw an initial decrease, then increased, presumably as people became more familiar with their new surroundings. An important suggestion was that more independent residents benefited least of all groups from moving, perhaps because resources for supporting and encouraging the development of independent living skills was seriously lacking. Some views from the movers themselves could perhaps have shed a little more light on this matter, as the authors do not expand on their notion of 'benefited'.

Weinstock *et al* (1979) go some way in supporting these findings, suggesting that relocation syndrome, or transition shock, could possibly be avoided if staff are supported in giving adequate time for transferring people, and perhaps more controversially, if people with learning disabilities were able to move voluntarily. Staff would perhaps observe less anxiety, withdrawal or sudden changes in behaviour in residents moving house if they were provided with more effective training and resources. The preparation time, it is argued, needs to consist of informing the person concerned of the date of the move, ensuring they are fit and healthy before moving and explaining the purpose of the move.

This might seem obvious, and indeed it is; however, it is argued here that the methods adopted by staff to convey this information need to be meaningful for the individual concerned, and here is where communication can break down. It is vital for staff to grow sensitive to the needs of each resident in terms of how they are going to react to change. Weinstock *et al* continue by reporting that sharing information will be of little use to people with profound disabilities (i.e. those categorised as untestable using the WAIS IQ scale), but sadly offer no recommendation as to how this difficulty could be addressed.

From this early body of research into quality of life, the two main recommendations are concise but are equally non-specific - to maintain staff morale and to develop a careful, systematic approach towards planning the integration of people into the community.

The 'tyranny' of quality?

Edgerton (1990), possibly envisaging the future of research in this area, suggests that quality of life for people with learning disabilities is the "challenge - or the shibboleth - of the 1990's", while Goode (1991), in a similar vein, wonders whether professionals in the field are replacing "the tyranny of normal" with "the tyranny of quality". The degree of debate appears comparable to that of defining other important concepts in the development of learning disability research - for example, "normalisation", "self-determination", "independent living". It seems fair to say that the concept of quality of life will be subjected to as much scrutiny as the term "community care", possibly for the similar reason that both terms are used freely both with and without context, and assume a certain degree of background knowledge for them to make any kind of sense at all. Parmenter (1992:247) comments that the phrase "quality of life" for some people

> ...embraces the notion of liberating people with disabilities from oppressive restraints, both physical and psychological, that have limited their opportunities for active participation in a community. To others, it is an index to assist in the scrutiny of health and welfare budgets where value judgements are made regarding the relative quality or worth of one individual's life compared with another's.

He expands this approach by arguing that:

> We are faced with the problem, possibly not restricted to the disability field, of having terms and concepts that have emerged as a result of philosophical debate losing their intrinsic meaning as we search to operationalise them and have them articulated into public policies.

This cautious view is again supported by Goode (1991:5) who claims that such terminology serves "rhetorical, political and professional purposes but [does] not help people with disabilities achieve a better quality of life." (p5)

Attempts at moving forward with researching quality of life have begun to realise the importance of stable and reliable definitions, now that services for people with learning disabilities are readily incorporating the terms "quality of life", "quality assurance" and "quality action" into their training strategies. Such developments might be derived from policy implementation, although Landesman *et al* (1987) argue that policy is likely to arise from the current philosophical, social or economic forces rather than from research - which itself serves to assess the effectiveness of such policy once introduced into a service (Parmenter 1992).

Understanding the 'quality of life' debate

One way of tackling the complexities of quality of life research is to understand its origins. Studying quality of life in the learning disability field has its foundation in many other disciplines. There are studies which look at the effect of policy on the lives of specific groups of people, using an index of measures which give an overall but implicit "sense" of their quality of life. More recent research has tried to stop avoiding the difficult question of what is meant precisely by "quality of life", and has begun to recognise the weaknesses of earlier work which failed to provide any workable definitions.

It is generally accepted that the root of modern research is Thorndike's (1939) study of the quality of life in American cities; this used social indicators to assess a broad view of life in an American community. Other fields that have used quality of life when studying service delivery are gerontology (e.g. Adams 1941), head-injury (e.g. Klonoff *et al* 1986), and mental illness (e.g. Lehman 1983).

Economic considerations became paramount in the last decade, as Government sought to constrain public expenditure, and health economists began to look at how they could evaluate medical procedures in terms of their monetary efficiency (Drummond 1981).

Ethical issues were raised when approaches recommending that less financially demanding practices should receive a higher percentage of available funding in order to increase the total number of life years gained (Zaner 1986). Critics argued that such approaches assume that all life-years afford an equal level of quality of life. This failure to account for quality in any meaningful context led to the introduction of Quality of Life adjusted years (QALY's); essentially, a year of healthy life expectancy is equivalent to 'one', whereas a year of unhealthy life expectancy is 'less than one' (Williams 1979). QALY's are used in a similar way to the analysis of medical procedures (Drummond 1981), in that they are utilised as evidence of cost-effectiveness for specific medical interventions or techniques, as well as for determining who should be treated. Understandably, QALY's have been criticised for being too simplistic (e.g. Loomes & McKenzie 1989) and ethically undesirable, as they focus on time rather than the life of an individual (e.g. Harris 1987). One can see how such thinking could also provide substance both for the abortion debate and for the adoption of foetal scanning.

Disillusioned with this emphasis on economics but noting its importance regarding the allocation of resources, other researchers have attempted to measure quality of life using a wider base of evaluation. Goode (1988) devised a series of seven categories which are felt to constitute quality of life: social (community and individual) considerations; life domains; life events; psychological and psychosocial factors; overall quality of life; outcome behaviours. Dossa (1989) is not as specific, suggesting one needs to identify objective, subjective and combined measures.

In general, disability studies tend to be led by legislation for the services being studied, often looking at independence, productivity and degree of integration with the community. Legislation also has a significant impact on the way that the population views quality of life for people with learning disabilities (Parmenter).

Deciding on relevant measures in quality of life research

A series of research models for quality of life research has been established, with specific measures:

(i) Social indicators

Social indicators can include income, marital status, race and sex, as well as other measures that are usually quantifiable but not necessarily so. They provide a useful counter to problems with direct measurement (Scott 1987). However, their relevance depends upon the context in which they are used, while the appropriate selection of social indicators is crucial.

Objective measures, or social indicators, have been criticised with the observation that the relationship between objective living conditions and subjective well-being is tenuous (Zapf 1985). Similarly, Schneider (1975) argues that objective measures need to be supplemented with more subjective material.

(ii) Psychological indicators

Psychological indicators are subjective and reflect an affective dimension of data, how people feel and experience their lives (Rodgers & Converse 1975). Illustrative studies include Zautra & Goodhart (1979), who suggest that happiness is short-term, whereas satisfaction is a longer-term, cognitive component. Research has tried to develop dimensions for accessing people's satisfaction (e.g. Flannagan 1982), using large samples in order to attain credibility for their results. However, Parmenter (1992:146) responds that:

...the effects of each individual's quality of life should be evaluated in terms of his or her personal values and needs rather than those that some central national authority believes all people have or should have.

Zautra & Reich (1983) suggest a relationship between a person's perception of their well-being and specific life events - moving house, a new job, the death of a partner. Headey *et al* (1984) feel that the way a person reacts to such life events or the way that people perceive their lives is possibly influenced equally by their personalities, personal resources and ability for adaptation, as well as the nature of the events themselves. This supports Parmenter's (1992) view above, demanding a need to examine the interaction between events and personal resources. Dalkey *et al* (1972) add to the debate by remarking that quality of life assessments are rarely longitudinal in terms of their methodology, thus omitting possible temporal changes in attitude.

Perhaps then, subjective indicators go some way in nearing the crux of what quality of life can mean as perceived by individuals. This is surely the state of the art approach to researching quality of life, as its principles and methodology appear to be in accordance with the concepts of normalisation and ordinary living as described previously.

As with all methodologies, subjective indicator research has its critics: Andrews (1974) questions four assumptions, namely validity (is the person able to answer the question?); the interpretation of the results; the completeness of information obtained; the utility of such research - data is expensive to obtain at policy level, as policy-makers could be unsure as to the relationship between individual satisfaction and societal welfare. Other criticisms, such as the possibility of people giving socially desirable responses, the possibility that responses reflect a momentary whimsical state of mind due to lack of a longitudinal approach and the prospect that psychological indicators might not provide a valid reflection of the effect of external conditions (Zautra & Goodhart 1979), are also useful in illustrating the multidimensional character of the 'quality of life' concept. Considering social class also seems to have been omitted.

Combining objective and subjective measures of quality of life

Attempts have been made to create the "person-environment fit" perspective (e.g. Murrell & Norris 1983). This proposes that a unit, be it an individual, family or community, can be exposed to stressors or traumata, and is protected to some degree by resources. This leads to the conclusion that the "larger the gap between what people have and what they need and want, the poorer their quality of life" (Brown *et al* 1988).

For Schalock (1990:144), such a discrepancy

> conceptualises quality of life as both an outcome from human service programs (application of additional resources should improve a person's quality of life) and the criteria for establishing the goodness-of-fit between a population and its environment. Thus, the better the fit, the higher a person's quality of life.

The importance of this philosophy cannot be underestimated: Brown *et al* (1989) suggest that quality of life is "a philosophy without an appropriate and functional technology", even though they accept that it represents an approach that increasingly contributes to the shaping of policy.

These developments are occurring in the context of a paradigmatic shift: people with learning disabilities are taking a more active role, expressing their own opinions in terms of shaping their own lifestyles. Symbolic-interactionist theories look at the interaction between affective components of quality of life (feelings), cognitive aspects (values) and behavioural components (actions), concluding that the three elements combined determine a person's level of perceived well-being or quality of life. Bearing in mind that people with learning disabilities in the community need to be interviewed indirectly according to recent philosophies, Andrews & McKennell (1980) designed a questionnaire which aimed to measure a person's behaviour in response to a number of ecological domains that affected him or her - namely, general well-being, interpersonal relationships, organisational activity, occupational activity and leisure and recreational activity. The authors used factor analysis to reveal five factors - occupational well-being; social well-being; family well-being; personal well-being; physical well-being. This supported the view of Parmenter, that:

> ...functional or rewarding and enriching life experiences are necessary for an individual to report a high level of perceived life satisfaction or subjective well-being (p254).

Milbrath (1982) feels that there is a "natural marriage" between objective and subjective indicators, formed by studying quality of life; Parmenter supports this view:

> A model of quality of life should reflect the values, aspirations, self-perceptions and other factors of the individual, but it also should accommodate functional behaviours in a range of life domains. There

should also be opportunity for societal variables to be incorporated (p255).

Summary

Deinstitutionalisation and community care have greatly boosted the search for an empirical definition of quality of life (Landesman & Butterfield 1987), and development has been in three phases. Between 1965 and 1975, institutional reform set out to establish minimal standards of care, while 1976 - 1986 was the era of deinstitutionalisation, with local and health authorities striving to create quality care programmes.

The present period of research is looking at people's membership of the community, concentrating on integration, quality of life and the progress of individualised support systems (Knoll 1990).

Studying quality of life: Established theoretical models

Such a complex area needs acceptable theoretical models for guidance, as there have been many criticisms of the evaluative approach. Emerson (1985) suggests that evaluation studies fail on three points: they fail to attend to crucial elements, ignoring the social nature of research and failing to overcome methodological difficulties.

Bronfenbrenner (1977) attempts to list the "crucial elements" for assessment studies as client satisfaction, happiness, social and interpersonal relationships, activity patterns, degree of self-determination and socio-economic factors. Although these are obviously very complicated entities to access, they are said to reflect a person's interaction with his or her environment, and are thus a more valid index of the success or failure of community living. With regards to empiricism in this research, Knoll (1990) reflects:

> The definition of program standards and quality is a process that transcends empiricism. This process ultimately appeals to the fundamental values of a society (p235).

Parmenter (1992) and Emerson (1985) disagree over the role of quality of life research. Parmenter feels that legislation underlines the way that services are funded and evaluated, and believes that research must therefore question the way that such legislation is implemented. In other words, the research can provide a framework within which problems can be identified along with potential solutions, thus progressing towards the formulation of future legislation. In contrast, Emerson argues that research is in reality merely symbolic - that the "non-functional use of data [is to] justify predetermined positions." This supports Goode's (1991) 'tyranny of quality' referred to earlier.

From the knotty problem of which the conflicting ideas described above provide a mere taste, at least five models of quality of life have been postulated, and each will be described briefly here. The first two have attained some support from the field of psychology, while the latter three remain to be supported with empirical evidence (Parmenter 1992).

(i)   The model of community adjustment

(Halpern *et al* 1986) has an empirical base. It is an integrated model which includes occupation, residential environment, social support and personal satisfaction. A battery of tests are used, along with exploratory and confirmatory factor analysis, providing strong support for this model. Its main premise is that opportunities for people with a learning disability to integrate with the community are generally found in a vocational setting. This is also true of the rest of the population, who are in a position to build a social life around their occupation. This is however, dependent upon class and nature of occupation, and there is a continuum running from a situation where people are interacting with others by virtue of working alongside them, to environments where employees socialise and form strong relationships with their colleagues.

The model has been criticised on two levels: the number of variables within each dimension of the model is relatively small, while the location of community integration within the occupation dimension may not be appropriate across other areas of disability. From a more positive angle, the model does make a useful contribution to the body of quality of life research, and incorporates a person's interaction with the environment, as well as combining both objective and subjective variables.

(ii)   The multidimensional model

Established by Schalock *et al* 1990, this model suggests that a person's perceived quality of life results from a combination of their personal characteristics, their objective life conditions and their perception of other service users, particularly people significant in their life. The model reflects these in its chosen indicators of independence - productivity, community integration and satisfaction - which the authors derived from legislation. The crux of the model is the assumption that aspects of a person's life experience are inseparable from cultural considerations, namely values, legal foundations and the way in which society thinks about people with disabilities.

This approach views the macrosystem (cultural and societal trends), as well as the microsystem (aspects relating to the individual), a paradigm supported by research in Sweden (Drugge 1990), which uses as its premise integration and normalisation.

Shalock *et al* found that quality of life scores, obtained using a 40 point questionnaire, increased consistently as environments become more normalised. It is noted by Parmenter (1992) that although the study has attained cross-cultural credibility and reliability, sample sizes used were quite small.

(iii) *Quality of life model for disabled persons*

This model is described by Brown *et al* (1989), who suggest that quality of life is the discrepancy between a person's achieved and unmet needs, as well as the degree to which people are increasingly controlling their own environment. The model combines objective and subjective measures, and similarly to Schalock *et al* (1990) above, is concerned with both macro and micro levels of an individual's environment.

The model has been criticised for its apparent failure to draw all of the variables together to form an overall quality of life index, but has been lauded for responding to Emerson's (1985) suggestion that quality of life research needs to look at the issues around specific environments.

(iv) *The ethnomethodological perspective*

The fourth model, devised by Goode (1991) follows logically from Brown *et al* (1989). It too concentrates on the impression that quality of life is specific to environments. Goode argues that quality of life is the product of relationships between people in each setting or environment, and emphasises that an individual's quality of life is very much influenced by the quality of life as experienced by people with whom that individual interacts. This is perhaps evidence in support of the need to utilise data provided by staff concerning their stress levels and attitudes to work.

This approach warns of the danger in quantifying a person's quality of life, though does not undermine the approach completely. Goode feels that quality of life is a very personal construct, and that there should be a bias towards the observational method, as this apparently reflects a more accurate picture of the individual's subjective experience of life, as well as their "real" social identity. The aim is to look at the depth and 'colour' of a person's relationships with others, rather than adopting carefully validated empirical tools. For Goode, producing 'standards' of quality which measure across the population are in danger of judgmental associations, hence his phrase the 'tyranny of quality'.

(v)   Interactionism: The impact of 'disability' on people

A fifth model, developed by Parmenter (1988), suggests that there is an absence of sound theoretical bases in the field of disability, despite the range of perspectives which have made attempts in research. For this reason, he forwards the symbolic-interactionist approach, the main premise of which is that "human experiences are mediated by interpretation (Bogdan & Kugelmass 1984), and that we come to know ourselves and what we are through the responses of other people (Stryker 1959). An illustration of the premise is provided by Bogdan & Kugelmass, who suggest that the word "disability" is not a symbol for a condition that is already there, but is part of a *mechanism* with which disability is created. An individual's psychological or physical 'differences' set parameters in which a definition develops; people develop their own definitions, or self-identity, according to the prevailing personal and community attitudes towards people who possess such 'differences'. Here, the labels attributed by the community depend upon the opportunities that people have had to interact at a personal level with people with learning disabilities.

Parmenter develops this discussion, suggesting that there is often a disparity between an individual's desired personal identity and their assigned social identity. The strength of Parmenter's argument is that he blurs the boundary between the able and the disabled as, potentially, everybody with or without disabilities has this experience.

The effect of this disparity for people with learning disabilities, is that they often fail to develop as 'authentic' people, fulfilling the roles ascribed by others, and thus reinforcing the stereotypes that initiated the process. As the person's self-perception assimilates the role assigned by society, they possibly develop 'secondary deviance' (Burbach 1981). Individuals with primary deviance are at a stage of still being able to see beyond their 'differentness' as a determining factor in their identity, whereas those with secondary deviance see only their 'differentness'.

Professionals are accused of contributing to this process (Finkelstein 1980). The implications of labelling for quality of life research are that researchers must be aware of the negative aspects of the personal condition as well as the effects of stigmatising (Burbach 1981), and acknowledge the conflict that potentially exists between the nature of the individual and the social nature of their human experience.

A further strength of the symbolic-interactionist approach is that it emphasises the viewpoints of the participants in social interaction under observation, and looks at aspects of the social experience which have previously been ignored (e.g. Barton & Tomlinson 1984). Parmenter (1992) acknowledges the importance of structuralist-neo-Marxist and Marxist class-conflict models which look at the imbalance of power between the disabled and non-disabled, and recommends that quality of life theories cannot be mutually exclusive.

Summary

The symbolic-interactionist model looks at three components of quality of life:

1. The person's perception of self.
2. His/her behaviour as response to ecological domains affecting him or her.
3. The responses that settings make to the individual.

These components interact, suggesting that the development of self is inter-dependent on functional and societal factors. The model's strength lies in its emphasis on how well people perceive themselves within a community.

Applying models of quality of life research to people with learning disabilities: Methodological issues

Heal & Sigelman (1990) suggest four dimensions for researchers:

(a) Objectivity or subjectivity of measures.
(b) The degree to which measures are absolute or relative (i.e. deciding on direct or comparative measures).
(c) The effect(s) of third party reporting on reliability and validity, when service users need others to speak on their behalf.
(d) The origin of the measures used (are they generated by the researcher or by the participants?).

With this framework, a number of difficulties for learning disability research become apparent. Firstly, subjective measures of well-being do not always correlate highly with objective indices of quality of life. Secondly, some responses need comparisons with past or future life - this can be difficult for people with learning disabilities (Parmenter 1991). Thirdly, reliability of research must always be doubted when respondents other than the participants themselves are involved - although the use of independent participative techniques goes some way towards resolving this issue. Goode (1991) is concerned with the generation of the life circumstances under observation - the fourth element in Heal & Sigelman's (1990) taxonomy outlined above. Fifthly, acquiescence amongst people with learning disabilities can be extremely high, which leads to the next concern that people tend to refer to a quality of life above a general or neutral point, despite the way in which this neutral point is described (Andrews & Withey 1976). Lastly, interviewing can be interminably difficult, and Heal & Sigelman recommend adopting a range of methodologies for a more accurate collection of data.

The intensity of such methodological difficulties might lead one to question the validity in researching quality of life for people with learning disabilities. Without providing adequate and workable context-based definitions, there is a danger of quality of life becoming a term of evaluation (Luckasson (1990), c.f. Goode 1991). Conversely, using an arbitrary and too rigid measure of quality of life could all too easily be applied to areas where resources are rationed.

What such research does seem to have invoked is an awareness that disability is a phenomenon with roots in the social, political and economic forces of society - rather than just a blanket term or clinical label assigned to individuals (Bowles 1988). It has also stimulated an emphasis on the importance of informal support, friendships and relationships with both disabled and non-disabled people (Turnbull & Brunk 1990). This is perhaps related to Fulcher's (1989) distinction between democratism, advocating the belief that those individuals affected by decisions need to take a genuine role in making those decisions, and professionalism, the view that experts are in the best position to make judgements. Parmenter (1992:280) remarks that:

> ...we have yet some distance to go in ensuring that people with developmental disabilities become *of* communities, rather than simply *in* them.

From a political perspective, Parmenter goes on to warn of the possibility of:

...value systems being misused by policy planners should make us vigilant concerning the possible ossification of the concept of quality of life.

The future for quality of life research and people with learning disabilities

There are two views of the future for people with learning disabilities. The pessimists suggest that:

...the optimistic and active ideology of the 1960's is changing as a result of economic difficulties into a pessimistic and passive one which is contributing to making the need the mentally retarded have of special resources disappear from sight (Soder 1984, p16).

The optimists, however, here represented by Mercer (1991), feel that approaches towards the learning disabled will become increasingly paradigmatic, in turn creating an appreciation of the need for treating people as individuals. Recent research supports this, and work has begun on viewing people within the framework of their personal needs and requirements. Significant breakthroughs could be achieved when this framework is itself generated by the people for whom it is designed to support.

3 A Qualitative Approach: Research Design and Methodology

Introduction

According to Parmenter (1992), social science research is experiencing a situation where

> ...terms and concepts that have emerged as a result of philosophical debate [are] losing their meaning as we search to operationalise them and have them articulated into public policies (p.247).

Terms such as normalisation, self-determination and independent living have served

> ...rhetorical, political and professional purposes, but [have not helped] people with disabilities achieve a better quality of life (Goode 1991).

The intention here is to explore the quality of life experienced by people with learning disabilities who have moved from institutional care to supported accommodation in the community.

For the purposes of this study, Parmenter's (1988) approach to quality of life has been adopted. The three components of the symbolic-interactionist model are considered, with the viewpoints of the participants in the setting under observation being of paramount importance. Structured interviewing aims to access these perspectives. The responses of settings to the individual will be studied using participant observation of interaction between tenants and between support staff and tenants, while the environment's response to learning disability will be revealed by analysing service documentation – such as operational policies – and the nature of service planning.

The main interest, then, is to assess the effects of social policy which seeks to

> [promote] ways of improving [the] quality of life for people in residential care (H.M.S.O. 1989, p.44).

Goode's argument (1991) will be assessed using the following research design:

1. *A case study* which compares the lifestyles of two groups of adults with learning disabilities who have recently moved from institutional care to housing in the community. One group live in an Inner London borough, receiving a service based on the principles of normalisation (Wolfensberger 1972). The other group live in Milan, Italy, where services adopt a philosophy based on the family model and status attainment through genuine employment, as opposed to work experience or other mini-projects.

2. *An in-depth analysis of two systems*, each designed to enhance the quality of life for people with learning disabilities:

(i) Life Planning, sometimes known as Individual Personal Planning(I.P.P.) or Personal Service Planning (P.S.P.), operates in many learning disability services throughout Britain. The system sets out to afford service-users control over their own lives, and is based around regular, person-centred reviews.

(ii) An individual planning service operating in Milan, Italy, which takes a multi-disciplinary, phenomenological approach to the service user's current situation, assessing the needs arising from a set of given circumstances rather than individual needs out of context.

These methods together form a *qualitative* assessment of the services participating in the study. Before the procedures are detailed, it is important to first examine the rationale for taking a qualitative approach, and discuss the implications and considerations that such a framework has for this study.

The qualitative method: Foundation and approach

The latter half of this century has seen the qualitative method become firmly established as a credible perspective in social science research, and this chapter will attempt to trace its history and development.

Introduction

The term methodology refers to the process, principles and procedures used to tackle research questions and problems (Bogdan & Taylor 1975). Scientific method was at one time dominated by the quantitative approach, which conventionally addresses measurable entities - often in the form of formalised laboratory experiments. Modern society has raised discussions which demand methodologies that are both holistic and descriptive. Debate over the selection of research method usually concerns any assumptions that need to be made, the theoretical perspective that is utilised and the ultimate goal or goals of the project.

Two main theoretical perspectives have been prominent: positivism, the origins of which stem from the works and ideas of Comte (1816, cited in Lenzer 1975) and Durkheim (1938), and phenomenology, which for the purposes of this discussion will be linked with the writings of Weber (1968).

Positivism, according to Durkheim (1938), seeks the facts or causes of social phenomena, ignoring the subjective states of the individuals being studied. Durkheim develops this by arguing that these "social facts" are to be related to as social phenomena which serve to influence human behaviour. In marked contrast, phenomenology focuses on understanding the nature of the behaviour under study from an arguably more relevant reference point - that of the person or persons of interest themselves, referred to as "the actor" or "actors" (Weber 1968). The rationale behind this perspective is clarified by Douglas (1970):

> The "forces" that move human beings as human beings rather than simply as human bodies.....are "meaningful stuff". They are internal ideas, feelings and motives.

For phenomenologists, then, the matter of importance and interest is not just the nature of the scenario, but how it is experienced, with emphasis placed upon not 'the truth', but rather on reality as the individual perceives it.

Quantitative or qualitative?

One needs to be aware that social science research does not culminate in selecting either qualitative or quantitative methods because it is more scientific or more accurate. It is more the case that phenomenologists and positivists tend to explore different problems, seeking different solutions to these problems. These differences, for obvious reasons, demand differing methodologies (Bogdan & Taylor 1975).

In practice, the positivist approach seeks facts and causes of social phenomena with the aid of survey questionnaires, inventories and demographic analyses, all of which produce quantitative data. These data can then be used to provide statistical evidence to support the existence of relationships between operationally defined variables (Cicourel 1964). In contrast, phenomenologists have as their goal an understanding of the actor's experience from his or her viewpoint, and seek to attain this by means of participant observation, open-ended interviewing and personal documents.

The fact that positivists are able to use qualitative methods under some circumstances, perhaps as indicators of social norms or other influential social forces, supports the earlier assertion that positivism and phenomenology are not opposing philosophies, but differ in the fundamental questions they address.

Symbolic interactionism and ethnomethodology

Within the phenomenological perspective are two main approaches - symbolic interactionism and ethnomethodology.

Symbolic interactionism has been widely reported (e.g. Blumer 1967, Hughes 1958). Essentially, symbolic interactionists argue that people are constantly in a process of interpretation and definition while moving from one situation to another. Every situation consists of actors, others and their actions, and physical objects; some situations are familiar, while some are new, but situations only have meaning via people's interpretations and definitions of those situations. Any actions which take place are derived from these interpretations and definitions, and therefore for symbolic interactionists, the interpretation and defining process acts as the mediator between the potential to act and the action itself.

The nature of the interpretation is dependent upon the specific life experiences and ways of interpreting brought to the situation by the actors. Other factors, such as gender or ethnicity, also need to be considered. In addition, actors in similar positions with similar life experiences might interpret an event in a similar way, referred to as a shared perspective.

Ethnomethodology has an equally well-reported foundation and background literature (e.g. Douglas 1970; Cicourel 1964). Much of this material refers to the subject matter of the inquiry, rather than the research methods themselves. Ethnomethodologists feel that people do not find the meanings of actions straightforward, and therefore need to apply abstract rules and common-sense understandings in order to make specific situations explicable. Meanings are referred to as 'practical accomplishments'; Garfinkel (1967) suggests that ethnomethodologists suspend their own common-sense assumptions to instead look at how common-sense is used in everyday life, hoping to understand how people "go about the task of seeing, describing and explaining order in the world in which they live."

Origins and development of the qualitative method

The research literature suggests that the qualitative method in its present form was developed in the 19th Century, the first reference being LePlay's observational study of European families and communities (Bruyn 1966). Nisbet (1966) remarks:

> But the "European working classes" is a work squarely in the field of sociology the first genuinely scientific sociological work in the century...Durkheim's "Suicide" is commonly regarded as the first "scientific" work in sociology, but it takes nothing away from Durkheim's achievement to observe that it was in LePlay's studies of kinship and community types in Europe that a much earlier effort is to be found in European sociology to combine empirical observation with the drawing of crucial inference - and to do this acknowledgedly within the criteria of science.

Qualitative methodology became readily accepted as a legitimate tool for research, primarily in the field of anthropology, and particularly in Europe and America. Bogdan & Taylor (1975) suggest that this could be because anthropologists were unable to utilise other techniques - for example demographic analyses or survey questionnaires. During the period of observation, data are collected by the researcher in as unobtrusive a way as possible. The main advantage of adopting this technique is the benefit of observing the organisation, relationships, interpersonal dynamics and conflicts from an original and unprecedented frame of reference. As Blumer (1967) states, research anthropologists are usually unfamiliar with the everyday lives of the people they study, this ignorance stimulating the main focus of interest. In contrast, sociologists at this time worked from the premise that details of the everyday lives of the actors in the study were well known and understood. Thomas & Znaniecki (1927:1832) suggest that qualitative methodology emerged as a popular approach for social science research at the beginning of this century, remarking that:

> We are safe in saying that personal life records constitute the perfect type of sociological material, and that if social science has to use other materials at all, it is only because of the practical difficulty of obtaining at the moment sufficient number of such records to cover the total of sociological problems...

Early studies such as this one are invaluable when establishing the foundations of contemporary qualitative methodology. It is equally important to note that despite such assertions, interest in qualitative approaches diminished and were more or less replaced for a period by positivist theory and the quantitative method. The qualitative approach eventually emerged as a reliable and valid perspective with Peter Townsend's team in the 1950's, with further support in the 1960's and 1970's, and has remained so to the present.

The qualitative method is concerned with settings (and individuals within those settings) in an holistic sense; the subject of the study, be it people or an organisation, is not reduced to an isolated variable or a single hypothesis (cf. the quantitative method), but is instead considered as part of a whole. Bogdan & Taylor (1975:4) comment:

> The methods by which we study people of necessity affects how we view them. When we reduce people to statistical aggregates, we lose sight of the subjective nature of human behaviour. Qualitative methods allow us to know people personally and to see them as they are developing their own definitions of the world. We experience what they experience in their daily struggles with their society. We learn about groups and experiences about which we know nothing.

Suggestive of an unrestrictive paradigm, qualitative methodology allows the researcher to examine concepts which are often ignored by or are more accessible for other approaches. Examples include love, beauty, pain, suffering and hope, all studied and recorded as defined and experienced by real people in the context of their everyday lives.

Assessment tools in the qualitative method

There appear to be two main tools in common use which fall under the umbrella of qualitative methodology.

(a) Participant observation
The first, participant observation, has no precise or clear definition. It is usually taken to imply a period of intense social interaction between the person conducting the research, and the person or persons in the setting.

The people involved in the interaction are usually referred to as the participant observers - those who have no direct relation to the setting, be it in terms of their career status, the past or the future - and the participants, those who are linked to the setting and are consequently able to see the situation only from their respective viewpoint. Participants are related to each other by means of shared assumptions about the context in which they are participating.

Another important difference between participant observers and participants concerns the allocation of time. Observers determine to allot a specific amount of time to working in the field, whereas participants are 'in passing'; the time spent in the field is in a sense coincidental, for they are preoccupied with their everyday lives. Thirdly, following from the previous point, researchers are trained in observation, or are at least aware of specific criteria which need to be met if reliable and useful data are to be collected. A unique vantage point for understanding is attained by the observer, thus fulfilling the basic aim of qualitative methodology.

It can be noted that while it would be most difficult and demanding in terms of time and energy required, it is not impossible or always undesirable for participants in the setting of interest to themselves become participant observers.

(b) Personal documents and unstructured interviewing

The second tool, or rather group of tools, utilised by qualitative researchers are personal documents and unstructured interviewing. These are materials where the person of interest describes in their own words, their view of life or a specific aspect of themselves. Examples include diaries, letters, autobiographies, transcripts of open-ended interviews. The main aim of adopting such methods is to acquire a more meaningful understanding of people, events or settings which are not readily accessible or easily observable. The researcher is able to become familiar with an intimate aspect or impression of an organisation, relationship or event from the very person or people experiencing the phenomenon.

Bogdan & Taylor (1975:7) comment that "personal documents offer a cutting edge by which we can examine our most basic common-sense assumptions about the nature of reality".

The person under study is seen by the researcher in the context of his or her time or history, and the researcher is enabled to consider the influence of a variety of external forces be they social, political, economic or religious. This assertion is validated by Mills (1959):

> The overall questions of the social sciences come readily to the mind that has firm hold of the orienting conception of social science as the study of biography, history and of the problems of their intersection within the social structure. To study these problems, to realise the human variety requires that our work be continuously and closely related to the level of historical reality - and to the meanings of this reality for individual men and women.

Bearing these considerations in mind, it would be useful to consider the stance of the researcher in ethical and philosophical terms. A lucid account is provided by Cottle (1972:16):

> For a method as fundamental as visiting with people, listening, speaking and

allowing conversations to proceed as they will, means that one's own life is implicated in the life of another person, and one's own feelings are evoked by the language, history and accounts of this other person.

Researchers need to both identify and empathise with their subjects, if they are to be effective in gaining any degree of understanding of their frame of reference. Weber (1968) called this "verstehen" - the ability to reproduce in one's own mind the feelings, motives and thoughts behind the actions of others. Blumer (1967) suggests further that attempting to achieve objectivity by remaining distanced from the setting often results in what he terms "the worst kind of subjectivism". There is a risk that by remaining external to the actor or actors, the observer will supply their own information to compensate for inevitable gaps in their interpretation, rather than attempt to understand the setting from the actor's viewpoint.

The qualitative method: A critique

Social science research often compartmentalises the people it purports to study. This arguably invalidates the perspective of the individual, a consideration particularly relevant to the case of people with learning disabilities. People labelled as members of this group are rarely allowed to be regarded as individuals, and research has often focused on how policies come to be written on the specifics of various organisations (Parmenter 1992).

Effective participant observation and appropriate utilisation of personal documents can result in a situation where the observer doesn't view the observed as "true" or "false", "good" or "bad", but acquires understanding. Bruyn (1966) feels that while one views events as happening for the first time, inaccurate judgements are avoided. Furthermore, the data obtained build a multifaceted impression of a setting, possibly with individual viewpoints contradicting each other. This reiterates the phenomenological concept that one need not be preoccupied with obtaining the "truth" about a particular setting, but rather begin to consider "truth" as being comprised of many opinions, experiences and personal interpretations.

Criticisms of the qualitative method tend to focus on the nature of the data collected, and it could be argued that observers selectively collect and analyse data which are non-representative. Bogdan & Taylor (1975) maintain, however, that techniques are built into the data collection and analysis stages of the research to avoid the presence of bias.

Secondly, there is the issue of generalising findings to other settings, but again, Bogdan & Taylor (op. cit.) defend the method by claiming that "all settings and subjects are similar, while retaining their uniqueness" (p12)-

general processes are observable in a variety of circumstances. Thirdly, one must consider the effect of the observer's presence. Webb feels the presence of the researcher is in danger of being underestimated (1966):

> Interviews and questionnaires intrude as a foreign element into the social setting they would describe, they create as well as measure attitudes, they elicit atypical votes and responses, they are limited to those who are accessible and will co-operate, and the responses obtained are produced in part by dimensions of individual differences relevant to the topic at hand.

Bogdan & Taylor (1975) can only respond by noting that all researchers face these dilemmas, whatever their philosophical foundation, and that the honesty of admitting such difficulties in any written reports is the price to pay for gaining a wider and deeper understanding of what amounts to various, complicated social settings.

With this background established, the procedures undertaken here can be presented in detail.

Methodology

The case study

(i) Subjects

12 men with learning disabilities took part in the case study, 5 men living in London and 7 men living in Milan. All men are described as having "moderate" learning difficulties. The English service-users are aged between 27 and 61 years, the Italian service-users between 28 and 54. The essential criterion for selecting the groups was recent change of accommodation from institutional care to housing in the community: for the Italian group, their previous home was a 50-bedded mental handicap institution, for the English group, a 23-bedded social services hostel.

(ii) Data collection

Two main methods were adopted:

1. Interviewing
2. Participant Observation

1. *Interviewing*

Interviews were held with service-users and members of support staff. While it is essential to obtain the views of service-users themselves, it has been suggested that obtaining information from others involved in a person's life can provide valuable insight. Powers & Goode (1986) argue that quality of life is the product of relationships between people in a particular life setting. While this refers to the interpersonal relationships that develop in residential accommodation, the argument can be extended to include all of those people who have close involvement in people's lives.

This made it necessary to devise a questionnaire for support staff, which aims to draw out important and relevant themes - motivation, job satisfaction and attitudes towards learning disability.

(a) Devising the questionnaires

Background
Government documents emphasising the importance of service-users' opinions have led to organisational changes in services, the aim being to enable users to work as partners with professionals to achieve a better quality of life. Consultation exercises have become more and more commonplace, an effective example taking place between North West Thames Regional Health Authority (N.W.T.R.H.A.) and the self-advocacy organisation for people with learning difficulties, People First. The results of this collaboration provide the basis for the questionnaires used in the present study. The Health Authority wanted to obtain service-users' views on moving from institutional care to "ordinary" houses in the community. The project co-ordinators had three main concerns:

(1)   The nature of current lifestyles experienced by service-users.
(2)   How service-users feel about their current accommodation and lifestyle compared with their previous, institutional care.
(3)   The nature of needs or hopes that service-users have for the future.

N.W.T.R.H.A. wanted People First to be involved as an organisation run by and for people with learning difficulties, having originated in the USA and established in the UK for over 9 years. The organisation's national focus is to encourage and develop self-advocacy, with members acquiring skills in speaking up for themselves and for others with learning disabilities. The independent status of People First was an important advantage.

An evaluation team was formed, consisting of representatives from

People First, N.W.T.R.H.A. and Hillingdon Social Services. This team recognised its unique status as a group which was enabling people with learning disabilities to evaluate a service developed for their peers. A questionnaire was developed, covering all aspects of people's lives both at home and at work or the day centre. This formed the basis of the questionnaires created for the London and Milan case study.

Adapting the N.W.T.R.H.A./People First/Hillingdon Social Services Questionnaire for the London/Milan study

This collaborative project attempted to record the views of service-users by means of questions which were in the main developed by people with learning difficulties. It was considered here that this was a useful starting point from which to gain some sense of the quality of life experienced by participants in the study.

Some questions were felt to be unclear, and these were either re-worded or expanded upon, whilst retaining their original line of enquiry. It is important to ensure that questions are as unambiguous as possible - perhaps by providing prompts or suggesting answers to the respondent, adding context to the question - but it is also necessary to be aware of acquiescence. The pitfalls of interviewing people with learning disabilities has been widely researched (Atkinson 1988), and a fuller discussion follows later in this chapter.

(b) Interview technique : "What do you think?"

As with any interviewing, the main concern here was clarity for the respondent. Time was given after asking each question, with a rewording of the question after an appropriate time lapse.

If still no response was offered, or if the respondent was distracted, moving on to another subject or appeared confused, the interviewer reassured the respondent before suggesting two or three possible answers. In this case the "possible answers" were followed by the statement "These are just ideas - what do **you** think?" This attempted to provide prompts without leading the respondents away from their own views.

All respondents participating in the case study communicate using speech, except for one. This man uses Makaton sign language and some personalised signs known to the researcher. His style of communication thus proved to be no more difficult in this situation than that of the other men.

Individuality was also a concern. One person's understanding of a question can differ radically from that of another. The interviewer took time to build rapport with each respondent, trying to gauge his pace of response and get some sense of how that person makes connections between different statements. This task was much easier with the English users, with whom the researcher was very familiar.

(c)   Building rapport : The English service-users

Both groups of service-users participating in the case study were given a standard explanation regarding the nature and purpose of the study, its aims and especially the level of confidentiality involved. Although the format aimed to be identical both for the interviews in English and in Italian, there were some important differences.

The English respondents were all known to the interviewer, which helped significantly in terms of the levels of co-operation that were achieved, as well as giving the interviewer confidence that he had been able to obtain responses that were a fair representation of what the respondent actually felt. The disadvantage of this prior knowledge was that for some individuals, time was needed to either reassure the respondent about the nature and purposes of the task, or to persuade him to concentrate on the particular subject in hand. Throughout the process it was borne in mind that talking to people with learning disabilities on a one-to-one basis can result in them feeling under pressure, or that they have done something wrong.

(d) Building rapport: The Italian service-users

The approach adopted with the Italian service-users was slightly different. The interviewer had not met the 7 men before, and thus more effort with building rapport was required prior to interviewing. The ethnomethodological research literature suggests that a true sense of a particular setting can only be gained by sharing and experiencing all aspects of that setting, particularly mealtimes (e.g. Strauss 1987). This happened without request, thanks to the wonderful hospitality of the service-users and their support team.

Staff allowed the men to introduce themselves during the first visit, and no interviewing took place during the entire session. It was felt far more important to spend time getting to know each other and allowing the men to ask the research team questions about the purposes of the project and what their participation would entail. Much of the conversation was led by the service-users, the aim being that as the researchers were guests in the participants' house, it seemed appropriate that particularly during that first visit, they did not feel pressurised or under scrutiny.

During the second visit, staff were interviewed, after which more time was spent with the service-users. They appeared, as a group, more relaxed than on the first visit, and asked questions about London and the researcher's work since the previous meeting. The evening was spent at the local pizzeria, which was a valuable occasion for important reasons: not only did the research team take the opportunity of being welcomed once more into the group, they were also beginning to see how the tenants interacted both with staff and with each other. This served as a useful foundation for the participant observation work which was to take place on future visits.

The interviews themselves were held at the house, individually, but differed from those with the English tenants in that they were held in a small sitting room leading off the main dining room. This was due to the fact that 6 of the 7 tenants share a bedroom: when asked where they preferred to be interviewed, none chose the room in which he slept. The other important difference with the Italian interviews is that each participant was effectively interviewed by two people at once - namely the researcher and an interpreter. The perceived effects of this are discussed below.

(e) The interpretation process

A great deal of time was spent between the researcher and the interpreter, establishing the aim of the interviews and approach to be adopted.

A native Italian from the Lombardian region, the interpreter is a research neurologist who has no real academic experience in the learning disability field, but has much social contact with service-users where he lives in London.

For the purposes of this study, it was felt that being at ease with people with learning disabilities and having a basic understanding of how to communicate in a flexible and sensitive manner is of greater benefit than specific academic expertise.

The Italian interviews took considerably longer than those held with the English tenants, mainly due to the interpretation process. The use of regional dialects by some of the tenants coupled with speech that is a little incoherent in some cases, meant that responses had to be translated verbatim on occasion. It had been anticipated that this process might confuse, frustrate or even frighten the participants - and that the prospect of being asked a series of questions by two relative strangers would be completely overwhelming. In reality, it appeared to have the opposite effect. Each interviewee seemed fascinated by any English that was spoken, and one individual insisted on being taught the words "thank you" and "yes". Rather than hinder concentration or limit attention spans, the presence of a foreign language seemed to evoke nothing more obtrusive than interest and curiosity.

Credit must be given here to the preparatory work done by the support team, who had spent time with the men reassuring them before our visit.

"Getting to know you": Safeguards and considerations when conducting interviews with people with learning disabilities

As it is recognised that quality of life research needs to obtain service-users' views (Sigelman et al 1982), the challenge is to do so effectively. Opportunities need to be available for people to express their views, which in turn will be represented accurately in subsequent reports. Qualitative research is concerned with subjective experience (Taylor & Bogdan 1981), a way in which one can understand people by viewing them in their social situation and exploring their view of it (Bercovici 1981). Although interest is growing about how people with learning disabilities live their lives in the community, the published literature on methodological issues is small (Sigelman & Budd 1986). Flynn (1986) believes that more sharing of experiences among researchers is needed.

Theoretically, the involvement of service-users in research about their own lives is straightforward; they are in the best position to describe their social situation, their personal experience and their feelings about it (Wyngaarden 1981). How the involvement occurs does raise many issues. Brost & Johnson (1982) suggest what they term the "Getting to Know you" approach, which means investing time with the participants in the research within the context of a relationship, allowing a sense of that person's life to gradually develop.

The argument here is that the majority of problems in research can be overcome given a generous allocation of resources, frequent and regular contact over a long period, whilst taking advantage of a wide variety of opportunities for both conversation and observation (Edgerton, Bollinger & Herr 1984). This is referred to as the "naturalistic" approach, and is usually unworkable for small projects or pieces of research with limited resources.

Most contemporary research is based around interviewing. The small but growing body of literature has created a consensus regarding the sorts of questions to be asked; how they should be asked; who should be involved; the safeguards to be built in. Atkinson (1988) suggests that the following considerations apply to participants in a variety of contexts and from different backgrounds.

1. Questions to ask
These need to be open-ended (e.g.Sigelman et al 1980), as this avoids acquiescence and over-reporting which is associated with yes/no questions,

and any tendency to choose the second option in either/or questions (Sigelman & Budd 1986).

2. Conducting interviews

As with all interviewing, the interaction between researcher and interviewee should be relaxed, unobtrusive and as informal as possible (Taylor & Bogdan 1981).

3. Who should be involved?

Individual interviews maintain confidentiality (Wyngaarden 1981) and it could help to be aware of any communication skills needed when there are known limitations (Flynn 1986). Using tape recorders reduces the chances of the interview being seen as a test, as well as there being less writing for the interviewer.

4. Safeguards

(i) Questions can be asked in a number of ways so that answers can be cross-checked (Wyngaarden 1981).

(ii) Beginning the interview with easy questions can build confidence in both the respondent and the interviewer. Difficult questions, or questions that are sensitive, can be placed in the middle or at the end of the interview (Atkinson 1988).

(iii) People closely involved in the respondent's life can provide information which can act as a "check" for any data gathered (Sigelman et al 1981) - although this is controversial in terms of breaching confidentiality, and needs to be handled sensitively.

Atkinson's "anticipated areas of difficulty".

Atkinson (1988) suggests four main areas of difficulty, potentially arising during the course of interviewing people with learning disabilities.

(A) The Respondent's characteristics

There are four considerations :

1. Institutional background

The interviewee might have limited experience of "ordinary" life, and have little to say. S/he might be inhibited by the fear of failure, which for them could suggest a return to the institution.

2. *Limited understanding*
S/he might find it difficult to comprehend the purpose of research or the questions asked, or might have difficulty in expressing her/his own views and experiences. Recalling events or names of people and communication in general can all present difficulties for those with learning disabilities.

3. *Trying to please*
- s/he might be preoccupied with trying to say what s/he thinks the researcher wants to hear. Great care is therefore needed to support respondents in giving their answers, without leading them, "influencing their choice of words or mode of expression" (Atkinson 1988).

4. *Communication difficulties*
- speech or hearing difficulties might present problems when the respondent and interviewer are trying to communicate. Knowing the respondent well and being aware of their own personal modes of communication help to alleviate such problems.

(B) Respondent's perception of research
People with learning disabilities have often lived segregated and stigmatised lives - this will possibly affect their perception of the research. One-to-one contact can lead them to believe that they're being tested or checked up upon. This might lead to non co-operation or reluctance to talk about certain issues.

(C) The need for feedback
Reassuring people during the course of interviewing can allay many fears - apart from explaining clearly the nature of the research, the interviewer can refer to the positive implications that the participant's help could have for others (Atkinson 1988).

(D) The respondent's perception of the researcher
Where the researcher is *known* to the respondents, it is essential that any data collection takes place outside any usual contact. A convincing explanation of the purposes of the research will help to ensure that respondents not only take the interviews seriously, but also will not be anxious about their implications. If the researcher is *not* known to the respondents, it helps if the person making the introduction is a familiar, trusted person.

With so many potential pitfalls, one can see the advantage of utilising data collected from other sources, to add context to service-users' responses. However, when respondents participate in interviews which leave them feeling valued - perhaps because somebody has spent quality time and afforded them respect - the extent of the difficulties can be limited.

The approach to participants now documented, it is important to acknowledge that the significant element of this study is its comparative perspective, and reasons for taking this approach needs to be explained and justified

The case for cross-national research

This sets the scene for an exploration of the key issues arising from the *comparative* approach to social policy adopted in this study. The pragmatic aspects of comparative work have been clearly established by Jones (1985). She maintains that:

1. Comparative work promotes a clearer comprehension of the home social policy environment.

2. It broadens ideas or "lessons from abroad".

3. The exposure to a wider variety of responses and data provides the potential for the development of theoretical constructs and social policy formation.

These basic tenets can be expanded further. To first look at the argument regarding the promotion of clearer understanding of the home social policy environment, in this case, learning disability services in Britain. Jones argues that social policy is relative to the time and place within the home country, that contemporary social policy is discussed in relation to that of other times. The performance and behaviour of local authorities is viewed in the light of observing local authorities elsewhere, which logically brings one to the conclusion that studying national policy needs the policies of other nations to provide a reference point. It seems reasonable to want to establish whether the perceived difficulties, problems or attitudes of the home country are peculiar to that country, or indeed exist to a greater or lesser extent in other similar nations. Jones remarks that with the advent of the E.U., academics, lobbyists and other professionals are liable to make comparisons at their convenience or support a personal cause, and 'intelligent' adoption of the method is necessary.

'Taking lessons from abroad' again demands caution. The temptation to lift verbatim from other nations' "good ideas", leading to the creation of an utopian society, is illusory:

> Social policies do not exist in a vacuum apart from each other and independent of the society within which and as part of which they have developed (Jones 1985:5)

Without due consideration, it would be all too easy to over-simplify another nation's policy. Jones continues

> ...lessons from abroad, both positive and negative, are there for the taking. The value of the lesson, however, depends very much upon how carefully and sympathetically it has been identified, defined and analyzed in the first place.

Thirdly, the development of knowledge regarding the theoretical underpinnings of social policy is limited by "natural" situations in which research takes place. Time and/or place comparisons therefore have the attraction of an additional dimension for study.

There are critics of cross-national research, but Jones believes that the difficulties existing are outweighed by the dangers of being unaware of the method's benefits. Jones suggests that all of those involved with social policy will encounter cross-national comparisons at one time or another, and that there is a need for what she terms "literacy" in handling material. Criticisms are divided into the practical and theoretical.

Practical difficulties are two-fold. Firstly, documentation: the use of similar terminologies can obscure meaning, while the methods of data gathering undertaken by respective nations will be more or less efficient. Researchers must therefore work with what's available or seek information themselves. Secondly, human limitations: in ideal circumstances, cross-national research would be conducted by someone with an equal understanding of and insight into each society concerned. While Jones acknowledges the existence of "bi-cultural" comparativists (e.g. Rose (1973), the U.K. and the U.S.A.), most researchers have a thorough comprehension of only one society. Being born and socialised in a particular country cannot be substituted by frequent visits or prolonged periods of study or employment; one view is, however, that new questions might be raised by somebody who is not an "insider".

Theoretical difficulties centre around the observation that nobody conducts research of any nature free from their own culture. Complete objectivity is an utopian ideal, and all questions asked by the research will be culture-specific. The issue here then, is whether to ask one's "own" or "other people's" questions: the stance taken by the present research is that of asking "home" questions, as this will attempt to answer questions about the home nation's policy using the other nation as a control group. If, however, one is seeking to formulate theoretical discussion, comparative work can present major difficulties. Controlled experiments cannot be conducted ethically, as relevant variables are virtually impossible to identify and hold constant in a naturalistic setting. Jones suggests that with enthusiasm, these difficulties can be of interest, rather than rendering the method as impossible.

The final area of criticism concerns those researchers who consider cross-national work as premature, in view of the research needed to bring further understanding to "home" social policy. Jones replies that cross-national analysis can bring a welcome dimension to research, and disputes the call for "scientific" and systematic approaches that establish theory on the basis of the accumulation of ordered, case study data. On the contrary, Jones argues, the body of social policy literature has not developed in a cumulative, "bottom-up" fashion, starting with local projects through to national and finally cross-national studies. Development is more piecemeal than pyramidal. Different types of research are able to coexist rather than serve to compete against each other, and different approaches in different settings produce, when executed with caution and consideration, a variety of valid aspects which can all combine to form a sense of the setting of interest.

The comparative approach is therefore useful in meeting the aims of the present study, as the intention is not to determine which of the local authorities - London or Milan - has designed the 'better' services. The objective here is to compare the outcomes and ideological underpinning of deinstitutionalisation in order to increase understanding about the influence of normalisation in services which have difficulty in ascertaining this by present means. Comparative research here is highlighting salient elements of services in Britain, as well as revealing interesting differences of approach.

Comparison of the present situation needs foundation, and this will now be provided by tracing four important histories:

- general discussion of the principles of normalisation to establish the main elements under scrutiny in this study,

- a history of psychiatry services in Italy, which will be used as an argument for the formation and influence of the present socio-educative model in Milanese learning disability services.

4 Supporting People with Learning Disabilities: Tracing the Development of Service Principles in London and Milan

Having identified important trends in research and the methodology adopted, the development of accepted service principles in both London and Milan needs to be outlined. This provides context for discussing differences between the experiences of the service users and staff taking part in the study, and describes the main influences which inform the services in each region.

In the case of London, and central to any debate about the model of 'ordinary life' for people with learning disabilities, the development and principles of normalisation will be outlined.

For the Milanese services, a key influence on the approach to learning disability is the development of psychiatric services in Northern Italy, and an account is included here.

(A) Service principles in London

Normalisation as implemented in Britain informs the services studied in London, and needs to be understood when regarding the impact that the approach can have on both people with learning disabilities and those providing the services they use. This chapter presents the Scandinavian origins of the approach, as well as the later American and British developments. Normalisation will then be placed within the frameworks of stigmatisation and integration theories, to look at the implications that it might have on the self-esteem and self respect of people with learning disabilities.

The Scandinavian origins

According to Emerson (1992), the principles of normalisation have their roots in Denmark's Mental Retardation Act of 1959, where the aim was to:

> create an existence for the mentally retarded as close to normal living conditions as possible (Bank-Mikkelsen, 1980).

This was later extended to include the objective of "making normal" housing, education, work and leisure, underpinned with a wish to establish equality of human and legal rights for all citizens. These early assertions resulted in major developments within learning disability services throughout the 1960's, both in Denmark and Sweden , where the aim became: "making available to all mentally retarded people patterns of life and conditions of everyday living which are as close as possible to the regular circumstances and ways of life of society" (Nirje 1980).

These statements appear quite reasonable: services need to increase and/or enhance the lifestyles of people with learning disabilities by "reproducing the lifestyle experienced by non-disabled citizens" (Emerson 1993). Nirje suggests that in practice, this requires enabling service users to experience the "norms" of everyday life:

1. The rhythm of the day - times for waking, dressing and eating.
2. The rhythm of the week - differentiating between weekdays and weekends.
3. The rhythm of the year - for example going on holiday.
4. Progressing through stages of the life cycle - experiencing the expectations of old age and childhood.
5. The development of heterosexual(sic) relationships, including the right to marry.
6. Economic standards - having appropriate access to benefits and fair wages.
7. Environmental standards - be it in workshops or in residential settings.

These criteria have implications if service providers are to accept them as being the benchmarks of good practice. Greater discussion will follow regarding some of the main arguments, but an initial observation is that the rigidity suggested by defining what is and isn't a normative lifestyle fails to take into account individual needs and characteristics. Culture is not addressed, neither is homosexuality, while it is unclear as to who or what determines the expectations at particular stages in a person's life. Self-determination - or support to explore the possibilities of informing the nature of one's own lifestyle - does not appear to be an option for those with learning disabilities, and as importantly, it is implied that those without disabilities uniformly contribute to these norms without exception.

The Scandinavian approaches, then, have three main areas of consensus: both make statements about "rights", equality is seen within the framework of quality of life and the issue of segregation with service design i.e. the need to close institutional accommodation and integrate people with the local community is not addressed specifically. Normalisation from the Scandinavian perspective is concerned with how learning disability services can reflect the basic rights of service users within an egalitarian society (Emerson 1992). It is important also to note that at no stage do the Scandinavian definitions refer to integration with society: only integration for those with severe disabilities with those with mild or moderate disabilities is considered, implying that it was thought that full integration with the non-disabled is not a requirement of equality.

It is important to reflect that while with hindsight normalisation can be criticised for its shortcomings and judgmental qualities, its advocates during the early stages of its development were working for an agenda of change, from a system of repressive, often abusive provision, to a system which they wanted to mirror the more liberal trends that were becoming more prevalent in western societies. The needs of some disadvantaged groups, who were perhaps more vocal than people with learning disabilities, were starting to be addressed. Normalisation did not evolve in isolation, developing in an atmosphere of growing awareness of a need for change.

The American development: Wolfensberger's definition

Three main influences are can be seen as providing an environment leading to widespread development of the principles of normalisation in the U.S.A. Firstly, the great decrease in the number of psychiatric patients living in state and county institutions which quickened during the 1950's (Brown 1985). Secondly, and linked with this, the rise of civil rights activism, which led to the acceptance in Federal courts of the rights of psychiatric patients to expect treatment within the "least restrictive alternative" (Castellani 1987). Thirdly, the often cited speech made by J.F.Kennedy in 1963 , here quoted from Scheerenberger 1983, is widely considered to have been influential:

> ...[we have a duty to] to bestow the full benefits of our society on those who suffer from mental disabilities...[and] ...to retain in and return to the community

the mentally ill and mentally retarded, and there to restore and revitalise their lives.

It is a fairly small step from this position to one where Wolfensberger (1972), who is now usually credited with developing the approach, was able to take the ideas from Scandinavia a stage further. His central definition of normalisation is the

> utilisation of means which are as culturally normative as possible, in order to establish and/or maintain personal behaviours and characteristics which are as culturally normative as possible.

Emerson (1992) observes that Wolfensberger has initiated two important changes to the approach. Firstly, there is a reference to the way in which society views and represents people with disabilities and other disadvantaged groups, while secondly, there is an emphasis on "socially valued roles" rather than

> culturally normative practices" (e.g. Wolfensberger & Thomas 1983). This later development led to the later renaming of normalisation by Wolfensberger as "social role valorisation (Wolfensberger 1983a, 1984).

As the principles of normalisation have such a central role in the present study, it seems appropriate to examine the seven main tenets or "themes" in detail.

Normalisation: Theoretical foundation

1. *The latent power of society*
Wolfensberger talks at length about social "intent", particularly with reference to the ability of social policy to target and undermine disadvantaged groups. It was his aim, therefore to raise this awareness in professionals working in personal social services

> [society has] made an identity alliance with death and...[is] working feverishly toward the destruction of life on this planet...[as reflected]...in a very well hidden policy of genocidal destruction of certain of its rejected and unwanted classes... Once a society has made a decision (explicated or not) to come down hard on a devalued minority group, it will transact this decision throughout whatever technical measures it may take toward this group, even those measures that are interpreted as being to the latter's benefit (Wolfensberger 1987:141).

2. *"Sociologizing" Normalisation: role expectancy and role circularity*

This refers to the links that Wolfensberger made with sociological theory during the 1960's and 1970's. Societal reaction or labelling theory was suggesting that so-called "deviant" groups, which includes people with disabilities, were greatly affected by the ways in which society reacted to them, to the extent that their behaviour and characteristics are largely determined by the labelling process, rather than by any psychological or biological factors that may have been originally behind the labelling. Ideas from authors such as Lemert (1967) and Davies (1975) were incorporated by Wolfensberger, resulting in his assertion that being described by society in a particular way will lead to the individual fulfilling the expectations that inevitably accompany those expectations. These Wolfensberger referred to as "self-fulfilling prophecies" (1972), continuing later to say that the phenomenon is one of the:

> most powerful social influence and control methods known... [and consequently]... these role expectancies have had predictably negative effects, i.e. devalued people by and large live up (or down) to these role expectancies, acting like animals or menaces (Wolfensberger & Thomas, 1983).

One of the reasons for conducting the present study is the concern that while there may be criticisms to be laid at the door of the approach's main proponents, it is during the interpretation process by service providers that the greater impact is felt by people with learning disabilities. Wolfensberger himself remarks that:

> overzealous proponents [of normalisation] are commonly guilty of the assumption that handicapped people are not handicapped, that retarded people are not retarded, and that every handicapped person could do and be almost anything if only provided with sufficient role expectancy and opportunity (Wolfensberger, 1980).

3. *The "conservatism corollary"*

This refers to the situation where the behaviours and characteristics of a devalued person - for example a person with learning disabilities - are under greater scrutiny by society by virtue of the fact that s/he has that devalued role. What might be considered an idiosyncrasy in a person belonging to a valued group in society would be emphasised and underlined as being an indication of subversion or abnormality in a devalued person. Services are therefore encouraged to almost overcompensate in some ways, trying to encourage behaviours and lifestyles which are highly valued, rather than just acceptable.

4. *Personal competency and development*

Building on the Scandinavian view that all human beings have the ability to grow and develop, Wolfensberger focused on personal competency, emphasising the role of developing valued characteristics and decreasing devalued behaviours. In practice, seen in many forms of service provision where normalisation has strong influence, this results in a concerted effort to teach service users the technical and social skills necessary to attain these acceptable standards.

5. *Role model learning*

One of the main underpinnings supporting the practice of integration, Wolfensberger and Thomas suggest that "imitation is one of the most powerful learning mechanisms known". This again links with societal reaction theory (see point 2 above).

6. *The role of "social imagery"*

Here Wolfensberger & Thomas refer to the "unconscious" power of images of deviant groups, particularly in the media, which both convey and then reinforce cultural stereotypes.

7. *Personal social integration and social devaluation*

Here lies one of the most central assertions of the approach, and probably the most heuristic in terms of the present study. It is best illustrated by way of a direct quotation from Wolfensberger & Thomas (1983):

> ...normalisation requires that, to the highest degree and in as many areas of life as feasible, a (devalued) person or group have the opportunity to be personally integrated into the valued life of society. This means that as much as possible, (devalued) people would be enabled to: live in normative housing within the valued community, and with (not just near to) valued people; be educated with their non-devalued peers; work in the same facilities as ordinary people; and be involved in a positive fashion in worship, recreation, shopping, and all the other activities in which members of society engage.

This builds on two concerns outlined previously: that devalued people need to be given the necessary support to acquire socially valued behaviours and traits, acquired through the processes of imitation and by experiencing "normative role expectancies", and that an environment is needed where social stereotypes can be directly challenged.

The British development: O'Brien's five accomplishments

The climate became right for the acceptance of normalisation in Britain in a similar way to events leading up to its establishment in North America. A series of scandals provoking investigations into living conditions in a number of long stay institutions enabled normalisation to influence the design of new service provision, as well as the modification of existing institutions. During the 1970's and 1980's, many organisations (e.g. Campaign for Mentally Handicapped People 1984; the King's Fund Centre 1980) and researchers (e.g. Tyne 1987; O'Brien & Tyne 1981) provided strong support for the approach's acceptance by those working with the learning disabled community.

Contemporary interpretations of normalisation in Britain tend to use O'Brien's (e.g. 1987) five service accomplishments to inform services:

1. **Community presence** - ensuring that service users are present in the same parts of the community as people without disabilities, be it at work or in recreational activity.
2. **Choice** - supporting people in making choices about their lives in as many areas and including as many issues as possible.
3. **Competence** - encouraging the development of skills and abilities that are meaningful to the immediate culture, skills which decrease a person's dependency and are valued by non-disabled people .
4. **Respect** - increasing the respect given to service users by other members of the community by ensuring that the lifestyles of people with learning disabilities encourage a positive image to be conveyed to others. This might refer to the clothes that people wear, the places they go to and the way that support staff talk to service users.
5. **Participation** - supporting people with learning disabilities in sustaining relationships with members of their family, as well as forming new relationships with others.

O'Brien's requirements of a learning disability service are only different from the writings of Wolfensberger in that they omit the references to sociological theory. Instead, O'Brien concentrates on defining normalisation in terms of quality of life and lifestyle, and for Emerson (1992), returns to the essence of the approach as set out by the Scandinavian writers Nirje and Bank-Mikkelsen.

The Implications of Normalisation: Contemporary analyses

With the principles of normalisation now firmly established, it is possible to consider how recent writers have reacted to its central ideas, particularly as in the middle of the 1990's, providers and academic observers are beginning to understand some of the impact that the approach is having on the daily lives of people with learning disabilities. Useful and relevant material for the present study centre around the critique forwarded by Szivos (1992), who is interested in the impact that normalisation has on the self-esteem and self-image of people with learning disabilities.

Self- image and self-esteem

Szivos begins her analysis by noting that words tend to have two meanings, one descriptive and the other emotive (Stevenson 1944). Known as "persuasive definition", words with positive emotive connotations can lead to the assumption that what is being referred to is inherently "good".

An example that Szivos refers to are "deinstitutionalisation", the inherent, emotive meaning being 'the provision of better services' while research suggests that it takes more to provide an appropriate service than a change of physical environment e.g. Bercovici (1981).

'Community' now suggests a "socio-political-geographical area" and a "friendship" network. And has come to imply a more positive place to be compared with an institution. Indeed 'Care in the Community' has become so widely used as to have lost much of its meaning. The danger for Szivos is that these two meanings become indistinct, with the former implying the latter.

Szivos' central argument against the benefits of normalisation settle around her ideas about integration and its effects upon the individual's social and psychological processes. Beginning with a debate on mainstreaming in schools, Szivos cites the work of Gresham (1982), who believes that the approach is inappropriate because it fails to achieve the objectives which advocates of mainstreaming claim are major benefits:

1. Those who are pro-mainstreaming argue that the practice increases interaction between disabled and non-disabled pupils: Gresham claims that research shows this not to be the case.

2. It is argued that placing disabled children in mainstream schools increases their acceptance by non-disabled children: Gresham suggests that the disabled need to learn the social skills needed to elicit that kind of response from non-disabled children. There is a danger, the author argues,

that the failure of this situation can lead to social isolation, perhaps even leading to being placed in a more restrictive environment.

3. Lastly, Gresham refutes the suggestion that disabled children learn from the modelling of appropriate behaviour by non-disabled children.

Using Gresham's writings, Szivos (1992) questions the degree of importance that Wolfensberger affords the role of modelling; while she agrees that it is an important learning tool, she suggests that "deviant" behaviour could arise for different reasons - reduced opportunities for people with learning disabilities to interact with others, for example. More importantly, Szivos observes that people with learning disabilities find learning in unstructured ways difficult, the very method of learning which needs to happen if people are to learn by modelling behaviour.

While acknowledging the value of people with and people without disabilities to interact with each other, such activity in itself can not be relied upon to either enhance the disabled person's quality of life or indeed lead to an increase in culturally valued behaviour. Additional support would almost certainly be necessary before any of the claims that Wolfensberger makes about such practice can be justified.

Szivos (1992) contributes to this debate with regard to self-esteem and people with learning disabilities:

> There is also a hidden assumption that dispersal of people with disabilities within the community will raise their self-esteem by enabling them to feel better, more valued or more "normal" about themselves. Although Wolfensberger does not mention self-esteem (Briton 1979), without some such reference to subjective self-experience normalisation sounds hollow.

Szivos continues:

> ...O'Brien's (1981, 1987) accomplishment "respect" is supposed to include self-respect and self-esteem. However, social comparison theory (Festinger 1954) implies quite strongly that there are psychological processes which might make people with disabilities who have been dispersed feel considerably worse about themselves.

The role of social comparison theory

Festinger's argument is central here, and warrants further discussion. The main assertion is that human beings develop in a social environment and tend to evaluate their own performance and competence with respect to that of others, usually selecting those who display similar levels of ability or experience. Szivos suggests that this is mainly due to the fact that it is often difficult to compare oneself with those who are too different. This results in our interactions tending to arise with people whom we perceive to be quite similar to ourselves, particularly if the context of the situation is perceived to be stressful (Cottrell & Epley 1977).

For people with learning disabilities, a stressful situation could quite easily be one in which there is interaction with non-disabled people (e.g. Levine 1985). Szivos therefore applies this idea by suggesting that:

> ...people with disabilities in an integrated setting may find themselves in a situation in which a large proportion of the social comparisons they make will merely serve to confirm in them a sense of inferiority.

Szivos supports this again with evidence from the literature. Studies by Coleman (1983), Gibbons (1985) and Oliver (1986) all suggest that people with learning disabilities have the ability to compare themselves with others, and indeed do so.

Adding weight to this argument one can refer again to Szivos (1989), where she claims that the experience of stigma needs to be linked with the act of viewing oneself as inferior when compared to significant others in the environment, rather than with the nature of the physical environment as has been thought in the past. The practice of integration is not being condemned altogether, rather it is the *priority* it is afforded by Wolfensberger (1972) that is being questioned.

Szivos concludes in her references to stigmatisation that normalisation has the inherent danger of 'denying difference' (p127), thereby encouraging the constant pressure on service users to aspire to a more acceptable level of functioning, in many ways dangerously and insultingly veiling the nature and extent of their disability. Szivos suggests that service providers need to cease asking whether or not an individual's behaviours conform to a pre-determined list of "social norms", and concentrate instead on thinking of ways in which the offered service is (or more importantly, isn't) encouraging the development and support of self-esteem.

It is the argument here that even if an individual **does** want to learn skills and behaviours that are considered to be "valued" for whatever reason, their ability to acquire that skill or behaviour will be somewhat impeded by feelings of insecurity or low self-worth. Effective learning can only really arise from confidence in one's own performance, and surely it is a priority for service provision to instil in people with learning disabilities a sense of security and safety, from which individuals feel able to develop at an individual pace.

If the definitions of normalisation as outlined above are studied in conjunction with an understanding of the ways in which staff are trained and supported in the implementation of the approach, the nature of the impact on individuals can be surmised to an even greater extent. This is the intention behind a discussion of training programmes detailed later in this study (see Chapters 9 and 10), where comparisons are made between training available in Milan and that commonly observed in British services.

(B) Service principles in Milan

The staying power of normalisation could be said to result from the lack of clarity over implementation, as well as the emotive dimension of debate about 'socially valued roles' for vulnerable people. Normalisation owes much to the opportunities arising from the reluctance to challenge what to many appears an equitable model of support. The approach has therefore acquired strength through the vacillation of service providers and other stakeholders.

It is suggested here that the ideology developed by Italian mental health services had a major impact on the ways in which community-based services for all groups of deinstitutionalised people have been developed in the north of Italy, and helps to differentiate further between the services selected for comparison in this study.

The approach to learning disability adopted in Northern Italy has its roots in the history of psychiatric services, which acquired strength through the very different process of conflict. This is an important contribution towards understanding differences between outcomes in the two services.

Basaglia and beyond: The development of psychiatric services in Northern Italy and their impact upon the approach to learning disability

The intention is not to consider the developments in Italian psychiatry in terms of their impact on mental health services, which has been explored elsewhere (e.g. Ramon 1981). It is the ways in which such developments have impacted upon and informed learning disability services which needs to be considered.

Italian psychiatry: A brief historical perspective

The unification of Italy brought with it many changes, one of which was the growth of the asylum system for the insane. Between 1875 and 1914 the number of institutions increased from 43 to 152, while the number of inmates grew from 13,000 to 54,000, peaking in the 1960's (Canosa 1979). The development of the asylum system contributed significantly to the professionalisation of psychiatry, which up to this point had been the bastion of asylum workers whose expertise comprised the more practical aspects of daily life in the institution, rather than familiarity with the medical model of mental illness.

A general focus on the medical model in Italian psychiatry became the aim of groups of psychiatrists in Milan and Reggio Emilia, which wanted to elevate the status of members of their profession as well as widen the extent of its influence (e.g. De Peri 1984). Proponents of these developments felt that they were contributing in an important way to the *Risorgimento*, or unification, in a moral as well as a professional way. Donnelly (1992) describes the approach taken at this point as positivist and organicist in orientation, following the concurrent trends in Italian pathology as set by anatomists such as Valsalva and Morgagni.

It could be said that psychiatrists were trying to surmount what they saw as the handicap of their historical roots, overshadowing their grounding in the pragmatic aspects of asylum-keeping with a concentration on and allegiance to anatomy and physiology. This orientation was adopted at the exclusion of all others.

In practice, psychiatry was able to connect with other disciplines, despite its rather conservative foundation. The use of clinical observation meant that the literature from the realms of anthropology and evolutionary biology could also be drawn upon, signalling a link between the rigidity of the medical model and the human and social sciences. In fact, what had at first been considered a handicap became an important advantage: psychiatrists, with their experience of practice in the asylums combined with the respect afforded to them by adoption of the positivist approach, were able to communicate with the wider scientific community with regard to aspects of the applied human and social sciences. At this early stage, the seeds of the eclectic, multi-disciplinary approach as observed in Milanese learning disability services was planted. Attracting public interest in their activities led to the conclusion that psychiatry was becoming:

> a discipline which was leaving behind the restricted confines of the asylum to include within its proper scientific ambit anthropology, forensic medicine, the law and social science (De Peri, 1984).

The impact of the *Risorgimento* again has to be considered here, as there was great concern that many problems were being presented by the fact that the total Italian population now comprised a variety of cultures. Psychiatrists and anthropologists became key figures in the development of a unified nation. The phenomenon of quasi-racial thinking (Donnelly 1992) became prevalent as a means of explaining the perceived differences in regional development, and incidents involving the insane, criminals and those with learning disabilities were liable to be explained in biological rather than social terms.

Early legislation

The first national legislation was enacted in 1904, calling for improvements in living conditions in asylums. Psychiatrists had been campaigning for the introduction of standards comparable to hospitals, but really only achieved the full recognition of their profession. In practice, the law concerned the role of asylums in protecting the public from the insane, and the admission of a need for the setting of general standards. Public safety was deemed of paramount importance, with all mental disorders treated uniformly if they were considered a threat to the welfare of the community at large: the law focused then on dangerous social behaviours, rather than on illness.

In 1909, further regulations explicitly addressed the conditions within institutions, including overcrowding, sanitation and the qualities to be borne in mind when recruiting members of staff. Progressive developments included the training of staff in both practice and theory and improvements in the care of inmates - work therapy was introduced (*ergoterapia*), restraints were largely abolished and those who were not self-injurious or dangerous to others were provided with separate accommodation.

Sadly, these regulations were at best implemented in a piecemeal fashion. As with other European nations embroiled in the chaos of the industrial revolution, asylums became something comparable to welfare institutions, housing those with learning disabilities and older people unable to work, as well as the insane.

Despite often vehement criticism, the 1904 law remained effective until 1968. Although many of its tenets were no longer adhered to in terms of restricting inmates, it was in effect still legally binding and symbolic of the distance that existed between those certified mad and the rest of society.

The winds of change: the 1960's and 'alternative' psychiatry

The psychiatric profession became increasingly aware towards the middle of this century of the extent to which Italian services had lagged behind the developments observed in the USA and Britain, as well as the incongruity of the situation when placed in the context of the fast-moving Italian economy and society. Italian practitioners compared the outdated 1904 legislation with the perceived progressiveness of the 1959 Mental Health Act in the UK and the proposal for community mental health centres in the USA in 1963. Frustration with the Italian system had been mounting due to previous failures to modernise the 1904 Act in both 1951 and 1953, which had attempted to shift the focus of mental health services from prioritising public security to identifying medical need (*Centro nazionale di prevenzione e difesa sociale 1956,* cited in Donnelly 1992).

A major turning point was the conference organised in 1964 titled *'Processo al manicomio'* ('The asylum on trial'). A number of participants called for the modernisation of mental health services, but in practice results were rather disappointing; many of those voting on the motions proved to be conservative in their outlook, and were unwilling to recommend national initiatives.

The positive outcome of the conference was the germination of ideas concerning local projects, which were adopted by some of the more radical psychiatrists. This development of pilot schemes led to the 'alternative' psychiatry that made the all important break from traditional approaches to service provision. Such progressive thinking was not peculiar to Italy alone - other nations were experiencing similar situations - but the difference here is that the initiatives were concentrated on public schemes, rather than on private schemes such as in Britain (Kingsley Hall as supported by Laing for example).

Perhaps the most famous and heuristic of the local initiatives took place at Gorizia under the direction of Basaglia in 1961. The group working at Gorizia had no model for guidance in their attempts at reform, and acquired the majority of their ideas from abroad, but it is generally recognised that certain important aspects of the work carried out to change the conditions at Gorizia were original (Donnelly 1992). First, straightforward practical changes were made to create the look and feel of an 'open' hospital - patients were given cupboards for personal belongings and were allowed to wear ordinary clothing; the use of E.C.T. was suspended. Such changes led to a feeling of alienation in support staff, who felt undermined by the new ways of thinking instigated by the psychiatrists; this in turn led to the psychiatrists spending more time on the wards, helping to create more unity in the team and to ensure that all were supportive of the changed environment.

It is important here to consider the theoretical orientation of Basaglia: although there is great reluctance in ascribing major shifts in thinking to individuals, his influence on support services in Italy is significant, providing a major contribution to current approaches. A trained medic, Basaglia became influenced by phenomenology and existential psychiatry, the only real alternative to the dominating bio-determinism. The significant aspect of the approach is the way in which it values the patient's subjectivity while requiring staff to be 'among' the people they are supporting, which at that time was rare. Basaglia wanted to know the inmates of the hospital as individuals rather than as patients, attempting to understand their subjective world rather than seeing them in accordance with sets of objective diagnostic criteria. In order to do this, Basaglia argued, it is necessary to 'place in brackets' the person's diagnosis, 'since that diagnostic label hung fixedly on the patient like a performed value judgement' (Basaglia 1968, cited in Donnelly 1992). This approach is prevalent in present day learning disability services (Cassaro 1994), but is not to be confused with the denial of a person's disability or illness - an accusation that has been made of Basaglia's work. Further resonance is found in contemporary services administered by the *Comune di Milano* for people with learning disabilities when Basaglia (1968) talks about the importance of assessing an individual's *situation* as well as their disability or illness:

> It is not that we leave out of consideration the illness...it is necessary to establish [a relationship with the person] independently of the label by which the individual is defined...What is important is to become aware of who is this individual for me, in what social reality he is living, and what his relation is to that reality.

Although the adoption of the phenomenological existential approach proved difficult pragmatically, its influence spread from Gorizia to other 'alternative' psychiatry projects. This development is central to present day thinking, its influence being two-fold: phenomenology provided a rationale for interacting directly with the service user, for valuing his/her subjectivity and for viewing him/her as existing in a social world. Secondly, advocates of the 'alternative' approach saw it as providing a foundation from which to criticise the traditional positivist view of psychiatry, which they saw as upholding and justifying the poor conditions in institutions.

The beginnings of the therapeutic community in Northern Italy

Basaglia initiated a technique which aimed to bring together both staff and residents in the institutions. Referred to as 'group assemblies' (Donnelly

1992), the practice offered for a which discussed problems and difficulties of daily life as well as providing opportunities for the discussion of individuals' personal experiences and past lives. This helped to focus attention on the damage caused by the environment of the institution *per se*, an approach taken from the Britain and the USA. From this, Basaglia again looked to Britain and the experience of therapeutic communities, but altered the focus in a key way. In Britain, therapeutic communities tended to look at the interaction on the ward, taking the energy produced from existing dynamics and channelling it into therapeutic work. It was seen as humanistic and communal. Basaglia took this concept and changed the focus: while accepting that the therapeutic community was a place for all - staff and residents alike - it was the *conflict* between individuals rather than the union and consensus that was seen to be therapeutic (Basaglia 1968). The permissiveness seen in the Italian system highlighted the anomalies within the institutional system, as well as criticising the British system for not taking the concept far enough: if the institutions became 'humanised', why were people still excluded from society? Basaglia wanted to extend the idea of conflict arising from the meeting of the supported and the supporters into the wider community and society itself.

Perhaps here a central difference between approaches in the two countries can be seen in its early developmental stages. While in Britain, the coming together of staff and residents is intended to provide a therapeutic atmosphere which focuses on the needs and adaptability of the individual service user, the model as developed by Basaglia and his supporters, which is prevalent in Milanese learning disability services at the time of writing, views the coming together of service users and service providers as a milieu which enables the *system* to be scrutinised in preference to the individual. Taken to its logical conclusion, this means the scrutiny of society at large, rather than expectations for change and adaptability being placed upon service users.

Castel (1971) refers to the 'contradictions' within society - namely, that asylums were established and justified in order to conceal the conflicts between society and its deviants.

Other experiments (e.g. that in Reggio Emilia in the mid-1970's) built upon the experiences acquired at Gorizia, becoming therapeutically eclectic so as not to become confined to one approach, as well as ensuring that individual situations could be addressed using the widest array of resources available. Again, it is important here to recognise the beginnings of the present Milanese approach to needs assessment and service provision:

The model of intervention was more like a collective politics than individual therapy. It was typical for the team to try to collect together a whole set of people who were part of a 'situation', including, for instance, a whole family but also neighbours and relatives, or teachers and local government officials. The style of intervention with such assembled groups was rather low-key, a matter of trying to link the given problems at hand with the characteristic problems of everyday life in similar social milieux (Donnelly, 1992:50).

As with any radical change in human services, the approach met with opposition and considerable difficulty. Shifts in both local and national political climates led to instability, and public opinion of the permissive approach was still low. However, the central message remained - individuals could be assessed in the community, and services could be introduced to meet individual needs, although scepticism became accelerated when the approach was applied to people perceived as posing a threat to public welfare.

Confronting society: The role of activism in the development of community based services in Northern Italy

For Donnelly (1992), Basaglia's pioneering work is full of contradictions: while condemning the existence of the institution, it was not completely abandoned, and although an individual's illness or disability was placed in brackets, its presence was never denied. After the 'experiments' of Gorizia and Reggio Emilia, Basaglia wanted to generalise the ideas that his team had developed; this he achieved by writing in terms of exclusion and segregation. Using Sartre social psychology, Basaglia was interested in thinking about the processes involved in developing the roles of psychiatrist and madman, and the role played by society in the formation of those roles. The interpersonal dynamics of psychiatrist and inmate were played out in the asylum, but for Basaglia, had been pre-programmed by society. The person's individuality is subsumed by the label of mental patient, so that the public is not required to confront him or her in every day life (Basaglia 1973). The conclusion drawn from the work at Gorizia was that:

> society had to be brought into collision with the problems it had tried to lock away in the asylum (Mollica, 1985).

The idea here was not to encourage the general public to sympathise with those with mental illness or learning disability, but to condemn the very existence of the category 'mental patient':

...only when the problem [of the mental patient] has become part of the experience of each and every one of us, will society feel obliged to come up with real solutions through the establishment of truly therapeutic measures (Basaglia, 1973).

Democratic psychiatry

The tension that had appeared in Britain and the USA concerning the appropriateness of organic or social models of mental illness led to a split between the two factions which is present today, still resulting in a tendency to oversimplify both stances. This division did not occur in Italy, although there was, however, a split within psychiatry itself, with those advocating social treatments speaking out against the more traditional medical model supporters. In 1973, both sides were beginning to reach something of a *rapprochement,* and the psychiatry movement eventually published its manifesto.

The aims of democratic psychiatry: A pledge for the support of vulnerable people

The manifesto clearly describes the principles of any service which focuses on the support of vulnerable people, be they those with mental health problems, children or people with physical and/or learning disabilities:

- The stress is on 'interventions' in the normal environment - where people are living and working.
- The needs of service users hold priority over organizational or bureaucratic concerns.
- *People* are to be treated, not illnesses or diagnoses.
- The aim of social assistance is to meet the needs of ordinary people - workers are to fight against the stigma of seeking for assistance.
- People in need of support have a right to that support in a way which does not interfere with or disrupt their daily lives.
- Service users have a right to treatment which respects and enhances their normal functioning.[1]

---

[1] It is important to note that this in an acceptance of what is normal *for that person,* rather than any comparison with socially defined norms (cf. normalisation in Britain).

The implications of developments in the Italian psychiatric system for learning disability services: the main signs of influence

1. The first issue to consider here is the similarities between the thinking behind both the psychiatric services and learning disability services in Northern Italy. Both groups of people are considered as individuals whose lives are multi-dimensional and therefore require multi-disciplinary interventions. Those interventions are introduced in the person's own environment in a way which respects their level of functioning and capability as a potential in its own right and not linked with any notional social norm.

    The survival of the dual framework approach - medical and social models appear to co-exist without conflict- has seemed to strengthen and further justify the ways in which individual programme plans devise a programme with a heavy emphasis on social and psychological development and enhancement from the starting point of a medical diagnosis.

2. The eclecticism of the approach to mental illness also laid foundation for learning disability services; although this had stemmed from a reluctance to become too tied to any one ideology, it proved to be successful and gained in credibility as an holistic rather than just a cautious methodology.

3. Local initiatives such as those carried out at Gorizia were very much in the realms of experimentation, but that tradition appears to have transferred in to learning disability services. Examples of community experiments currently underway include an educational scheme which is encouraging people with learning disabilities to run workshops for school children, hoping to increase awareness at a young age and thus enhance acceptance of the learning disabled by the rest of society as a result of early intervention. A second scheme is an advertising project calling for volunteers on the local television and radio network, as a means of providing extra trained support. This is thought to help address difficulties over the issue of the imbalance of power that inevitably accompanies relationships between paid staff and service users.

4. The adoption of a phenomenological approach to support services as initiated by mental health services appears to have been transported directly into learning disability services, perhaps as many of the key issues are similar: people have a personal perspective on their world,

which will be influenced by a number of important and individual factors. Both mental health and learning disability services emphasise that their task is to assist vulnerable people in making sense of those perceptions.

Current learning disability services in Milan: Main structures

The political and cultural jump that transformed the Italian welfare state began in 1978, with the enactment of National Law 833: together with the Regional Law of 1980 (No. 76) and of 1986 (No.1), it attributed the major role in health and social welfare provision to local authorities. This has been implemented in Milan in a variety of ways, one of which is the creation of a central office for the co-ordination of disability services. Responsibilities for this resource include the following:

1. The creation of programmes for service users across the area served by the *comune*, or local authority.
2. The development of relationships with other sectors of the *comune* - health services, private and voluntary services, who have interests or functions in the areas of disability.
3. The implementation of regional law, in terms of contacting and evaluating specific projects that serve the *comune* as part of the voluntary sector. Similar standards are set as demanded of statutory services.
4. Setting criteria for the admission and discharge of people using particular services, be they residential, respite or day-care services.
5. Overall management and administration of a disability service.

The Central Office strives to achieve the above tasks using specific structures, called *"unite operative"* or operational units. They include the Social Services Secretary - comparable to a Principal Officer in English Social Services; an officer for home care support; services for the deaf; transport services; Centres of Social Education (C.S.E.'s or day centres for people with learning disabilities) and holiday services; an officer for residential services; work and training services. Learning disability services are thus part of a comprehensive disability service, and individuals are referred to this generic service before being provided with services to specifically meet the needs of their learning disability. These specific services are outlined below.

Learning disability services: the C.S.E.

The Italian approach to disability is concerned with enhancing potential, and views an individual's "pathology" from biological, social and psychological standpoints simultaneously. All service users are deemed to require medical and social treatment: quality of life cannot be enhanced without "rehabilitation". Assessments reveal the functional abilities of each person, suggesting the appropriate services to be accessed. Work and training opportunities do exist, but are only considered for people with appropriate levels of functioning; it is readily accepted that for some service users, their level of disability means that "work" or indeed "training" are not meaningful, and therefore not offered. Instead, the C.S.E. (Centre for Social Education) provides for those who have completed 14 years of obligatory education. The main aim of time spent at the C.S.E. is development and enhancement of ability using socialisation and education. Three main levels of disability are recognised by organisers of the C.S.E.:

1. Potentially independent - be the impairment sensory, motor, psychomotor, psychological or a combination of all of these.
2. Potentially secondary damage - autonomy and independence are impeded.
3. Total dependence, or third level damage - this could derive from birth complications, multiple pathologies or progressive pathologies.

Development for each person attending the C.S.E. is monitored annually, at the beginning of each Social Year, which runs from September to July in a similar way to the British academic year. The team of professionals working at the centre meet and produce an individual programme for each centre user, which establishes the person's level of potential and development in all areas, and the corresponding appropriate level of social integration - which itself is very much deemed to be linked with the individual's ability to respond to and benefit from experience of and exposure to the wider community.

Centre managers are responsible for the implementation of the individual programmes, and assess the professional involved regularly. The team itself consists of the following:

1. The *educatori* - support workers in direct contact with service users.
2. A social worker - supporting the *educatori* in implementing the programme.

3. The *fisiatra* - a general practitioner with a learning disability specialism, who assesses the social, biological and psychological nature of the specific disability or pathology, gives a diagnosis and prognosis and lays the foundation for a programme of rehabilitation.

   It seems appropriate to note here that the central role afforded the *fisiatra* perhaps indicates that while learning disability services appear to adopt a multidisciplinary approach, its foundations can be identified as following a medical model in the main, although service providers maintain that ideas derived from the medical model are always placed within a wider context of the individual's personal social, psychological and experiential history, resulting in what could be described as an holistic model (Cassaro 1995). It is also important to realise that "rehabilitation" as used in this sense refers to an enhancement or fulfilment of potential, rather than any attempt to eradicate either the extent or the effects of the person's disability.

4. A **clinical psychologist** - who evaluates the psychological nature of the person's disability, looks at the familial environment and his or her other interpersonal relationships. A programme of psychotherapeutic rehabilitation arises from this. (Again, the definition of rehabilitation as outlined above is applied here.)

5. The *psychomotricistra* - perhaps comparable to the role of an occupational therapist in British services, also helps with a programme of rehabilitation, designing appropriate activities to fulfil and develop the person's potential.

6. A **rehabilitation therapist** applies the best available technique to enhance the person's neuromotor function, being aware of cognitive and psychological considerations.

The above list suggests much overlap of roles within the team, but all are deemed to have essential value by service managers (Mazzini 1994; Cassaro 1995). Perhaps the detailed description of each reflects the multi-faceted, "gestalt" approach taken by Italian services: each professional can only fulfil his or her role in conjunction with others, as working in isolation or considering only one discipline at a time does not result in constructing an accurate picture of the service user's potential.

The individual programme

The individual programme has specific aims:

i)   To enhance development and potential.
ii) To address any psychopathology that accompanies the disability, or indeed, exists independently of the disability.
iii) To reinforce development and avoid regression.
iv) To enhance self-esteem.
v)   To encourage acceptance of a person's pace of development and level of competence, both by the person and by other people in his/her life.
vi) To intervene in the "micro-social" environment
   •   by reducing feelings of guilt
   •   by reducing anxiety
   •   by addressing denial
   •   by resolving conflicts between and within the service user and members of his/her family that have arisen as a result of the person's disability.
vii) To encourage interaction with the community.

There is a great emphasis on the person's psychology and general mental health in relation to his/her self-perception and self-esteem. With no expectations in terms of a general level of independence - each person is encouraged to aim for a state of independence and pace of development that is pertinent to his or her specific level of ability - effort is placed on supporting people in viewing themselves positively.

This is a major departure from the principles underpinning services in Britain. Despite recent criticism from proponents of social comparison theory as advocated by Festinger (1954) (e.g. Szivos 1993), service managers are still briefed to encourage people with learning disabilities to integrate as fully as possible with the wider community, claiming that this is the most effective way of increasing self-esteem and self-worth.

In Milan, however, it is felt that acceptance both within and without the person, is of primary concern. Professionals are also involved routinely - their skills are applied as a matter of course, unlike in Britain. where a referral system is commonplace. This perhaps accentuates the vulnerability of the individual, contrasting with the British approach of identifying strengths - as well as needs - which can be nurtured and built upon to attain ever increasing levels of independence. The perception of the Milanese services, then, is of a drive to fully describe the nature of a person's disability and enable him or her to accept the related ability, rather than hide the true extent of the disability by completely abandoning the medical model.

In 1994, twenty C.S.E.'s were operating in Milan, providing a service for 363 people. Half of these centres were managed by private organisations on contracts from the *Comune* itself. The average worker to user ratio is 2:1, while service managers feel that the ideal ratio is 3:1 (Mazzini 1994).

Other services offered to people with learning disabilities by the Comune di Milano (Local Authority of Milan)

i   *Social services*

General social services are in charge of strategy in the field of disability, as well as more personal services, such as funding low-income families or providing in-home support. Social services also fund provision that the Health Service is unable to meet - this might include aids and adaptations or holidays.

ii   *Home help*

This provides support to enable people with learning disabilities to remain in their personal context - usually the familial environment - as this is felt to be essential for the maintenance of self-esteem and general well-being. These services are usually tendered by the *comune*, and are managed by organisations with expertise in the field of learning disability. The success of resettlement with services users' families is discussed elsewhere (see p206), but it is important to note here that support given at home is deemed to be far more appropriate than that provided in the form of a small group home and which is more commonly found in Britain.

iii   *Transport services*

As in many countries, public transport in Italy is not completely accessible, although since 1980, many initiatives have set out to address parking, transport planning and street layout issues. Taxis and networks of small buses equipped with tail lifts also operate, with a grant of L6,000 for each journey given by the *comune*. Again, service users are assessed according to their level of need, and allocated a specific number of "journeys" accordingly. Alternatively, money can be presented as petrol vouchers, enabling relatives and carers to escort service users to where they need to be.

Summary

The salient observation when comparing the development of normalisation in Britain with that of the community support model in Northern Italy is the *mode* of evolution in each case. Normalisation appears to have sneaked in the back door and quietly asserted its authority in an atmosphere which is unchallenging and offers no viable alternative - perhaps because the language used to describe the approach talks about respect and valued roles, resonating in the minds of many people. In contrast, the development of community services for vulnerable people in Northern Italy arose from debate and conflict, originating in psychiatric services, where splits among professionals forced services to confront and question their aims and objectives.

The legacy of this debate culture is a detailed legislative framework which not only sets out the purpose of learning disability services and other support frameworks in the community, but also details the role and responsibilities of those employed to implement policy. Such clear guidelines are not evident in British legislation, and the unquestioned prevalence of normalisation, or social role valorisation, is now clear.

Despite this strong divergence, there is one tenable point at which the approaches in London and Milan converge. In each case, services are delivered by means of a central plank, the analysis of which not only illustrates the ways in which staff are enabled to create individual support programmes, it also reveals and explains more about differences in the two models. These individual planning processes are designed in each case to help the service provide the support needed to meet the needs of the person with a learning disability, therefore having major implications for the way of life prescribed for individual service users. Such is their importance in understanding the implementation of policy, that detailed analysis of two systems, one in London and one in Milan have been conducted.

The next chapter provides an account of this analysis, with brief descriptions of the individual planning systems and their basic modus operandi.

5 Individual Planning in Learning Disability Services: Implementing Service Principles in London and Milan

Background: Individual planning in Britain

Individual programme planning has become widespread in British services for people with learning disabilities, having its origins in the USA during the early 1970s (O'Brien & Lovett 1992). It has been supported on the grounds that by using a three stage process of assessment, goal-setting and review, appropriate and individualised services can be provided with co-ordinated input from multidisciplinary sources (Blunden *et al* 1987; Mallinson *et al* 1995).

The Department of Health (1992) has advocated the widespread adoption of individual programme plans as a way of ensuring that service users are encouraged to access ordinary facilities in the community.

In practice, it has been noted that there exists a considerable lack of clarity as to the nature of effective assessment and planning (Greasley 1995), with many studies raising concerns regarding the ways in which individual programmes systems operate and the assumptions made (Sutcliffe & Simons 1993; de Kock *et al* 1985). These issues include a tendency to set 'service-related' rather than 'service user-related' goals (O'Brien & Lovett 1992); inadequate involvement and consultation of service users and carers in the process (Crocker 1990) and a tendency to focus on the person's needs rather than strengths (e.g. Wilcox & Bellamy 1987). This is the context within which the present research was conducted.

While a single service is studied here, its operation and objectives are characteristic of the majority, if not all of the individual planning services in Britain which are influenced by normalisation.

The key objectives were to:

- examine the extent to which the service's claims that the individual planning process is service user-led can be supported,

- explore the ways in which individual planning serves as a tool for implementing the main principles of the overall service for people with learning disabilities,

- compare the process with the individual planning service operating in Milan.

Background: Individual planning in Milan

The principles inherent in individual planning in Lombardia, Italy provide a clear contrast to practice in London. The Lombardian system is not built upon the principles of normalisation, despite evolving as a result of the deinstitutionalisation of people with learning disabilities and their consequent resettlement into the community (Cassaro 1995). The functional aspects of the Italian and British systems are comparable; both determine the strengths and needs of service users and set goals and tasks which form the individual programme, contributing both at the micro-level as well as to the overall planning of learning disability services.

A key difference is that service users are not involved in the Milanese process in the way that the London service aims to involve its service users. The comparison made therefore looks at policy and practice in the London case, and uses interview material with documentation to describe the approach in Milan . After each process has been described - and in the case of the London service, data summarised - the similarities and differences, along with their implications for understanding the underpinning models of support, can be discussed.

Evaluation and analysis of an individual planning service for people with learning disabilities in London

Introduction

The individual planning service operating in the London borough targeted for this study is called Life Planning. It aims to:

...make sure that we look at each person we work with as an individual with his or her own unique needs...the key individual...in the process is the person whose Life Plan it is. We should respect that person's views so that they can decide as far as possible how their lives should develop (from The Keyworker's Role in Life Plans: service training document 1992, p5).

Service users are told that:

A Life Plan is a way of helping you choose what you want in your life. Those close to you will find out what you want and what you need. Then they will plan with you what to do to help you (from Your Life Plan, Life Plan Project document 1992, p1).

These principles are here taken to represent the approach to the study and enhancement of quality of life for people with learning disabilities as discussed by Parmenter (1992), whose model suggests that the essential components of an acceptable quality of life are satisfaction, happiness and decision-making, along with increasing levels of empowerment. Involvement with, and in many cases, control of the decision-making process, is central to the Life Planning service.

The analysis here attempts to explore the extent to which Life Planning can enhance the quality of life for participants by interviewing keyworkers and involved family members, as well as the participants themselves. These data are supplemented with those obtained from participant observation of individual Life Plan meetings.

Evaluation and analysis design

The way in which the research was to be conducted was established in conjunction with the Life Planning team, which consists of a Life Plan Co-ordinator and two Life Plan workers. The research's aim as stated above was harmonious with that of the team, who wanted to look at how users of the service experience Life Planning, and explore ways of incorporating specific individual into the system.

The elements and procedures of Life Planning are detailed in the discussion of the system's history and function. In usual circumstances, there are three main components:

1. The "Pre-Life Plan" - during which the service user, Life Plan worker and keyworker discuss the organisation and content of the imminent Life Plan meeting.

2. The Life Plan meeting - attended by invited family and professionals, and based around the needs and goals of the service user, which are as far as possible generated and established by the service users themselves.

3. A follow-up period - during which all persons concerned work on the agreed tasks set out at the meeting.

It was agreed that one way of gaining some sense of what participants are experiencing would be to ask a series of questions to a random sample of people with learning disabilities living across the borough. Interviewing keyworkers and involved family members would add context to data obtained from service users (Schalock et al 1990).

The central role played by the Life Plan meeting itself was acknowledged, and participant observation was used to look at how, and to what extent, people with learning disabilities are involved in this important stage of the process, and whether or not the system could be said to be meeting its established objectives.

The relationships between participants in the process are represented in Figure 1.1, the pre-meeting, and in Figure 1.2, the meeting itself. Directional arrows show the ways in which input to the meeting is established, while dotted lines represent possible or partial sources of support for those concerned.

The interviews

(i) Service users

A total of 21 service users were involved in the service analysis, 10 men and 11 women. The local NHS trust manages accommodation for 12 of the service users, 6 live in local authority accommodation and 3 live with their families.

All participants were sent a letter requesting their consent to taking part in the study, assuring them of the degree of confidentiality adopted and the nature of their involvement.

Only 9 questions were devised in total, and covered important areas of the process ("Who makes decisions in your meeting?" and "Do people listen to what you say?") as well as the concepts of Life Planning ("Who is a Life Plan for?" and "What is a Life Plan?").

A full list of the questions asked are shown in Appendix 2.

Interviews were to be as unobtrusive as possible, taking place in the homes of service users during the scheduled "Pre-Life Plan" visits made by members of the Life Plan team.

Method

Service users were encouraged to choose a place within their house where the interview was to take place. In reality, keyworkers usually made suggestions, either because no choice was forthcoming from the service user or the nature of the situation required their intervention.

The researcher introduced himself and explained the nature of the interview. In theory, this would be the third explanation offered - the first given by the Life Plan team when the initial contact was made, and the second by the keyworker prior to the visit.

A similar technique was adopted as with the residential lifestyle questionnaires (see chapter seven). All of the questions were open-ended, and where alternatives were given, the order was altered and the question asked again to check for accuracy.

People with communication difficulties constitute a considerable proportion of the sample interviewed, and the techniques adopted here warrant separate consideration. Where possible, somebody who knows the service user well, apart from the keyworker, acted as an advocate - the intention being that they could speak frankly on behalf of the service user while being reassured that their responses would be treated with confidence. In practice, this did not always work, and in some cases the keyworker also assumed this role - either because of staff shortages or because there was no other member of staff available who knew the service user sufficiently well. In the majority of cases (but particularly when interviewing people with communication difficulties) a photograph album was used to prompt responses to questions and promote discussion about Life Planning generally. This album contains pictures of the Life Plan team working with service users, with representations of the service user being asked questions, and then saying what s/he wants to do. The scenes represented include people planning meetings and writing invitations; discussing the organisation of the meeting with a keyworker; people engaged in a meeting.

(ii) Keyworkers

The keyworker interviews were always conducted in the office or the staff sleepover quarters of the residential establishments involved in the study. The nature of the research was explained, as well as the confidentiality observed and the importance of honest responses. Questions aimed to obtain a sense of what the support staff understand by Life Planning ("What do you think are the aims of Life Planning?"), as well as how they feel it benefits their Key-client ("Who is Life Planning for?" and "Do you think the process is effective for [service user's name]?"). The research team were also interested in the keyworkers' perception of how service users are involved in the system, and how supported staff feel, both by management and by the Life Plan team.

(iii) Interviewing involved members of the family

Family members were involved in 8 out of the 21 Life Plan meetings used in the evaluation. Five agreed to be interviewed - this took place after the Life Plan meeting. It had been hoped to interview more relatives, but including older service users, as well as those whose families were either not involved or lived far away, made this very difficult.

Areas of interest which the questionnaire aimed to explore were the relatives' perceptions of the Life Plan process in terms of aims and objectives; the support they receive in participating and their opinions as to the effectiveness of the process.

Participant observation

The Life Plan team, view the Life Plan meeting itself as the central component of the process:

> Once you have thought about all the things you want and need in your life, you will have the chance to plan how to get them. This happens at a Life Plan meeting. You and the important people in your life decide:
>
> 1. What are the most important wants and needs you have now?
> 2. How you can be helped with them.
> 3. Who will help you.
> 4. When people will be able to help you.
>
> The decisions made will be written down by the person chairing the Life Plan meeting. (Disability Service publicity leaflet, 1994).

The Life Plan meeting is therefore an important time for data collection and observation, as once again control of, or involvement in, decision making is seen as quintessential to the enhancement of quality of life.

Method

Consent was requested for the observation of individual planning meetings, and the procedure and nature of the observation was discussed at the pre-Life Plan meeting, or interviewing stage.

Life Plan meetings take the following form:

1. Introductions : each participant introduces her/himself.
2. Reviewing of actions/tasks set at the previous meeting; the chair reads through each task set and the relevant named persons offer feedback on what has been accomplished.
3. A discussion of the service user's current health and lifestyle.
4. Establishing future actions/tasks, with the relevant persons agreeing and making a commitment to work with the service user in that area.
5. A final review of the meeting, establishing deadlines for the actions/tasks set.

The researcher's role and purpose was established before the introductions were made - this aimed to confirm that he was not a participant in the actual meeting, that he would not be contributing and was there solely to observe. Assurance was given that only the **nature** of the interactions and the service user's involvement is of interest, as opposed to the **content** of what is discussed. All participants were given the opportunity to ask questions once the meeting was over.

Recording

The following information was of interest:

(a) The total number of interactions.
(b) The frequency of interactions directed towards the service- user.
(c) The frequency of interactions between participants other than the service user, which discuss the service user and/or his/her behaviour.
(d) The length of the meeting.
(e) Significant non-verbal communication between participants.
(f) Obvious changes in the service user's behaviour - noting the topic of discussion at those points in the meeting.

(g) The nature of pauses in the proceedings - the extent to which service users are given time to think and/or speak.

(h) Other behaviours or events occurring in individual meetings which provide interesting anecdotal data.

A series of notation was developed to ensure accurate recording in what were very difficult and at times stressful circumstances.

The total group of service users was sub-divided to explore other themes:

(i) Social services and health authority residents.

(ii) Verbal and non-verbal service users.

(iii) Very high dependency users/users with profound disabilities and those regarded as having "moderate to mild" learning disabilities.

(iv) Those service users with a high number of professionals attending and those with predominantly immediate staff and/or family members attending.

As well as statistical findings, data of this sort provide opportunities for looking at how Life Planning addresses particular "traits" present in the sample.

For example:

• Are the topics discussed similar for older service users compared with younger service users?

• How are people with additional sensory disabilities involved in their meetings?

• Are some issues too sensitive to discuss at Life Plan meetings?

• If these issues are broached, how do participants react?

• Does this vary according to the user's ability in self-advocating?

Results

The data have been analysed by dividing the participating service users into two groups: those who speak for themselves (Group A) and those who need others to speak on their behalf (Group B).

The key finding from the observation data is that people needing others to speak on their behalf (Group B) were *excluded* from discussion in their meeting more frequently than they were *included*. In contrast, the service users who speak for themselves (Group A) were *included* more than they were *excluded*. Details of this finding can be found in Tables (i) and (ii).

Table (i): Average percentage of total interaction in meetings held by service users who speak for themselves.

	INTERACTION WITH PERSON		SPEAKING ABOUT THE PERSON	
	INITIATED BY SERVICE USER	DIRECTED AT SERVICE USER	PERSON EXCLUDED	REFERRED BACK
Person stayed in meeting throughout	25.5%	41.6%	16.7%	3.2%
Personal left for part of meeting	14.3%	34.3%	26.0%	3.5%

Table (ii): Average percentage of total interaction in meetings held by service users needing others to speak on their behalf

	INTERACTION WITH SERVICE USER	SPEAKING ABOUT THE SERVICE USER	
		PERSON EXCLUDED	REFERRED BACK
Person stayed in meeting throughout	27.0%	36.8%	5.2%

Individual planning and people who speak for themselves: An overview

It appears that in general, the individual planning process studied here works well for this group of people. They are involved in discussion to a fairly high degree (about 69% of the time) while just over half of those interviewed feel the meeting is there for their own use ("..to try and help me improve my life...get me involved in different things"). Most of the group (64.3%) felt comfortable in their meeting, with 28.6% feeling comfortable for some of the time. It should be noted, however, that those people who do feel uncomfortable with the issues discussed said they can find it difficult to say so at the meeting.

Half of this group were unclear as to the aims of individual planning meeting, saying they didn't know (28.6%) ("I haven't got the faintest idea") or that it is some kind of case conference where decisions are made (21.4%). Explanations about the process seem to be given mainly by support staff (71.4%) using a specially produced pack (35.7%) or simply sitting talking (64.3%) ("[They] sit down with me...like we are now"). Half of this group feel that they make decisions in their meetings, with decision-making also thought to be by staff (50 %) or people who the service user knows well (28.6%). The majority feel they have space to think during their meetings (78.4%), and are listened to (92.9%). While 57.2% of those interviewed think that things change after their meeting ("Some things do change"), 28.6% feel that things stay the same.

Individual planning and people needing others to speak on their behalf: An overview

The greatest contrast between interview and observation data can be seen with Group B. The majority of those advocating for this group feel that enough time and space is afforded service users during their meetings (85.7%), while the observation data suggests that this group of service users are excluded from discussion more than they are included. The majority of those advocating (71.4%) also said that they feel the process is for service users. Explanations are given verbally (71.4%) and to a lesser extent using physical prompts (28.6%), by members of staff (57.1%) or members of the IPP team (21.4%). Only 14.3% of those advocating feel that the service users in this group have any understanding of who or what the process is for ("It's a token gesture for the profounds"; "I don't think she knows what a Life Plan is for"). Most of the respondents report that decisions are made by staff (71.4%), while all of those interviewed think that the process is enjoyable for the service users taking part.

Speaking to staff, parents and carers

Staff are able to see the benefits of individual planning - for service users (35.3%), staff themselves or the service user and staff together (41.2%) ("..it *should* be for the service user - the keyworker benefits in that I know what she's doing, that she gets a little bit of quality") or the service (23.4%) ("...the 'house' benefits - the image presented to others") - and 64.7% of those interviewed feel supported in their role either all or some of the time. Some (23.3%) feel that the process is tokenistic for those service users who need others to speak on their behalf, with pressures being felt if goals set are unrealistic or if demand is placed upon resources ("..people sometimes have high expectations...[you] need to be realistic").

The sample of parents and careers interviewed was very small. All feel valued in their contribution, and believe the process benefits both service users and support staff.

Observing meetings and interviewing participants: Comparing and contrasting the findings

This comparison between interview and observation data is not designed to imply that people are saying one thing and doing another intentionally: the aim is to see if service users and staff can be supported in attaining the maximum involvement of service users possible in the individual planning process.

There seem to be three main differences in perception:

(1) A high percentage of the staff interviewed feel that service users needing others to speak on their behalf are given adequate space in meetings for thinking and absorbing discussion. The observation data suggest that this is not always the case.

(2) 71% of the keyworkers interviewed who support people needing others to speak on their behalf feel that the individual planning meeting is for the service user. This sits uncomfortably with the observation data which suggests that during the meetings observed for this group, 42% of interaction *excluded* the person for whom the meeting is held.

(3) Just over half of the people interviewed who speak for themselves feel that their individual planning meetings are for them. However, during the observation of the meetings, it was felt that service users had no influence on the format of the meeting or on the proceedings generally. It was also noted that for this group, 20% of discussion *excluded* the person for whom the meeting is held.

Conclusions and Possible Recommendations for the Future

The following ideas are forwarded in response to the main findings, suggesting ways in which individual planning in this service could be even more meaningful for service users, members of staff and participating relatives.

Individualisation

Based on observation of the two groups above, it appears that a very similar approach to individual planning is taken with all participating service users, whatever their level of need or experience. The findings of this study suggest that this can exclude a large number of people: service users who need others to speak on their behalf seem to be directly involved to a much lesser extent than people who speak for themselves.

It is suggested here that the process could be made more individualistic, focusing on ways of communication for each person, with the support and consultation of speech and language therapists at the development stages to avoid tokenism and frustration on the part of both keyworker and service user.

The observed sample of people needing others to speak on their behalf suggest there is a danger of meetings becoming like reviews or case conferences, or that the service user is not the key person in the process. Interviews with staff reveal that they *do* want service users to feel that it is their meeting, and with support, it is hoped that this effect could be increased. For people who speak for themselves, it seems that both service users and keyworkers are working together in ensuring that the meeting is seen as being held by the service user: this could perhaps be reinforced by giving service users more control over both the format of the meeting and the nature/order of agenda items.

Individualisation would also ameliorate the inclusion of people from minority ethnic groups, older people and those with additional physical and/or sensory disabilities. These particular needs all question the usefulness of a single approach , and demand the development of creative strategies to ensure that involvement is maximised.

Support for staff and managers

The concept of support is difficult to define - often a service relies on individuals to ask for support as they need it, as well as offering it more formally. Some staff say that they feel unsupported in their role as keyworkers in the planning process: managers and home leaders will have their own ways of providing support, as do members of the individual planning team. It is essential to maintain motivation and enthusiasm for the process, and this can only be achieved if keyworkers are encouraged and enabled. Courses could be offered for residential and day-centre managers to equip them with skills that would assist keyworkers in individualising the planning process for the person with whom they are working. These would complement those already offered to keyworkers. This joint responsibility for the success of individual planning - between the service user, the keyworker, the manager/home leader and the individual planning team - would hopefully create an approach that does not attempt to "slot" service users into a process, but facilitates the joint working needed to meet individual needs and enhance involvement.

Every role in the individual planning process is important. By asking team leaders to reassure keyworkers and service users in developing appropriately paced individual plans which concentrate on involving and empowering, a culture of shared responsibility could be achieved.

If individual planning aims to involve and empower all service users, it cannot rely on the reporting of unmet needs alone as a measure of quality: the danger of such a system is that the qualitative nature of valued interaction between the service and the service user can be lost as a result of the pressure to establish lists of completed tasks. It is recognised here that the reporting of unmet needs has many uses; it is suggested, however, that in isolation it cannot present a natural picture of how individual planning is experienced.

Evaluating and monitoring the process

This is the first major evaluation of this individual planning service that has not centred around the reporting of quantitative data. It is suggested here that a more accurate sense of what happens can be obtained by more regular, perhaps less detailed evaluations, which would build up a profile of the views of service users, keyworkers and relatives. A small, random and rotating sample of service users and other participants could be interviewed on a regular basis, to look at some of the issues raised in this study as well as any others that might occur. With the consent of all participants, members of the individual planning team could sit in on meetings chaired by one another, attempting to gain an overview of what happens in practice. This information would be most useful as material for training courses, as well as providing the chair with an objective insight into the standards of their own chairing.

Involving service users in the development of Life Planning

If the views of service users are to be respected to the extent suggested by the Statement of Intent (see page 90), it also seems appropriate that there is a role for service users in developing the service they receive. Representatives from service user groups could attend a steering group or planning forum, which would provide an important voice for the population of people with learning disabilities.

Individual planning in Milan: Primary sources

The majority of the material was extracted from Local and National Government legislation, Local Authority documents, other guidelines and papers from the archives of the *Commune di Milano* (Local Authority) Social Services Department. Other sources include interviews with the Director of Social Services, the Director of the Regional Learning Disability Institution, group home and day centre managers, *educatori* (support workers) and service users.

The foundations of individual planning in Milan: The Cartella Clinica

There are two distinct day services provided for people with learning disabilities: full employment with support, and day centres comparable in some ways with those operating in London. The decision as to which of the services people will use is made using data collected by an assessment called the *Cartella Clinica*, or Clinical Paper, which is an assessment of the person in the context of his or her situation, rather than just a strengths and needs list. The family and environment are considered in as much detail and with as much gravity as the person with disabilities. The assessment is not carried out by a care manager or social worker (as is likely to occur in London) but is the product of various contributions from a team of professionals, each giving a slightly different perspective.

Individual planning meetings

The information gathered by the *Cartella Clinica* forms the basis of discussion which takes place at the service user's individual planning meeting. These take place annually in the autumn, and it is widely recognised that such meetings serve an organisational purpose for professionals and are not intended to involve service users (Mazzini 1995), making it rare for service users to attend their planning meetings. Examples of the reports written for individuals can be found in appendix 3.

The main aim of the meeting is to assess the person's current situation, using the *Cartella Clinica* as a means of understanding important factors in the person's life such as intra-familial dynamics, the nature of the person's physical environment, health, psychological state and the significant events that have occurred during the past year. This breadth of information is felt to contribute towards an holistic picture of the service user's circumstances, including present needs and state of mind, which are inseparable from the needs and welfare of the family. The holistic picture is referred to as the person's *ambiente* (atmosphere or environment), revealing to professionals *Il bisogno* or personalised need (Cassaro 1995). The nature of individual planning in Milan is represented in Figure 2.

There are two technical terms which are crucial to understanding the theoretical framework of the individual planning system in Milan, and hence the approach to supporting people with learning disabilities in Lombardia. Explanation needs to be given here to help clarify the aims and objectives of the service.

Ambiente

This refers to the person's atmosphere, the personal environment as introduced above and illustrated in Figure 2. During the training for support workers, students are encouraged to think of people with learning disabilities not only as people with individual levels of need, but as people who are part of a family, who are affected by their physical environment and who will be influenced by the nature of the role ascribed to them by wider society. The interaction between all these considerations is termed the *ambiente*, and while there will be some commonality for all people with disabilities, many of the factors will be highly individual. It is also recognised that a person's *ambiente* is fluid in nature, and needs to be monitored continuously in order to maintain some sense of how the person's overall well-being and general welfare can change with time and new experiences (*Bolletino Ufficiale della Regione Lombardia* 1989).

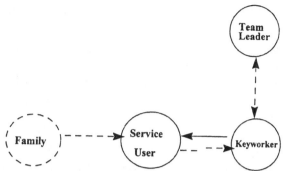

Figure 1.1: Individual Planning - Stage One: Identifying Strengths and Needs

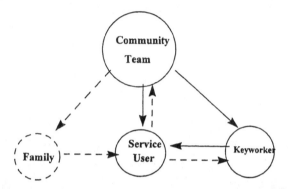

Figure 1.2: Individual Planning - Stage Two: The Planning Meeting

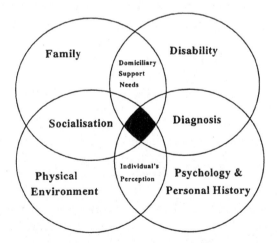

Figure 2: The Model of Individual Assessment and Planning in Milan

Reabilitazione

The term 'rehabilitation' is used frequently. It is considered that a person with disabilities has a potential in every area of life, but that this potential is often not fulfilled for a variety of reasons. These are usually linked with inappropriate levels or nature of support or the result of other relevant factors forming the person's *ambiente*. The objective is to 'rehabilitate' or enhance faculties and the capacity for understanding within the 'ceiling' recognised and described by the *Carta Clinica*. Expectation is levied at progress in terms of the current achievements and circumstances and how this compares with the 'ceiling' discussed with the multi-disciplinary team. This is therefore central to understanding any differences between the two systems: in London, a process which has the goals of integration and competence at its heart, compared with the Milanese approach which takes the cue for setting goals from an assessment which combines developmental limitations with sociological and environmental influences.

Comparing processes: Important issues and implications

There are several key areas in which the Milanese process differs markedly from the majority of approaches taken in Britain. Looking at these issues raises the profile of assumptions about the appropriateness and efficacy of certain aspects of individual planning practice, using the case study of the London service here as a point of reference.

High involvement of professionals

The Milanese process involves a large team of people meeting at the day centre, all of whom contribute to the final programme developed for the service user. This team consists of a psychiatrist, psychologist, *fisiatra* (a medically trained practitioner specialising in psychiatry), *psicomotricistra* (a therapist specialising in the development of psycho-motor skills e.g. hand to eye co-ordination), rehabilitation therapist, keyworker from the day centre or workplace and a keyworker from the home support service or residential placement. The service user and family representatives are conspicuous by their absence. Interviews with service professionals indicate that decision-making is felt to be too stressful for service users, and the process of planning in groups too abstract, even for the most able people with learning disabilities.

Evidence is needed to support the view that the involvement of such a large number of professionals does not lead to confusion and lack of clarity over roles in the planning process. What is clear is that the aim of the process is to achieve its objective of designing a service for each individual without any participation from that person.

In contrast, the study of the London service suggests that while the service purports to include and involve all service users in the planning process, this does not always occur, particularly for those needing others to speak on their behalf (Tables i and ii - see page 96). The role and nature of involvement of professionals seems to be reliant upon a referral system in London (McGrath 1991), compared with what appears to be a situation where professionals contribute to the assessment process as well as the planning of the person's individual programmes itself in Milan. The assessment procedure in the Milanese system adopts this strategy as an attempt to gain an holistic view of the person's personal and familial situation and needs, while in London goals and tasks are set according to the principles of normalisation, particularly with reference to O'Brien's Five Service Accomplishments (O'Brien & Tyne 1981) and an Ordinary Life (King's Fund 1980).

Staff involvement and resources

The involvement of professionals at such an intense level has implications in terms of resources, and also impacts upon practice. The programmes set by the team in Milan are very detailed, and need commitment from staff to ensure their successful implementation. Feasibility is enhanced by the fact that day centre staff-user ratios are set at a minimum of 2:1, with service users who present with difficult behaviour or who have complex needs, such as additional physical and /or sensory disabilities, being allocated the support of three workers (Mazzini 1995). This would suggest that support staff have more opportunities to ensure that many of the issues raised during programme meetings can be addressed, and that the annual reviews are more meaningful in terms of the feedback given by involved staff.

Such a ratio is higher than that of many services in London, where the day centres participating in the pilot study have a working ration of one member of staff for every six service users. The consistent training of staff resulting from the three year course supported by the University of Milan and the Central Disability Office (see Chapter 10) provides support workers with professional training, which helps them to work with more confidence and on more equal terms with other people in the multi-disciplinary team (Cassaro 1995). This ascribed status along with the fact that programmes are set by all team members results in a greater shared responsibility for the content as well as the success or failure of a particular person's programme (Mazzini 1995).

Another interesting contrast concerns the expectations placed upon staff and service users. In Milan, the goal is to fulfil a pre-determined potential related to diagnosis and other information gathered on the *Carta Clinica*. For people living with learning disabilities in London, in theory the only ceiling for progress and development is that set by societal norms, the ultimate goal perhaps being independence and integration with the rest of the community. For Milanese service providers, activities serve a more specific, therapeutic function.

One way of viewing the London system of individual planning would be that of leaving support workers to interpret the aims of individual planning as it applied to any one service according to a set of principles. By providing little in the way of consistent support from other professionals it is understandable that staff can feel that the process is a service audit or tool for monitoring their practice and the behaviour of the people they support. This attitude was expressed by 35 % of the keyworkers during the evaluation of the London service. The Milanese system does not consider the involvement of service users and their families in the initial and formal decision-making process, but tries to place their experiences and needs at the centre of the programme as part of an inextricable whole.

The role of the family

Following on from this, the family is seen in Lombardia as the most appropriate place for people with learning disabilities to live (Ferraro 1995; Cassaro 1995), and has potentially the greatest influence on a person's psychological well-being. The emphasis placed on the role of the family in London appears to be quite different. While relatives are involved where appropriate, it is the person's choices which are prioritised and elicited where possible - despite research suggesting that choice-making can be stressful and complex for many people (Fischoff *et al* 1980), particularly those with learning disabilities (Jenkinson 1993). Criticism has also been aimed at individual planning processes in Britain for the way in which they fail to account for cultural (ethnic, class or lifestyle) differences in terms of how families might perceive a programme's aims and objectives. Some cultures would find the discussion of personal matters as a task for the family with the exclusion of professional 'outsiders', for example (Baxter *et al* 1990). Perhaps an approach which assesses individual situations, rather than one which places families within an established process, can be more sensitive in this respect. It is important also to recognise key cultural differences between Italy and Britain in terms of the role that the family takes within society. Writers such as Barzini (1964) and Haycraft (1985) use the phenomenon of the family to explain many aspects of the society's characteristics and idiosyncrasies.

The uni-dimensional vs the situation specific approach

This refers to the way in which the Milanese approach differentiates clearly between those able and those unable to work, as well as other levels of ability. Objectives for people needing support to understand their immediate environment are infinitely different to those for people with lower levels of dependence, and programmes are designed accordingly. This contrasts sharply with the situation in British services where processes are established for all people with learning disabilities, with support workers in the main being allocated the task of involving all of the service users they support, whatever their level of understanding of the process, and how it can be used. The pilot study which evaluated the London planning service found that 47% of the keyworkers interviewed who support people with complex needs in the individual planning process feel unsupported in their task, and have concerns regarding the meaningfulness that the process in its current form has for this group of people.

Conclusions: Challenging the assumptions

The process and central principles of individual planning for people with learning disabilities in Milan provides an interesting contrast to systems operating in London.

A comparative approach to studying individual planning in Britain raises important issues and highlights key concepts which are influential and often applied without question by service providers.

The central differences between the two systems are summarised in Table (iii).

Table (iii): Key differences between individual planning processes in London and Milan

KEY ITEM	LONDON	MILAN
User Involvement in individual planning meetings	Service mission statements record the importance of involving service users without concrete guidance for supporters. The evaluation study showed that involvement is more successful for service users able to speak for themselves.	Service users are not involved in their planning meetings.
Effect of service user's ability on approach taken by individual planning service	The same approach to planning is taken with all service users, whatever their level of ability or understanding.	Those deemed able to work are supported in doing so; other people are allocated programmes aimed at enhancing a potential as established by a multi-disciplinary assessment (*Carta Clinica*).
Staff Resources	Keyworkers are usually given the role of co-ordinating the process and ensuring the implementation of decisions. Input from professionals relies on a referral system.	Decisions are made jointly by the multi-disciplinary team, who take joint responsibility for programme implementation. High staff-user ratios enable attainment of highly intensive, therapeutic work.
Family involvement	Members of the person's family are invited to attend planning meetings as appropriate. Staff receive no formal training in how to value or understand their involvement in the process.	The person's family are included as a key component of the assessment, and staff are trained during their 3 year course before graduating as a support worker to view familial interaction as central to the development of self-esteem and general well-being.
Underpinning philosophy	Individual planning uses O'Brien's Five Service Accomplishments for staff to use as signposts when setting goals and tasks with service users. Issues of integration and competence inform much of the decision-making.	Support workers are encouraged to help service users to understand their immediate environment and their role in society as a disabled person. The person's needs are viewed holistically, with activities having a therapeutic focus and integration being contingent upon the strength of the person's ability to cope with a social environment.

The experience and influence of the family in the lives of service users, the role of professionals, the central purpose of the process and the appropriateness of uniform implementation are important domains and are central to discussion which uses individual planning systems as aids to understanding the principles underlying learning disability services. It would appear that while wanting to approach each service user as an individual, the London service tends to have one method of involvement for all levels of disability. This call for involvement illustrates the emphasis which normalisation places on participation. The nature of the goals and tasks which service users are encouraged to set are also explicitly based upon the Five Accomplishments (e.g. O'Brien 1981). The apparent low-key role of professionals (for more able individuals) and high responsibility for the keyworker, supports the approach where 'ordinary' people, who are inconsistently trained, develop 'ordinary' lives for people with learning disabilities.

In Milan, service principles are also well illustrated by the individual planning process. Decisions are made for people by a co-ordinated professional team which includes the keyworker as a peer, supporting the emphasis on training and qualifications for staff. Assessments are made of the individual's situation, focusing on relationships with family members and others, as well as looking at skill attainment. Again, this supports the model which places the family and close relationships at the centre of development, in contrast with the London service which is primarily concerned with the individual.

These two systems for implementing service principles lead to two very different ways of approaching the individual with learning disabilities. It is important to know how these differences affect everyday life, and this concern will form the following part of the study.

A comparative approach is taken throughout, and the data are presented in a way which attempts to illustrate similarities and differences between the two projects, as well as how effectively practice reflects the principles stated in operational policies. Two groups of men described as having moderate learning disabilities took part in a comparison of daily life as a user of a residential service. Both groups moved into the community from large institutions, at about the same time. After they talked about their lives in a wide number of areas, support staff were interviewed. Participant observation of interaction between staff and residents also gives a sense of how service principles affect individuals. These data are also placed in the context of the operational policies in place for each project.

6 An Ordinary Life or Substituting for the Family?: A Case Study Exploring the Impact of Learning Disability Service Principles on Daily Practice in London and Milan

Introduction

The most direct way of assessing the ways in which theoretical models of social care inform practice is to sample the services which have adopted the models of interest. In this case, the influence of normalisation has been explored by taking an approach as argued by Goode (1991), which attempts to gain some sense of the approach's effects by collecting data from three angles:

1. Interviews with service users themselves.
2. Interviews with the staff who support them.
3. Participant observation of daily routines and interactions between all of the people living and working in the residential setting.

Using a case study in this way also fulfils the three criteria established by Parmenter's (1988) symbolic-interactionist model of assessing quality of life (see chapter 3), as here the views of the participants, along with observation of the ways in which the setting reacts to their behaviour, is compared with the documentation policy describing service objectives.

The main focus of interest is specifically the impact of the principles of normalisation on services for people with learning disabilities, and hence the impact of the approach on the lives of service users themselves. The comparison with services operating in Milan, Northern Italy, was made in an attempt to highlight key aspects of the normalisation approach. These aspects become more lucid when the framework of analysis steps outside the value systems prevalent in the home country to create a contrast. A case study focusing on domestic life is essential, particularly as normalisation is concerned with 'ordinary living', integration, independence and socially valued behaviour. Gaining some sense of the experience of people supported by this framework could reveal how these values impact on practice. The model supported by the Milanese services emphasises the importance of the family, to the extent that anyone unable to live with their natural families is provided with an environment which attempts to substitute everything that a family life can offer - for example if the person with disabilities is orphaned, or presents with difficult or unmanageable behaviour. This is the responsibility of Social Services, in this case the *Comune di Milano.*[1]

The data that have been collected are detailed, and will be presented in a summarised format. Findings will be discussed for each service, after which a discussion of that particular area will highlight the interesting similarities and differences; this will then provide a series of issues which can address the question of how far the respective theoretical models inform and influence each service, and how clearly the connection between service philosophy and practice can be made.

Background to the findings: Services and environments

London

The project targeted for this study provides a residential service for five men with moderate learning disabilities. At the time of conducting the research, they had lived together in the purpose-built, five bedroomed flat for a year, having previously lived in a 23-bed hostel for people with learning disabilities for between 4 and 18 years[2] funded and supported by the local authority. Prior to living in the hostel, four of the men had sporadically lived in either large mental handicap hospitals or with relatives; the fifth man had lived with his family and a in number of short-stay respite care placements.

---

[1] This is supported with the observation that individual care programmes are designed around the needs of the *family* with a learning disabled relative, rather than focusing on the strengths and needs of the individual.

[2] Four of the men had known each other for at least 18 years - the fifth man had originally moved to the hostel for respite care four years before the hostel closed, but this developed into a long term arrangement.

The hostel: Service design

The hostel had originally provided support in an open plan environment, similar to a mental handicap hospital but, as a result of plans for reprovisioning which began in 1988, the building was divided into four self-contained flats. At the same time five residents moved into a house with their own support team, while two others moved into a flat of their own. This left 16 people living in the hostel, in the following compositions:

Flat 1: Home for 2 men, supported by 2 full-time equivalent support workers[3] working alone on alternate 8 hour shifts. While living at the hostel, one of the service users was very independent, using public transport without support and needing support with personal care in the form of occasional verbal prompting. The second man is also quite independent, but had some mental health problems which tended to present by him being withdrawn and sometimes displaying inappropriate sexual behaviour.

Flat 2: Home for 4 men, supported by a staff team of 3.5 full time equivalent workers. This group of men formed the basis of the group now living in the project participating in this study. The men have moderate learning disabilities; one has additional physical disabilities, and a second has mental health problems. While living in the hostel, their needs centred around support with cooking and all domestic tasks, handling finances, going into the community and almost all of the practical daily tasks of living. Emotional support was particularly important for the man with additional mental health problems.

Flat 3: This was home for three men and one woman, supported by a staff team of 3 full time equivalent members of staff. Two of the men needed a high level of support, while the woman needed support in terms of some challenging behaviour and assistance with personal care. The third man had additional mental health problems, which presented a very low-resourced staff team with considerable difficulties when he was particularly dependent.

---

[3] 'Full time equivalent' typically refers to a person working 37 hours a week as part of a rota which includes 'early' shifts (usually 7.30am - 3.00pm), late shifts (usually 1.30pm - 9.00pm) and "sleep-ins", where the worker is required to sleep at the hostel between working late and early shifts.
Weekends are also included in the rota, with staff expected to work 3 out of every 5. In this hostel, 2 'waking night' staff were also employed to work with those service users who needed support during the night.

Flat 4: Many of the staff referred to this flat as the 'SNU' or 'Special Needs Unit'. It was home for five people (one man and four women) with severe learning disabilities and/or complex needs - including visual impairment and physical disability. One of the women had very challenging behaviour, while two of the residents used wheelchairs. One of the resident also had severe self-injurious behaviour. Staffing for this flat was set at 5 full time equivalents.

Each staff team were in theory required to work only with the groups they were assigned, but in practice, the response to covering sickness and annual leave was often to move people around to ensure that minimal levels of cover were maintained. The hostel was managed by a senior member of staff who had four deputies, each one responsible for the management and support of a staff team. As plans for reprovisioning were confirmed, those deputies became the co-ordinators of resettlement programmes for each group of individuals.

The resettlement process

This did not begin in earnest until 1991, when organisations were identified as providers of community housing for those service users still residing in the hostel. Two projects were purpose-built - one for those people with physical disabilities who needed adaptations to their environment to 'increase' their levels of independence (Flat 4), and one for the men participating in this study. Two individual voluntary housing organisations had agreed to provide accommodation, with the staff support being funded by the local authority.

An assessment process was initiated by the Hostel Manager and the Resources Manager to enable staff at the Hostel to identify friendship groups and relationships amongst the residents. These relationships were taken as indications of the social groupings in which people feel most comfortable. The format of this assessment was based on keyworkers' knowledge of individuals and informal observation of group interaction; while it was recognised that needs can change, it was thought essential to establish initial compatible groups as starting points.

The second stage of the resettlement process began in 1992, with contracts drawn up between the local authority and the voluntary organisations which had agreed to provide accommodation and housing management. The time period between the first and second stages was looked upon by management as one of encouraging residents to think about moving house: the process by which this was done is unclear, and no formalised documentation exists as to the thinking and policy envisaged by either management or direct support staff. As recommended in the literature (e.g. Booth *et al* 1990), it appears that those service users who were able to either visit their prospective new accommodation or contribute to planning their new lifestyles did so, but in such a way as to rely entirely on the commitment and creativity of individual keyworkers, rather than being a result of adherence to any shared and consistent approach. Service users with profound disabilities and/or complex needs - the people described above living in Flat 4 - were excluded from this process altogether, confirming the culture prevalent in many institutions such as this hostel which argues that people with this level of understanding are not capable of making sense of any attempts to include them in a consultation process. Furthermore, trying to do so is not only fruitless but possibly results in that group of people becoming more distressed than if they were just resettled without a planned, cohesive preparation programme.

Assessments were conducted prior to the moves: the Hampshire Assessment for Living with Others (HALO) aimed to enable staff to identify residents' short- and long-term needs and the levels of support required. Again, the extent to which service users were actively involved in the assessments is unclear. The information was referred to Care Managers, who then made recommendations regarding certain individuals with difficult behaviour or certain difficult lifestyle characteristics on the basis of this information. This is a powerful mechanism: key, heuristic decisions were being made about people of whom the Care Managers had no in-depth knowledge and no established relationships.

The one consultation process which is more straightforward to report was that involving parents and carers. Discussions were held by keyworkers as well as regular meetings with the Resource Management team; the main concern raised consistently at these meetings was the vulnerability of people who would not have the protection - as perceived by families - of a large building with more members of staff around. The strategy taken to allay fears centred on explaining and spending time discussing the particular staffing levels in each of the new projects. No other palpable or documented formalised methods of supporting parents and carers have been recorded.

Meeting needs: liaison with the Registration Department and Inspection Unit

Considerable time was spent before the moves on contractual arrangements between the local authority and the housing associations providing accommodation. In fact, it appears that more time was spent on this stage of the process - and more space allocated in records documenting the resettlement process - than on the consultation and preparation procedures conducted with service users.

Avoiding the need to register the new projects as Care Homes under the Registered Homes Act 1984 was important to the local authority, as it was felt that not only did this make a statement in terms of the status of service users - that they were no longer 'in care' and were living semi-independently in the community - but advantage was also to be gained regarding the level of benefits that service users would be able to claim. Many people had been extremely impoverished for a number of years while living in the institution, and attaining a higher level of income would enable them to access individualised packages of day care if appropriate, as well as allow them to afford holidays which the local authority was no longer in a position to subsidise.

The issue of registration was resolved for the project detailed in this study by introducing the concept of contracts between the residents - now to be referred to as 'tenants' - and the housing association and support workers respectively. At the time of conducting the present research, the contract between the tenants and the housing association had been completed (before they moved into the new house), but the contract between the tenants and the support workers had yet to be drafted.

This suggests two important perceptions of the idea of service users having meaningful contractual arrangements with the providers of the services they use in this instance:

1. Although the move from the hostel was seen symbolically as an elevation in status of the people with learning disabilities it involved, in reality there has no been no significant shift in how they are viewed by support workers or by the community. If any lasting effect was to take place, there would have to be significant developments in the working strategies adopted by staff to enable the service users to realise and make sense of the changes that they experienced on leaving the hostel. Although such thinking might have been incorporated into the new operational policy (see below), there is no evidence of how staff are to either interpret or implement such a strategy.

2. The fact that the completion of organisational contracts was prioritised over the contracts involving service users perhaps illustrates the importance and real status afforded to the involved parties. It would seem more appropriate for the contracts and agreements involving and consulting service users to be established and agreed before those delineating organisational responsibilities, if the service were to be truly led by the needs of its users.

The conclusion here then, is that the potential for meaningful change of status in society for the service users moving to the community was minimised due to the lack of a coherent, planned and service-wide strategy. All that could really alter for people - on paper at least - was their physical environment. The same staff teams moved with the tenants, and the only input and training given was a three day course in raising some of the issues that were coming up for service users, and asking the staff themselves in the main to devise strategies for managing these issues. The greatest assumption on the part of management of the service was that individual supervision and team meetings would enable support workers to develop the ways of working required in the new environment, but again, no clear guidance was offered on how this could be carried out in practice. The service users have become tenants in name but apparently not in status, particularly in the eyes of the service supporting them.

The new building

The purpose-built ground floor apartment is located within an inner-city borough within reasonable distance of key bus and railway routes.

The building consists of a number of flats, most of which are home for people once on the local authority's housing list and who have often been disadvantaged in some way. The flat allocated for the five men is the largest, with a bedroom for each tenant, a bathroom, toilet, kitchen, living room and staff 'sleep-in' room.

An assessment of one of the tenant's mobility difficulties led to certain design features, such as rails for support from the lounge to the patio, and a handrail in the bathroom.

Service Design in the new project: staffing levels

Resource Management papers document the process which took place involving the Registration Unit, the respective Housing Associations and the Principal Officer to establish the staffing structures needed to support each project. The Wagner Report (1988) and Health and Safety guidelines were combined with the service's individual assessments to design the team needed by each group of users. In the case of the project which took part in this study, an adequate team was identified as consisting of a team leader (NJC6), a Senior Support Worker (NJC5) and five Support Workers (NJC4). At that time, no waking night staff were deemed necessary. This expanded the existing team, and so extra funding was provided from the deletion of obsolete posts at the hostel. All of the posts had to be upgraded, with corresponding job descriptions drafted to reflect at least the realisation on the part of service management that supporting people with learning disabilities in small group homes in the community should carry with it new responsibilities and in many ways a totally new landscape of tasks, commitments, priorities and underpinning thinking.

However, it is interesting to note the way in which this recognition is documented by Resource Management. While there is no doubt that a commitment was established by Service Providers, the ways in which this commitment was filtered down to direct support staff is described as follows:

> The current RSO [Residential Service Officer] job description was updated to reflect the tasks in the small houses and the job titled to Support Worker. Any amendments to the job descriptions were taken on board and implemented.

There is no indication as to who was responsible for ensuring that the modifications were "taken on board" or as to how this could have been or has been achieved. There is also little evidence to convey to staff the significance of the move in people's lives; by referring to "amendments" to job descriptions, the implication is surely that the substance for the working practices was already in place, and that staff skills were merely to be enhanced rather than assessed thoroughly. Here is one significant difference between the Milanese and London approaches to resettlement: in Milan, the task was viewed with such gravity that specific professional training was deemed necessary to ensure success. In London, there may have been comments and plans laid out to illustrate a commitment to the size of the project, but without the consequent investment in human resources and required thinking, this surely amounts to nothing more than rhetoric.

Key roles within the housing projects

(a) Team leader
Amongst the duties described by documentation is a responsibility for staff development and training and the implementation of policies and procedures, emphasising the importance of this position in the project. There is also a reference to "maintaining the quality of care", but this is not elaborated upon. Again, this would appear to support the view that the quality and nature of the service offered is contingent upon the interpretative skills of the team leader, and reliant upon his/her commitment to the same values as the service provider.

(b) Senior support worker
This post was designed to "take on as much devolved responsibility from the Team Leader as is required to ensure the smooth running of the unit".

(c) Support worker
Confirming the observation that the nature of the job description did not undergo significant changes to match the task of resettling people into the community, the role of Support Worker is outlined by the comment:

> Although the job description remains basically the same, it is envisaged that the Support Worker will enhance the role by becoming more involved in the day to day management of the residents' affairs and general administration of the unit.

The London residential project in the community: Operational policy

(A) Main objectives

These are described in the Operational Policy document as providing a home for life for 5 people with learning disabilities and some degree of "special need", be it physical disability or some degree of challenging behaviour.

An emphasis on integration with the local community is illustrated in the document:

> The proximity of this house to other housing and public amenities will be exploited in order to give the feel of an ordinary home in the community.

(B) Service philosophy

Explicit reference is made to the fact that the service is underpinned by the principles of normalisation, and the ways in which O'Brien's Five Service Accomplishments are interpreted are indicated:

> The philosophy of the house is] to enable the tenants to live by the principles of 'ordinary life' as outlined by the King's Fund in 1982 and takes as its framework the Five Service Accomplishments outlined by O'Brien in 1985.

PRESENCE: Refers to the proximity of service within a local community.

PARTICIPATION: Refers to the full participation of service users in all aspects of their life in the local community. The service will actively encourage participation through the on-going development of systematic and comprehensive Life Planning.

COMPETENCE: Refers to the degree that service users feel and are seen to be competent in as many aspects of their life as possible. The service will actively strive towards this by developing a wide range of teaching and non-teaching plans and opportunities for integration, self-development and growth.

DIGNITY AND RESPECT: Refers to the extent to which people are perceived treated and engaged as valued human beings in their own right. The service will adopt a strong value base deeply rooted in the notions of respect and dignity for the people it serves."

(C) Profile of tenants and prospective tenants

The Operational Policy also defines the criteria for referral in the event of a vacancy occurring at the project, and is very clear about the people who are considered unsuitable as prospective tenants:

1. People suffering from pre-senile or senile dementia.
2. Those whose primary diagnosis is that they are suffering from mental health problems.
3. People with severely disturbed or violent behaviour.
4. People who need nursing care due to long term, acute or life threatening illness.
5. People whose primary need is for treatment for alcohol or drug misuse.

6. Wheelchair users.
7. Those who are regularly incontinent.
8. People whose needs can only be met by 24 hour waking support.
9. Those who are unable or unwilling to meet the weekly charge.

It is important to note that the operational policy appears to imply that if the needs of the people currently living in the project fall into one of the above categories at any time in the future, their tenancy would be at risk of being terminated and alternative accommodation in a project deemed to be more appropriate in terms of meeting those needs would be identified. This questions the accuracy of the statement used to describe this and similar projects as offering tenants a 'home for life'. What might be a more meaningful account is a 'home until your needs change to a point which falls outside the design of this service'.

(D) Outline of the service offered to tenants

This describes in some detail the more practical aspects of the facilities offered to tenants in the project, covering issues such as telephones, pets and receiving visitors.

Again, there is evidence of normalisation underpinning the service's framework, in this case presence in the community:

> In order that tenants do not become divorced from the community, particular emphasis will be placed on contacts from family, friends, volunteers and advocates.

(E) Tenants' involvement in their service

This section of the Operational Policy outlines how the tenants are to be involved in making decisions about the running of the house, mainly with reference to complaints procedures and the administration of relevant information regarding what are termed "Rights and Responsibilities". There is no reference to how or whether such information would need to be adapted to account for the varying levels of understanding.

A commitment to tenant involvement is stated:

> The effectiveness and implementation of user participation will be regularly monitored.

Again, there is no indication as to how this could be achieved, or any comment on the appropriateness of this for those individuals who might find such an expectation either difficult or undesirable. One example of this is very real: a tenant currently residing in the project has autism, which by definition results in that person finding it difficult to communicate with others - particularly with those outside his immediate family.

Rights and responsibilities

This section comprises a large part of the Operational Policy, and has been allocated more space than both the section outlining the service and the description of contractual arrangements.

The 43 points are not arranged in any particular order; many are specific in nature (e.g. Point No. 32 states that tenants have the right to purchase their own clothing), while others are more conceptual and give no real guidance as to how tenants could be assisted in understanding the full implications of such a responsibility (e.g. Point No. 25: "Tenants have the right to independence, choice and to take responsibility for their actions")

Again, many of the points made directly refer to O'Brien's Five Accomplishments. What is less clear is the ways in which staff are introduced to the main concepts of the policy: while they might have individual perceptions of how normalisation needs to be applied to a residential service, it appears that the only fora for those perceptions to be shared and debated are team meetings and individual supervision sessions. It is suggested here also that the way that the rights and responsibilities are presented, particularly the lack of precision and clarity in the more general points, allows for a great deal of flexibility which could be positive in the sense where team leaders are able to encourage a culture of sharing ideas and approaches amongst team members, but could also be negative in cases where there is no clear direction or guidance in terms of what is and isn't appropriate support.

Perhaps more fundamental than these concerns is that of how the term "responsibility" is interpreted by management and support workers, and the nature of the expectations accompanying those interpretations. More importantly, the ways in which tenants might or might not understand the nature of "responsibility" is not addressed - surely if such a large section of an operational policy is devoted to the ways in which tenants are required to think and behave, there would need to be some indication as to how their ability and capacity for this could be assessed? Further, they could be assisted in seeing taking responsibility in its various forms as a positive experience. This is particularly relevant in the case where tenants are expected to become responsible for the consequences of their actions (see

Appendix 2: Rights and responsibilities - point 25).

Milan

The seven men living in the residential project in the community (*communità allogio*) which took part in this study had all previously lived in a large mental handicap institution not far from their current home. National Law 482/68 called for the resettlement of all people with learning disabilities into the community, but was specific in reference to those who are able to assume some form of employment. More able people with learning disabilities were expected to rejoin their families wherever possible, the intention being that they would be able to maintain a lifestyle that is based upon work in a supportive, and most importantly, social context.

While it is the belief among Milanese professionals that the most beneficial and *therapeutic* environment for a person with learning disabilities is his/her own family home, it has been recognised that this is not always achievable. Although an astonishingly high number of hospital residents did move back with their families,[4] a minority were unable to do so. This could have been due to parents and other relatives moving away or dying, or significantly, because of the poor quality relationship existing between the service user and his/her family. While the importance of family support is widely advocated, it appears that the *nature* of that support is viewed to be crucially influential in the process of enabling people with learning disabilities to attain an acceptable quality of life.

For the seven men living in the project which agreed to participate in this case study, a residential service was provided for them as a result of them being orphaned or having unsupportive or inappropriate relationships with their families. These are to be seen in many ways as exceptional, in that the majority of their peers in the institution are now living with their 'natural' families, and the service in which the seven men live has been designed and developed solely with their needs in mind. It has not been developed for 'a group of men with mild to moderate learning disabilities who are able to sustain part-time employment'; the men were identified as a group and instigated the conception of the project, rather than a physical space being identified which would be appropriate for a group of 'able' men with learning disabilities.

---

[4] Approximately 95% of residents (Ferraro 1995).

The resettlement process

Although originally accustomed to living in large groups, sometimes of up to 80 service users, the seven men living in the project had developed relationships among themselves and came to be identified by the staff at the institution as a group who seemed content in each other's company. As the resettlement process quickened and the task of tracing families became central to the work of the institution, it became apparent that for these men, alternative arrangements in terms of accommodation would have to be made. By consulting the men themselves, staff and the Director of the Institution felt confident that it would be agreeable and beneficial to provide a service which would keep them together. A living space adapted to resemble an apartment was developed inside the institution to enable the men to gain some sense of what living as a group would be like. After liaison with the local authority *(Comune di Milano)*, plans for a community service began.

An apartment on the outskirts of the city was identified and bought by the local authority. People already living in the area - particularly those living in the same building - were involved at this stage. Local authority staff consulted and informed residents of the aims and purpose of the project as an attempt at providing a receptive environment for the new tenants.

The apartment is on the third floor of a residential block near a key bus route which connects with the tram system. There are four bedrooms for the residents - six of the men share with one other flatmate - and a bedroom for one of the domestic staff (Assunta) who lives in. There is a large main living room/diner, which has an anteroom leading towards the toilet and bathroom. The kitchen leads from the other side of the living room.

The operational policy

"Setting the scene"

One of the most striking qualities of the operational policy is its emphasis on geographical context. Considerable time was spent on detailing the precise location of the project within Milan, perhaps to help establish some of the factors which supporters would need to consider when assisting the men with integrating into the local community. The aspects covered by this description include transport facilities; the presence of industry and nature of available housing in the area; a demographic breakdown which refers to other minority groups nearby - such as people from minority ethnic backgrounds and drug mis-users; details of facilities such as shops and recreational amenities. This account concludes with discussion of future plans for the area - the nature of housing developments and how this might impact on the lives of people already living in the area.

Acknowledging local resources

As an overview, this introduction to the project provides insight into the profile of the community, which becomes more specific around issues which have a potential to directly affect the men living in the project. One example of this is the mention of a community centre provided by Social Services which is aimed at younger people but welcomes people with disabilities.

Other voluntary groups and associations are listed:

- a community group which is commissioned by various industries for the production of ceramics, textiles and woodcrafts. The aim of the project is to provide social integration for people with disabilities living in the area.[5]

- a group which from cultural, religious and recreational perspectives, has attained notoriety in the field of leather craft and photography.

- a charity which works with people from minority ethnic groups.

- a scouts' group, which works with the local residents' association as well as the day centre for people with learning disabilities.
- a small residential project which provides a service for two people with Down's syndrome, supported by the *comune di Milano* (local authority).

All of these groups and projects are listed as a way of describing the local community and how it might impact upon the lives of the men living in the house. The Director of the institution also notes that despite some difficulties in the area - mainly the presence of drug-users - the well co-ordinated support programmes described above result in the location being

---

[5] It is important to note that in Italian, the word *handicappati* (the handicapped) is used in preference to *disabili* (the disabled). When questioned, service providers say that it is felt that people with disabilities are "handicapped" by society, and thus the terminology refers to the person's context - which is potentially limited by the reactions of the able-minded and able-bodied society - rather than to the nature of his/her disability per se.

deemed to be an appropriate choice.

Resident profiles

This refers specifically to the progress and characteristics of the seven men currently living in the house, and is not designed to generally describe potential groups who would be able to live in the project in the future. This section of the operational policy can be divided in to six main areas.

(1) Ability and disability

The seven men are described as having had a long period of institutionalisation and by means of a variety of therapeutic interventions, have attained or recovered a degree of ability in terms of life skills. This is termed *autosufficienza* which is thought to be enhanced with appropriate levels of support.

(2) Behaviour

These men are not thought to have challenging behaviour. Their central need is that of a role model which will act as a reference and provide help, guidance and stimulation.

(3) Application of legislation

All have family histories originating in the Milan region, and all had secured work in schemes outside the auspices of the institution, under the protection of Law 482/68 which lists the regulations applying to the employment of people with learning disabilities and the requirements demanded of employers and authorised by local magistrates. One of the reasons for the local authority choosing the present apartment is the opportunity for four of the men to live closer to their place of work.

(4) Developing an understanding of social responsibility

For some time, the men have been following a programme aimed at increasing their capacity to increase communication and develop relationships with others. Other work has been focusing on the experience of living in a group and increasing opportunities for developing responsibility for oneself and towards other people sharing the same environment, be it at home or at work.

(5) Developing life skills

Before moving to the community, the men led a life which is described by current service managers as regulated by norms and precise timetables. It was soon realised that moving out of the institution would disrupt that organised lifestyle and necessitate the formation of an alternative lifestyle appropriate for the new environment. The principle behind this was aiming to avoid the development of passive compliance. This is used to explain the energy expended on researching the available local resources, to encourage the men to find meaning for their free time. The keywords cited by the operational policy are recreation, interest, relationships and expression.

(6) Central reasons for establishing the project

According to service providers, the men showed that they wanted to leave the institution in order to lead a more autonomous life. Resettlement with relatives is not a viable option for any of the service users, either because of absent families or because intra-familial relationships are deemed to be inhibiting in terms of enhancing both quality of life and personal autonomy.

Staff profiles and responsibilities

The selection of staff is seen to be the fulcrum of the whole organisation of the project, and can determine its success or failure. Criteria for providing an adequate service have been derived from careful analysis of the functions of the support programme provided for the service users. This resulted in the identification of three main roles for *educatori* (support staff).

(A) The function of responsibility

(i) Staff must have the ability to work efficiently within the structure of the project, as well as with other staff.

(ii) They must possess sufficient technical and pedagogical skills.

(iii) Vast experience in the field of social education is essential.

(iv) Flexibility in terms of hours of work is very important - this was particularly stressed during the period just after the men moved into the house, and is extended until the present time when the men are considered to be still integrating with the local community as well as adjusting to the project itself.

(B) The educational role

Due to the great level of need identified in people with learning disabilities transferring to the community - particularly into a house such as this project - it is deemed that an educational approach is not only indispensable, but indeed the only way of providing adequate support.[6] The expectation is that this role is expressed in five key ways:

(i) Staff need to be able communicators with the potential for forming positive relationships with the service users.

(ii) Staff act as role models, helping, supporting and stimulating service users.

(iii) Staff need to have:

> ..the capacity to act as a 'point of reference', encouraging the service users'ability to trust and value others, stimulating in an educative way the potential for developing autonomy, but at the same time being clear and consistent. (Operational policy 1995 p.4)

(iv) Staff are also required to create and realise projects with the group which will develop over time.

(v) Emphasis is placed on staff promoting and stimulating relationships between the service users and the local community.

(vi) When the service users first moved into the house, their abilities and strengths in terms of autonomous living were unknown. Staff therefore performed all household tasks, so as not to place unnecessary pressures on a group of people who were experiencing major change and upheaval.[7]

This forms the foundation of the basic approach to interpersonal relationships with the residents: the approach to support work is said to

---

[6] This perhaps explains in part the use of the term *educatori* (educators) to describe support workers.
[7] Two other important strategies adopted when the men first moved in were the access to a psychologist whose task was to support the men at this time, and the briefing given to staff to expect to provide additional support during the night for the initial period if the men required extra support.

require:

> ...a *loving* presence which demands that at strategic moments, staff assume the role of providing good familial support in solving problems. (Operational Policy 1995, p5.).

Project objectives

The operational policy lists the community project as having 5 main aims.

Accentuating the value of living together

Looking at 'life in common' that arises from living in a group, and which is believed to make life more meaningful.

Understanding living in a shared building

Learning from the experience of living in a condominium, which is thought to provide a structure for understanding social relationships, 'good' neighbouring, mutual help, respect and solidarity.

Benefiting from the social world

Giving great significance to the fact that all people live in a social world and belong in a social context, within which one can play an active part. Being in the house provides opportunities for the *group* to participate in social life, primarily from the safety of the group and perhaps as individuals.

Valuing work experience

Work is a dimension which can facilitate social integration, but can also be an exercise in learning and understanding the social norms of behaviour by taking part and finding out what can be achieved.

Benefiting from integration

Seeing the move to the project as a potential introduction to more complete integration with the community at a later stage.

After outlining these points, the core of the policy is then revealed:

> ...in short, apart from enabling the service users to work, the programme provides the experience of family life, the reciprocal collaboration of living in

the house, participation in the local community and opportunities for using local recreational and leisure facilities...The programme has to be individual, and should be set annually with clear stages, periodically assessed to look at how the [person's experience of community life] is progressing (Operational Policy 1995, p5).

Supporting people with learning disabilities in London and Milan: Comparing operational policies for two residential services in the community

There are several key ways in which the two policies differ, and it is useful to outline these to aid understanding of the aims of each project. Further, comparison with the Milanese policy will highlight the important characteristics of what is assumed here to be a typical example of a British operational policy for a learning disability service which is following the principles of normalisation.

Identifying tenants

The London policy describes the criteria which tenants need to meet in order to be appropriate for living in the flat. Should the needs of the current tenants change significantly, there is a possibility that alternative accommodation would be found.

The service in London has therefore been set up to provide a service for any five people with learning disabilities whose needs can be met given the resources available.

The Milanese policy describes a service which has been set up only for the seven men currently living in the apartment, the implication being that should their needs change, the service would have to adapt in order to meet those needs.

Responsibilities

The operational policy for the London service details the responsibilities of the people living in the project, some of which are practical and palpable, others of which have wider implications for people who have learning disabilities (e.g. taking responsibility for their own actions). Less space is devoted to the responsibilities of staff, which are not presented in any detailed form. The converse of this true for the Milanese policy, which spends a great deal of time outlining the key roles and responsibilities of the *educatori*.

Providing context to the project

The Milanese service seems to consider it essential that the demographic and physical nature of the local community is acknowledged and incorporated into the service plan. This approach is not taken with the London operational policy.

Using a legislative framework

Discussion around valuing employment in the context of integration makes reference to Regional employment laws in the Milanese policy, in turn linking this with the development of self esteem. No real reference is made to the role of people with learning disabilities in society in the London policy, or to ways in which staff need to acknowledge the impact of the community on the tenants.

The pace of integration

The focus on group living in the Milanese policy conveys the idea of the men integrating *together* rather than as a group. Social responsibility is placed in this context, rather than emphasising the individual and his responsibilities as in the London policy. Integration is also coupled with an educational element of support in the Milanese policy, which does bear some relation to the issues of teaching appropriate skills described in the London policy. The key difference is that individual integration for the Milanese tenants takes place at the workplace, while at home, they are encouraged to integrate more as a unit.

Project objectives

Each policy can be summarised by using its core objectives. In the case of the London policy, these are simply the Five Accomplishments for ordinary living as described by O'Brien (1985). A similar five objectives can be derived from the Milanese policy, and a direct comparison is made in Table (iv).

Table (iv): Key objectives of the residential services in London and Milan as stated in their operational policies

LONDON: KEY OBJECTIVES	MILAN: KEY OBJECTIVES
Presence in the community	The experience of living with others
Participation in all aspects of local life	Integrating as a group, as well as individually
The experience of competence	Valuing work as a requirement for self esteem
To be treated with dignity and respect	Moving to the community as an *introduction* to integration, not integration per se.
Opportunities for making choices	Attempting to recreate family life and provide a loving presence

The findings

Speaking to service users: Background

The origin and development of the questionnaire which formed the basis of the interviews with service users has been discussed fully on page 54. The format was adapted with the intention of giving service users the space to make points and add comments freely and not feel overburdened with a continuous barrage of questions.

The results from the interviews with each group of men will be presented separately in the following text. The men from London are aged between 27 and 65, and are described as having moderate to mild learning disabilities. They are referred to as Matthew, Clive (who also has a physical disability which leads to difficulties with mobility), David, Peter and Alan.

The men living in Milan are also described as having moderate to mild learning disabilities and are from a similar age group to the men living in London. In the text, they appear as Alberto, Andrea, Paulo, Dario, Stefano, Riccardo and Roberto.

Full data sets with the exact questions that were put to the men can be found in appendix 5. Each response summary is followed by a comparison of the two accounts, highlighting similarities and differences between the replies given by the two groups.

The questions fell into 22 broad categories which together attempt to access in some way the lifestyles of the two groups of service users [Table (v)].

Table (v): Main question categories in the service user questionnaire

QUESTION CATEGORIES	
Where you lived before	Neighbours/Acquaintances
The building that you lived in	Friends & Relationships
House Rules	Religion & Belief
Privacy & Trust	How you feel about yourself
Relationships with staff	Making your own decisions
Relationships with other professionals	Time at home
Relationships with residents	Leisure: Weekends & Evenings
Solving problems	Getting out and about
Money	Hobbies
Clothes	Holidays

Speaking to service users in London and Milan[8]

Where you lived before: Thoughts on leaving the institution and preparation for life in the community

There seems to be no consensus in either group of men as to their feelings on moving into the community; while some are clearly relieved to have left behind their lives in the institution, others are less certain that it was a completely positive step. What is common is the evidence that both services saw their priority to be offering the men skills which they might need in their new lives, indicating perhaps that both the London and Milanese authorities felt that the change in living conditions and status would lead to a seemingly more independent way of life.

All of the men in both projects had 'help' or 'training' of one sort or another before they left the institution: the teaching tasks included washing up; drying up; working in a woodwork shop; washing clothes; cooking; help with moving itself; using buses ("travel training").

London: All 5 of the men said that they lived at the hostel for 'a long time'; 4 said it was good or all right living there, while Matthew said that he didn't like it. Clive and Peter found it difficult to leave the hostel ("It was a bit

---

[8] All names have been changed in the interests of confidentiality.

tricky - I liked it better than here" and "I was upset") while the other men either felt that it was "all right" or were pleased about leaving. Alan and David said that they prefer their present accommodation, Matthew and Peter think it's "all right" in the new house, while Clive liked the hostel more than where he lives now.

Milan: Four of the men lived in the same large institution for between 16 and 30 years, while the other three - Dario, Stefano and Paulo - moved to the institution having previously lived with their families. Roberto, Dario and Alberto thought that life in the institution was 'O.K', while the others didn't like it at all. Riccardo and Andrea said that they really hated it there.

When he lived in the institution, Andrea had to share with 70 other residents; Stefano talked about his life sharing a room with just three other people.

Dario and Stefano - who had lived with their natural families before moving to the institution - were not taught new skills which might help them adapt to life in the community. The other 5 men report that they did indeed engage in a number of activities designed to help them learn new skills, including money handling, cooking, using transport, how to find work and washing and cleaning.

When asked to compare their present home with life in the institution, Paulo said that 'it [the institution] was horrible'. Stefano said that it 'felt good' to leave, while Alberto felt sad on leaving the big hospital. Dario said that the fact that their new home is smaller means that it is better than living in the institution. All of the men conclude that they prefer living in the community house, with personal reasons for this being the opportunities for working outside the house as opposed to living and working inside the same building (according to Paulo) and feeling safe in knowing the other people who would be moving in (Dario).

The building that you live in: Moving in and living arrangements

The striking difference between the two groups here concerns ownership of space. The men in London have their own rooms, as in the institution, and were encouraged as far as possible to have control and choice as to how the rooms are furnished. The concept of choice is covered in the normalisation approach, as are individuality and independence; having one's own room is therefore a direct consequence for services which advocate these principles.

In Milan bedrooms are shared in pairs, a conscious policy instigated by the service managers as a way of gradually introducing the men to a more independent way of living. It was thought inappropriate to expect people who were used to living on large wards of up to 80 people to immediately sleep alone. The responses from two of the tenants that they need staff to be around during the night, supports the project's policy that security needs to be provided for the men during this important period following their move into the community. Such inter-dependence is a theme which permeates the entire support service, and is a clear illustration of the attempts at substituting a 'family' environment.

London: Four of the men said that they went to have a look at their new house before they moved in.

Matthew, Clive and Peter chose the colour schemes in their bedrooms, while Alan said that his was chosen by staff. "The builders" decided on the colours for David's room. In all cases, the men seem happy with the colours that have been chosen.

On the subject of pets, only Matthew felt that they are not allowed in the house.

Milan: Four of the men in the Milan project came to see their new house before they moved in . Six share a room with one other - only Roberto has his own room, a chance happening due to his moving in a little after his flatmates. This sharing of rooms is given as the main reason for the men not choosing the colour schemes - all indicated that the builders painted the walls without input from the prospective tenants. Riccardo commented that 'the ragazzi [the guys][9] like white', while Paulo remarked 'I didn't choose it, but I would have chosen white anyway'.

There are no animals living at the house, which is a result of a group discussion about the practicalities of keeping pets in a third floor apartment. Indeed, while all of the men expressed a liking for pets, particularly dogs, it was Alberto who commented 'Where would you keep animals in a flat?'

House rules: Making decisions and allocating responsibility

Differences do appear to exist between the two groups' perceptions of house rules and responsibilities. The men from the London project talk about certain activities which they feel are governed by rules - helping in the kitchen is one example - while the Milanese tenants do not appear to recognise the structures which they talk about as 'rules'.

Decisions regarding chores seem to include the London tenants

---

[9] The tenants refer to themselves, and are referred to by staff as 'i ragazzi' (the guys); this is an Italian colloquialism used by young people when talking to and about their friends or peers.

considerably, and they seem to be responsible for cleaning their own spaces as well as taking a share in communal chores such as shopping. Again, this could be seen as evidence that the model of individual and independent living is operating. The Milanese tenants seem to be clear that part of the role of staff is that of cleaning (when the men are at work) and shopping, and especially cooking.[10]

House meetings are formally arranged in the London project, a strategy which promotes participation in decision making as well as in daily life - a central tenet of normalisation. In Milan, meanwhile, the cultural institution of the Italian family evening meal appears to have provided a role model upon which the project has based its approach to supporting the men and giving them a recognised space for talking about their day and any issues they might want to raise - in a relaxed, informal way. Meetings are seen by the Milanese men as being the reserve of staff.

London: All of the men gave names of members of staff as those responsible for doing the cooking, while all of them clean their own rooms. Peter and David feel that the food shopping is done mainly by people living in the house by themselves, while Alan and Matthew said that the men do the shopping with the support of staff. Clive feels there are no clear rules about shopping - it can be done by anyone.

Decision making is a joint process between staff and residents as far as Matthew and David are concerned, with Alan believing that it is the residents who have the final say. Again, Clive feels that there is no real pattern - deciding on who is responsible for chores can be up to anyone.

House rules were mentioned by all of the men except Clive. They include helping in the kitchen, going to bed, deciding the frequency of visiting a particular relative and having a bath. Only Alan feels that there is a house rule stipulating a time for the residents to be home at night.

Peter and David feel that the men choose what music to play and which programmes to watch on television individually, while Clive , Matthew and Alan said that staff decide[11].

All of the men reported that they all sit down for a meal together every day.

Matthew and Alan said that house meetings are held where they sometimes speak - these meetings are not held very often. The other men either didn't know (in the case of David) or said that meetings are not held.
Milan: The men agreed that the two female staff, Assunta and Maria, do the

---

[10] See evidence from participant observation regarding the involvement of the Milanese tenants in cooking.

[11] All of the men have their own television and music playing equipment in their bedrooms.

majority of the cooking, while the residents are responsible for cleaning their own rooms. At weekends, the shared areas of the house are cleaned by everybody - staff and tenants - but during the week it is done by Assunta and Maria. Food shopping also appears to be left in the main to staff, who tend to decide who is to be responsible for completing domestic tasks.

The consensus is that there are no house rules; Paulo's comment was that he has 'never been told what to do'. Dario and Andrea said that they would call home if they were going to be out late, but the others feel that being late home is a situation that never arises.

Deciding what to watch on television is a group activity, and there do not seem to be any particular rules about playing music. Only Roberto and Riccardo talked about using their rooms for listening to their own music.

Mealtimes are communal, and are seen as important by all the men for the social aspect as well as the obvious satisfying of hunger. Later evidence suggests that the dining table provides an important space for talking and sharing thoughts and feelings (see page 292), perhaps indicating an informal channel through which the tenants are able to voice concerns and get support. Meetings are not formally arranged, although Dario did mention that a meeting could be set up for discussing what he termed 'formal problems'. An interesting comment was made by Stefano: 'Meetings are for staff - I don't know what they talk about'.

Privacy and trust

While both groups of men appear to believe they enjoy a certain degree of privacy, the physical layout of each project would suggest that the London project gives the men more private space. The extent to which the men feel they are able to trust one another seems to need more exploration to ensure that the definitions offered to the men are appropriate. The present findings would suggest that individuals have their own thoughts and interpretations, but the structures in place for the London men - personal locks and keys to bedroom doors and clear boundaries between the tenants' part of the house and that used by staff - would perhaps lead to more discussion between workers and residents about the nature of trust, privacy and security than an environment which tends more toward an 'open-plan' approach. The more integrated style adopted in Milan would support the focus on inter-dependence as set out in the operational policy.

London: The men were asked whether other people knocked on their bedroom doors before entering: Matthew said they knock sometimes, and

Alan said they never knock. The other three all report that people knock on their doors. Only Clive suggested that there is no lock on the bathroom door.[12] All of the men said they feel they can be alone in their own rooms if they so wish.

In terms of enjoying privacy with visitors and guests, the London men have chairs in their rooms for people to use when they visit - although David disagreed.

The more difficult and perhaps abstract concept of trusting flatmates led to Peter and Clive commenting that they feel able to trust people not to take money from their rooms, and can also tell them secrets. Matthew and David said that they do trust people - but yet replied in the negative to the two examples given. Alan said that nobody in the building can be trusted.

Milan: Only Andrea and Dario suggested that other people in the house are in the habit of knocking before coming into their bedrooms, and that there is a lock on the bathroom door. More general discussion about privacy did reveal that the men are able to be on their own in their rooms if they wish, although it remains unclear how this happens in practice, given the current sleeping arrangements.

Stefano said that visitors are welcome, and can stay overnight - this was not felt to be possible by the others. All agreed that chairs are available in all bedrooms for guests to use as they wish.

All of the Milanese tenants feel they can trust their flatmates except Riccardo, who said that he feels he can trust them 'a little bit'. As with the London men, the concept of trust could well have been too abstract for the men to comprehend: Roberto said that he trusted them, but 'you can't tell them secrets', while Paulo simply replied, 'yes, they're good friends'. This area would perhaps make an interesting research study, as it is likely that the concept of trust is bound up in numerous but important culturally and socially derived factors.

Relationships with staff

There appear to be some similarities here: both groups seem to agree on when they feel staff need to be around - indeed, there appears to be a realisation that they are people who need the support of others. Both groups talk about the significance of their keyworkers or identify one person as being of specific importance in the supportive role. One difference seems to be the emphasis that the London group gives to the help they are given in

---

[12] Time spent in the house during participant observation supported the majority view here.

completing tasks, while the Milanese men talk about support when they are feeling anxious or unwell. This observation would suggest that competence as advocated by the normalisation approach is being implemented in the London project, interpreted as requiring the men to learn and engage in tasks regularly. The Milanese men talk more about receiving psychological support from staff.

London: The tenants did not agree on the number of staff working with them. Clive and David said it is two, while the others said three, four and five respectively.[13]

All of the men reported that staff are with them all the time. When asked about the most important times for staff to be around, Clive, David and Alan said that staff should always be around, Peter said he felt mornings are most important and Matthew that both mornings and evenings are important.

None of the tenants were involved in the recruitment of staff, but Matthew said that he chose his keyworker and seemed to feel that this was a form of recruitment.

All of the men replied that they are able to talk easily with staff and enjoy being with them. It was not possible to encourage any expansion on this. More detail was provided in responses to questions asking how the tenants feel that staff help them. Three quotes - from David, Alan and Matthew respectively - illustrate the task-oriented nature of the replies: "..they tell me to have a shower"; "...if I can't do any cooking I just say 'staff will you come and help me'"; "...[they] tell me to wash things".. Other interesting comments came from Peter and then Clive: "...[the staff] don't help with things that are worrying me" and "...[the staff] tell me when I do well".

Milan: In perhaps a similar way to the London group, the Milanese tenants gave answers very much from their own perspective when asked about the number of staff supporting them. Riccardo said there are 7 (the total number of staff in the team), and Paulo and Roberto 3 - the number of staff on shift at any one time. The other men said they work with only one member of staff, giving the name of their keyworker. This perhaps indicates the importance that people place on the role of their keyworker, a phenomenon also observed in London.

All the men reported that staff are around the house all day. Dario,

---

[13] There are 7 people in the team altogether, with the number on shift at any one time varying between 1 and 4 depending on sickness, annual leave and the interpretation of the rota by senior staff. Each service user has two co-keyworkers.

Paulo and Roberto feel that staff need to be there all the time, while Stefano and Andrea said they are needed most during the night. Alberto and Riccardo suggest that either the morning or the evening is most important, depending on what is happening and what the 'ragazzi' need to do. The men were not involved in the recruitment of staff.

Most of the men named their keyworker as the member of the team with whom they felt most at ease. All except Dario and Stefano said that staff help them at times when they are worried about something. Dario said that staff are always helping him, but especially when he feels unwell. Stefano's response was that only his keyworker does anything which he recognises as being helpful.

Relationships with outside agencies and professionals

The two groups of men seem to have similar views about how they use specialist services. It is interesting to bear this in mind when looking at differences and similarities in the approach to individual planning in the two services (see chapter 6).

London: All of the men replied that they go to a GP. Alan and Clive chose their doctor, while the others said that a member of staff had made the decision. Peter and David receive services from a psychologist, and Clive visits a chiropodist. When asked whether he had special help from people other than the staff working in the house, Alan named two of his flatmates.[14]

Milan: All of the men in the Milan project use a GP, chosen by staff in the main and by themselves in the case of Dario and Stefano. The only person who talked about special help from people other than direct support staff was Riccardo, who regularly sees a psychologist.[15]

Relationships with other residents

There are certainly differences in perception among the London group

---

[14] None of the respondents made any reference to individual life plan meetings where professionals are said to be invited in order to meet individual needs and support residents in integrating with the local community.

[15] The men made no reference to the annual planning meetings at which decisions are made regarding their progress at work placements. While meetings are apparently held to discuss work at which the resident is invited to attend, the major meeting is exclusively for a multi-disciplinary team of professionals. Their exclusion from this process could perhaps explain why the men did not talk about professionals during the interviews, as it could be that they are unable to relate those regular meetings as having any bearing on their daily lives, even though the reports are fed back by staff.

concerning how well they get on together, and there is talk of conflicts - perhaps to be expected among any group of adults living together. The mention of violence does appear to be accurate - one of the men has been experiencing difficulties in coming to terms with great losses in his life, and according to the managers of the service he uses, appears to be expressing his feelings in this way at the time of writing.

If there are no conflicts between the Milanese men, it would not be appropriate to suggest reasons for this apparent difference in the nature of relationships between tenants. Further long term observation would be needed to establish the accuracy of the mens' perceptions and even then, too many variables exist in the living environment to draw any meaningful conclusions. Individual characteristics and interpersonal dynamics are obvious key considerations. It is relevant to note however, that the rationale underpinning the Milanese approach to integration - the socio-educative support model - would argue that encouraging peer support, particularly in terms of sharing rooms, develops a sense of trust and camaraderie that cannot be achieved when people with a limited understanding of their new environment are integrated individually. This concept will be explored further using other themes during the discussion of the participant observation data.

London: All of the men reported that they mostly get on well with their flatmates. Matthew and Alan said that there are never arguments; David and Clive feel that arguments do happen, while Peter said that such conflicts can be physical.

All of the men reported that they had known their flatmates for a long time before moving in with them.

Milan: All seven men reported without hesitation that they get on well with their flatmates and that there are no arguments. They all knew each other for a long time before moving into the project: Stefano is the relative newcomer, having known his flatmates for 6 years, but the others have lived together in the institution for 'a very long time'. This was borne out during discussions with the Director of Social Services (Cassaro 1995).

Solving problems and dealing with difficulties

The point of interest here is the role that each group appear to have assigned to their support staff. The London men would apparently not choose to go to staff working in the project in an emergency, or for solving problems - the

Milanese men say in the main that they would approach staff. While a complaints procedure does exist as a structure within the London service, the service users do not seem to be aware of its existence. Some of the Milanese men appear aware of their service's procedure.

London: The men were asked to name the people they would consult when minor problems arose. None of the group mentioned staff working in the project, choosing instead either a day centre keyworker, GP or the manager of the institution where the men used to live. All five feel they are able to make this choice freely; in terms of the results of the problem-solving, Matthew, Peter and David are often happy while Clive is not always happy.

In the event of a serious emergency, Peter and Alan would alert staff - in the case of Peter, his keyworker. David would call the police.

Discussion about the procedure for making complaints did not reveal any knowledge about using a specific procedure. Clive said that he would tell the manager of the project, Peter his keyworker and Alan said that he too would go to a member of staff. None of the men know what they would do should they have a complaint to make about a member of staff: indeed the concept seemed to be something that they had either not considered or were not able to understand.

Milan: When problems arise, Paulo talks to the house manager[16] and the others consult a member of staff. All seven said they are able to choose the person they consult, and all reported that they are happy with the results.

In the case of a serious incident - examples given by the interviewer were if somebody got hurt, or some money was stolen - Dario would go to a policeman, Alberto wasn't sure who he would contact and the others would talk to staff.

Four of the men are aware of a complaints procedure they can use, and feel they would be able to do so. Alberto, Paulo and Riccardo do not know about such a system.

Handling and controlling money

The systems for organising tenants' money is different in each project, and these differences can be traced to the level of legislation. The fact that people with learning disabilities living within the authority of the Milanese local authority are supported in securing contracted employment with wages comparable in value to the rest of the working population means that they

[16]This is the resident who often refers to the house manager as "Daddy".

are able to contribute in the usual way to the payment of bills. Employment is seen by the service managers as the corner stone of the project in many ways, as they feel it offers not only a structure and sense of purpose to the mens' lives, but also contributes to the development of self-esteem when they realise that they have employment status like any other citizen. Certainly, the men talk about their work with great pride, peppering their responses to interview questions with vignettes from the work place, and in the case of Paulo, illustrating his stories by miming the activities he is involved with during the day. The participant observation data suggests that returning from work provides the focus for the evening during the week, and often instigates conversation between the tenants and between tenants and staff.

The men in Britain receive benefits because any work that they are involved with pays a token amount - in Peter's case £3.00 for two day's work. A vicious circle seems to be in operation: if supported employment schemes were to pay much more to their employees, the men would experience a reduction in their benefit payments. The absence of employment legislation for people with learning disabilities in Britain means that such supported employment schemes do not have the funds to provide appropriate salaries. The direct link made between work and self esteem that has been established and recognised in Milan does not seem to be possible at the present time in Britain. This surely has implications when assessing the implementation of normalisation, as genuine integration cannot occur unless people have been assigned valued roles - attending day centres and working in part time sheltered employment schemes are minority activities when compared with the rest of the population, and do not elicit comparable salaries. This is a key area where normalisation is not being implemented in its most basic form, as service users are still tied to services and are financially dependent - even if services are striving to encourage emotional dependence and exposure to non-disabled activities and environments in the community.

London: Clive reported that staff accompany him to the post office to collect his DLA (Disability Living Allowance) and income support, while the others said that they collect their own money.[17] All five men said that they pay their own rent - Peter mentioned that staff accompany him when he

---

[17] All of the men need support when they collect their benefits from the local post office. This is a relatively new system: when they lived in the institution, monies were sent to the Social Services Department, where they were distributed to the various projects via senior staff, arriving in a security van and placed in individual lockable tins with service users having no contact or involvement.

does this at the post office.[18]

David, Peter and Alan said that they buy their own food; Clive said that staff are responsible, while Matthew said that Peter usually buys the food.

All five of the men said that they have money of their own to spend. "Staff give it to me" said Clive; Peter feels that "we [the tenants] only have a little bit of money".

The men said that they are able to go out alone to buy small items, except David who said that staff need to go out with him.

Milan: None of the men in the Milan project receive benefits which are comparable to those paid to people with learning disabilities in Britain. Their supported employment pays them a conventional wage the rate of which has been authorised by the magistrate's court to prevent exploitation. These salaries are paid directly to bank accounts, enabling the tenants to contribute to household bills in a similar way to any employed person. Food is purchased from a 'kitty' to which all the men contribute and the local authority provides a sum to cover the cost of staff eating with tenants. This practice is also observed in the London service.

After bills have been paid, the remaining funds are left in the personal accounts, and all of the men report that they feel they have control over how this money is spent. All seven also said that they are able to go into shops on their own and make small purchases such as a newspaper or can of drink. This was noted during participant observation: Assunta required some more milk to prepare dinner, and asked Andrea to go to the local grocery store with a note that she wrote for him.

Clothes

Both groups seem to have control other the clothes they buy and what they wear; this is an area of choice making where both approaches converge. Choice making does seem to happen in the Milan service, but clear boundaries are drawn between issues open to users and those which are closed. Choice making for the British service users is a less clearly defined concept in the sense that, ostensibly, no area of life is closed to service users making their own decisions. Perhaps this links with the service's aims to promote individual responsibility, which can only be acquired with exposure

---

[18] Rent is in fact paid directly to the Housing Association concerned, in the form of housing benefit from the Government. A 'top-up' is paid individually by each tenant, which guarantees the provision of services such as refuse collection, building maintenance and general housing management services. In conversation with service users, staff refer to this small fee as 'rent'.

to the decision making process. However, this observation needs to be placed in the context of the results from the analysis of the individual planning system: it would appear that staff are less skilled in helping people with more profound disabilities make important choices. Operational policies make no reference to the possibility of variation in these abilities between service users, while advocating the importance of 'needs-led' provision and 'individuality' in many other respects.

London: The five men choose their own clothes. Peter, Alan and Clive said that they buy their own clothes, David that he chooses his clothes but staff need to go with him to buy them. Matthew said that he doesn't buy his own clothes.

Milan: All of the men choose their own clothes. Roberto said that staff buy his clothes for him,[19] Paulo and Riccardo claim to buy clothes on their own and the others all said that staff need to be around when they buy their clothes.

Visitors

One issue here appears to be around privacy when receiving visitors. The London project places an emphasis on privacy and individualising of bedrooms perhaps enabling tenants to have more control over who meets or doesn't meet a guest. It is assumed that the guest has come to see one person in particular, and would want to spend time with him alone as a priority, rather than socialising as part of the larger group. Staff would ensure that the tenant and guest are afforded space away from both staff and other tenants, which does not seem to be important practice for the Milan project - where guests seem to be viewed as having come to see everybody in the family'.

London: People can visit the men in the London project whenever they wish. Discussion about visits from members of the family suggest that contact is varied.

David couldn't remember when he last saw his relatives; other responses included three days ago (Alan), last week (Clive) and two weeks ago (Matthew).[20]

When people visit one of the tenants, Peter, Clive and Matthew said

[19]At the time of interview this man had had an accident and was temporarily using a wheelchair - it is possible that he was referring to his inability to go shopping at that moment in time.
[20] Four of the men have relatives who are in contact. In three cases these relatives are parents.

that everybody meets them, but wouldn't necessarily spend a great deal of time in their company.

Milan: Five of the group said that people are able to visit whenever they want to, while Alberto said that his friends live far away, making it difficult to meet up very often.

When asked how recent was the last visit from a family member or friend, the tenants answered within the contexts of their individual situations. Paulo had seen his father two months previous to the interview. Riccardo replied that all his family are dead, and Roberto said that he visits his uncle and friend on the bus at weekends. Stefano has no family or friends 'outside', and Andrea said he had not had any visitors recently.

When people come to the project everyone meets them. This too perhaps raises important recognition of cultural factors influencing the service. Hospitality is central to the Italian way of life, and a place at the dining table is usually offered to guests without hesitation, whatever the length of their acquaintance. As mealtimes are viewed with such importance within the project as communal time, one can see how the tenants would be given opportunities to meet people very easily.

Neighbours and acquaintances

There seems to be more informal interaction between tenants and people in the local community in the Milan project compared with the experience of the men in London. This is important to note when one realises that time is spent in the London project's operational policy outlining the importance of making links with the local community. Presence in the community is also one of O'Brien's Five Accomplishments (1985) upon which the operational policy is based. If interacting with non-disabled people is as valuable as is stated by the normalisation approach (Wolfensberger 1972), advocates of the framework would presumably be concerned that the project appears to be failing in this area. It is also interesting to note that it was the Milan service providers and not the London service providers who decided to inform the local neighbourhood about the project before it was instigated, as they felt that acceptance of the project by local people was essential to its success. No comparable piece of work was carried out with the London project.

London: Most of the men speak to their neighbours. Only Clive had a different view, his response being "No, I just say goodbye, you aren't supposed to talk to strangers".

The men do not feel that they get help from neighbours, and none have been inside neighbours' homes.

Discussion then turned to other people living or present in the local community. Alan and David do not speak to people nearby. Matthew said that he likes meeting other people, but remarked "I don't speak to people I don't know". Clive's response was that he went into the local paper shop, but the woman who works there asked him to leave. Peter simply said "Don't talk to them!".

Milan: The men have contact with the family next door. Paulo feels that this family help him in one way or another - Dario, Roberto and Stefano see them as neighbours, perhaps implying that neighbours are not people who provide support as such. Riccardo views them as his friends, while Andrea thinks they are 'very kind' - but not people from whom help can be sought.

Andrea, Roberto and Dario have been inside their neighbours' homes at one time or another. All of the men talked about parties they hold at the house when neighbours are invited, usually at Christmas or for someone's birthday.

Informal interaction with people in the community seems to take place at the pizzeria, the bar or at the newspaper shop. Stefano and Riccardo said they do not meet or know other people nearby. The nature of contact in all cases appears to be in the form of greetings, although in the pizzeria, where the men often go as a group, there is much bantering between residents, support staff and pizzeria staff in what staff describe as a very relaxed atmosphere.

Friends and relationships

For both groups of men, the special friends in their lives are those with whom they have lived or worked. This can be placed again within the ideological frameworks adopted by each service. The Milan project states that group living and peer support are essential to the well being of people with learning disabilities, and that integration in the community can be more successful and appropriate if service users are integrated as individuals within groups. The London project, informed by normalisation, suggests that interaction with non-disabled people encourages development and enhances self-esteem, as people with learning disabilities become more valued. The experience of the British men here is that the important people in their lives, those with whom they have formed special relationships, also use learning disability services. As with the evidence from interaction with the community, it would seem that the policy to encourage interaction with non-disabled people has not managed to support the men in forming relationships which they are able to regard as meaningful.

London: Peter talked about someone whom he knew at the institution as his friend - this person was still living there at the time of interview, but would be moving out soon. David, Clive and Alan have friends at the day centre, while Matthew was unable to think of someone he considers to be a friend other than those people sharing the house.

All of the men have 'special' friends - in all cases either flatmates or people still living at the institution.

Milan: When asked about friends other than those living in the project, the tenants talked about people at work or from the past. Riccardo mentioned someone who lives downstairs, and only Andrea said that his only friends are his flatmates. Five of the men have a friend they regard as 'special': only in the case of Andrea is this person a flatmate.

Religion and belief

The Milanese tenants seem more able to identify and associate themselves with specific faiths than the men in London - although the British tenants still commented that they realise they are able to worship should they wish to do so.

London: All five men said that they feel able to worship wherever they wish. At present, only Peter chooses to do this. When asked about their experiences of meeting people from other religions or cultures, none of the group gave a reply.

Milan: The men gave responses according to their own religious predilections: Paulo and Riccardo identify as Roman Catholic, and Roberto as a Jehovah's Witness. Dario said that he does not identify with any particular religion, but does go to church every Sunday. The other three describe themselves as having no religion.

When asked about their experiences of other cultures, Andrea said he has met people from Sardinia and Germany; Riccardo has met people from Japan.

How you feel about yourself

There seem to be differences in how confident the two groups of men feel about asking for help, and more of the Milanese men seem able to assert themselves when asked to do things they don't like. This could of course be attributed to the individual personalities within each group or the way in which the questions were phrased, rather than resulting from the implementation of the operational policies underpinning the two services. However, it can be noted that the assumption that the work scheme in Milan develops self esteem could be supported by the comments made by some of the Milanese service users. Secondly, it is of separate concern that the London men are saying in part that they find it difficult to ask for assistance when required.

London: Questions in this section asked the tenants how they feel about doing things for themselves. Alan , David and Matthew said that they feel 'all right'. When asked about making choices or going out alone, the responses included "I feel a bit scared" (Clive), "I can choose things" (Peter) and "I look both ways to see if cars are coming" (David).

Moving on to talk about support needs, Matthew, Peter and Clive all said that they find it difficult to ask for help from staff. David said that he likes having help.

When it comes to being assertive and saying no to things that the men do not want, Alan and Matthew are the two who feel able to speak out. Clive's response was that he says 'go away' when people ask him to do things or say things that he doesn't like.

Milan: All of the men reported that they enjoy doing things for themselves. Responses included 'I feel good because I have my own work, I go by myself' (Paulo) and "It's good - I like T.V. and radio and going to work because I do it myself. I choose food at work" (Dario). When asked, all of the group said that they do not find it difficult to ask for help from the people supporting them. Equally, all of the men feel able to say no to things that they don't like. Examples were provided first by Riccardo: "I don't like cleaning, but it's part of my job - I'd say no to other things" and then by Roberto: "I'd say yes to cleaning the bathroom [at home] but not the other guys' bedrooms".

Making your own decisions

It would appear that both groups of men feel reasonably able to do things for themselves, as and when they wish. Access to keys is given, while the issue of consent when taking medication is not relevant for the people interviewed here.

London: Peter, David and Alan all replied that they feel able to go out when they wish, and Matthew said that his keyworker says that he needs someone to go with him. These men all said that they can return whenever they wish, and can also do other things without having to ask - having a cup of tea, having a bath or going to the pub. The issue of safety was raised by Clive, Matthew and David, who when asked about going to the pub alone replied respectively, "...no, it's too dangerous crossing the road on my own"; "...no, not really, no. I don't want to go on my own" and simply "...not on my own".

The issue of independence was raised again in the context of holding front door keys and taking medication. All of the men have keys - although Matthew was unsure on this. David, Clive and Alan also have keys to their rooms.[21] With medication, Alan, Clive and David regularly need support from staff, while Peter and Matthew said they are not taking medication on a regular basis.[22]

Milan: The men feel that they can go out and come back when they wish. All of the men said they can make themselves drinks and have baths at will except Paulo, who said he feels he needs to ask a member of staff first. Dario stressed that everybody eats together.

The men visit the bar on their own, and have their own front door keys, but not keys to their bedrooms. None of the men currently take regular medication.

Time at home

The groups are similar here in that in the main, they are engaged in established day activity which provides structure to their week.

London: Matthew spends all day at home. The others spend their weekdays at the day centre or at a combination of different day centres and supported workschemes.[23] At weekends, David, Matthew and Alan go out 'sometimes', Peter goes to clubs in the evenings and Clive spends time at home.

---

[21] All tenants are given keys to the front door and to their rooms. One of the men carries these with him, the others are kept in a special unlocked cabinet in the staff sleeping-in room.

[22] All of the men are prescribed medication for a wide range of conditions including epilepsy, psychosis and anxiety. Four of the men need support in administering this medication, and one man is engaged in a self-administration programme.

[23] This work scheme is designed for very able people with learning disabilities and is a small scale commercial enterprise. Involvement of service users does not seem to be individualised, and payment at the time of writing is £3 for 2 days work.

Milan: All of the men living in the Milan project work five days a week, and therefore talked about their time outside working hours. Roberto spends 'a lot of time at home', while Riccardo, Paulo and Dario spend time visiting people at weekends. Andrea and Alberto spend the evenings and mornings at home - Stefano goes out 'sometimes'.

Leisure: weekends and evenings

It is interesting to note when comparing the groups that two of the English men listed domestic tasks as the activities they are engaged in during their spare time, while the Italian men talk only of leisure pursuits.

London: In this spare time, David and Matthew watch television and Alan spends his time cleaning and vacuuming. Clive goes out "sometimes". Peter said that he goes to clubs and "I don't like washing my clothes but I have to do it".

Favourite television programmes included watching table tennis, football, sport generally, the news, films and "The Bill" (a television drama about the police).

Milan: Dario, Roberto, Riccardo and Stefano enjoy listening to music, and Andrea likes to visit the Cathedral or play cards. Paulo watches television and Alberto prefers to 'stay in'.

As far as television is concerned, listed favourite programmes include football, cartoons, comedies, anything on RAI Uno (a particular television channel) and circuses.

Getting out and about

It seems that both groups of men are fairly active, and able to enjoy the facilities their communities can offer, as well as travelling farther afield. Getting around, either independently or with support, does not seem to be an issue in either service.

London: Matthew, Alan and David do not go out on their own. Clive goes out sometimes, and Peter goes to his social clubs two evenings every week. When asked about issues with getting around, Clive said 'I don't like it'. Peter reported that he doesn't have any problems in this area. David's response was that 'We go in the van to the day centre' .24

The men were asked if there were any places that they particularly enjoy going to. The long list included shops, the cinema, restaurants - especially 'McDonald's - Hampton Court, Kew gardens, the Tower of London, Southend and airports. Five of these responses came from Peter, who is perhaps the most independent of the men in the London project in terms of going out.

All of the men said that they would like to go out more than they are able to at the moment. David feels that there is enough to do in the local area, but Clive feels there isn't enough. The others gave no clear response.

Milan: Paulo is the only one of the men who needs support when travelling to work - the others all travel independently. Dario, Roberto and Riccardo also travel on their own at weekends. The 'workbus' - provided by the local authority - is felt to make travelling around independently much easier.

The list of places that the Milanese group enjoy included the mountains, the cinema, the City centre, the Cathedral and Genoa. Riccardo and Dario feel that they already go out a lot, but the others would like to go out more often. All of the men also think that there is plenty to do in the local area - Riccardo and Paulo think that their current local community has more to offer than where they lived before.

Hobbies

Again it is interesting that some of the men in the London project talk about domestic chores in response to questions about hobbies and pastimes.

London: Clive enjoys sport, Alan's response was 'washing' and David said 'washing up and 'cooking' with his keyworker. Matthew said that a new hobby for him would be "making tea". If the men wanted to find out about new hobbies, they would approach the house manager, their keyworker or "do it myself".

Four of the men have been to the local library - Peter went once and took out some books, Alan went with his keyworker from the day centre. Only Matthew said that he doesn't look at books.

Milan: Hobbies among the group include music, books, Kung Fu, watching the news on T.V., singing, travelling around and eating at the pizzeria. Staff

---

[24] Day centre transport calls daily for three of the residents, usually in the form of a mini-bus which picks up day centre users from all over the borough according to specified routes.

would help them to try new hobbies, which might include body building, dancing and going to the mountains more often.

Only Roberto and Riccardo visit the local library, although Paulo and Stefano said that they also look at books.

Holidays

Going on holiday for the Milan group seems to be further evidence of the emphasis on peer support: the whole house usually goes away together, an idea which would not be supported by the managers of the London service.

London: Holiday suggestions named by Alan, David and Clive were a boat trip, Clacton and 'I'm going to see my mum'. The men were going to be accompanied by the house manager, a member of support staff and the handicapped people".[25]

David, Matthew and Clive have been abroad in the past. Usual holiday destinations include the seaside, Clacton and Wales. The three people who responded to these questions all said that they can choose where they go for their holidays.

Milan: Most of the men are going to the mountains on holiday - only Dario is going to Sardinia with his mother and nephew. Staff will be accompanying the others. Paulo, Riccardo and Stefano have been abroad - to Germany, Lourdes in France and Israel respectively.

The usual holiday destination for the whole group is either the mountains or the sea, with four of the men feeling that they are able to choose where they go.[26]

Speaking to the service users: A summary

The findings above can be summarised into main differences and similarities between the experience of daily life as reported by the service users. The main headings are presented in Table (vi) and (vii).

---

[25] This refers to holidays for people with learning disabilities organised by MENCAP which this service user now goes on. Holidays in the institution were often group affairs, but now staff are encouraged to organise individual holidays - sometimes with agencies such as MENCAP or The Winged Fellowship - or trips for perhaps 2 service users supported by staff.

[26] The staff suggest that decisions regarding where to go on holiday are made as a group and that the service users are given two or three options from which to choose. They usually all go away together.

Table (vi) Differences in response between service users in London and Milan during the lifestyle questionnaire

MAIN DIFFERENCES IN RESPONSE BETWEEN GROUPS	
Use of living space	Employment and financial status
Choice of bedroom decor	Receiving visitors and guests
House rules	Relationships with neighbours
Decision-making process	Perceptions of the role of staff
House meetings	Confidence in asking staff for help
Perception of peer relationships	Use of leisure time
Responses in the event of emergencies	Approach towards taking holidays
Understanding of complaints procedure	

Table (vii): Similarities in response between service users in London and Milan during the lifestyle questionnaire

SIMILARITIES IN RESPONSE BETWEEN GROUPS
Preparation for the move: learning skills
Perceptions of disability
Meeting special friends
Perception of specialist services
Perception of autonomy
Getting out and about

Similarities in experience

1. Both groups suggest that before moving into the community they were involved in teaching programmes looking at particular skills. This perhaps implies that both of the services saw the move as tending towards a more independent way of life for the tenants.

2. Both groups agree that they are people who need the support of others. They also agree generally on the times of day when this support is most needed.

3. Special friends are people with whom the tenants have either lived or worked. In the case of the Milanese group this supports the policy of peer support taken to develop self esteem for people with disabilities. For the

London project, the absence of evidence of relationships with non-disabled people as recommended by the normalisation approach would suggest that if using this as a criterion for success, the service is currently failing to meet its objectives in this area.

4. Both groups of men have similar views on their use of specialist services.

5. Most of the men feel they can do things for themselves as and when they wish.

6. The general feeling in both projects is that most of the tenants are able to move around the community without too much difficulty.

Differences in experience

1. Ownership and use of personal space is approached differently. The Milan project seems to emphasise a more communal approach, with shared rooms and activity founded upon principles of gradual integration after institutionalised living. The project in London has allocated a bedroom for each man and does not seem so focused on sharing and communality as lifestyle goals.

2. The London men appeared to have had more choice in decorating their bedrooms - the project in Milan painted all the rooms the same, before the tenants moved in.

3. The London tenants are aware of the existence of house rules, while the Milanese tenants talk about certain structures within their lives but do not consider these to be rules.

4. With regard to deciding on who will be responsible for completing household chores, it seems that the London men are more involved in the process - although the Milanese men are clear that certain activities are in the staff's domain, particularly cleaning the communal areas of the house and cooking.

5. House meetings are arranged for the tenants in the London project, while the discussion and sharing of thoughts for the Milanese men happens informally together over mealtimes. The use of 'we' rather than 'I' when talking about their lives perhaps further illustrates the reference to group

living in the Milan project's operational policy. 'Meetings' in the arranged, formal sense are viewed by the Milanese men as an activity engaged in by staff.

6. There appear to be differences between the projects regarding the use of private space. The Milan project could be described as 'open-plan', with shared bedrooms which look similar and a large space divided in to a lounge and quiet area. It is suggested here that the individual bedrooms and focus on tenants' personal space and privacy would afford staff in the London project more opportunities for raising issues of security and trust.

7. The London tenants perceive that there can be conflicts among them, while the Milanese tenants feel this not to be the case in their house. No clear conclusions can be drawn using solely this evidence, although again it contributes towards and supports the approach of group living described in the operational policy.

8. In the event of emergencies, the Milanese tenants would consult staff, while the London men feel they would go to professionals or agencies not directly involved with the support of the project.

9. The Milanese men are aware of a complaints procedure and feel they would be able to use it. The London men are less clear about any such procedure in the service they use.

10. A fundamental difference concerns the employment status held by the men in society. While both groups are recognised as being learning disabled, with similar levels of disability, the approach taken towards employment is clearly different in each project. Real employment status in terms of salary and ability to support oneself is available to the Milanese men, compared to a mixture of day centre attendance and part-time employment schemes offered to the London men. More importantly, the Milanese framework for employing people with learning disabilities has been supported with Regional legislation, where individual situations are monitored using the authority of the Magistrate's Court. The Milanese project's operational policy makes specific reference to the scheme, suggesting that valued employment recognised by the State is essential for the development of self esteem in people with learning disabilities.

11. The approach taken towards visitors seems to differ in each project. In London, people come to the house to see individuals, and hence the tenants are encouraged to spend time alone with their guests, usually in their bedrooms. While visitors might also visit the Milanese project to see individual tenants, there seems to be a recognition that they have entered a communal household and thus spend time with everybody, usually involving a meal of one kind or another. The physical layout of the house also means that the London model of individuality could not be adopted unless tenants are encouraged not to use their bedrooms while their sharing partner is entertaining a guest.

12. There appear to be differences in the way that the two groups of men interact with and perceive their neighbours, as well as the local community generally. The higher level of contact with neighbours reported by the Milanese men could be a result of the preparation work carried out by service providers, as well as the acknowledgement within the operational policy of the existing diversity of needs amongst people in the surrounding community. The men in London do not talk of any input concerning their relationship with the community, nor are strategies for implementing the policy of presence in the community detailed in the operational policy.

13. The London tenants report that they find it difficult to ask for help from their support staff, whereas the men in Milan do not seem to regard this as a problem . Possible factors contributing to this could be differences in perception of the role that staff play in each project, or perhaps simply the nature of the personal dynamics between individuals. One could be lead to consider, however, that if operational policies are influential, there could be a resulting difference between the projects in terms of the levels of intimacy between staff and residents. The Milanese operational policy not only suggests the recreation of a family environment for these men but also talks of the importance of 'a loving presence' and the provision of 'good familial support in solving problems'. In contrast, the London project, utilising normalisation principles, aims to encourage the formation of relationships between service users and other *non-disabled* people in the community - no specific reference is made to the formation of close relationships between staff and residents. Indeed, in many projects throughout Britain - including this one - keyworking tasks are rotated in order to avoid the development of what are thought to be inappropriate close relationships.

14. A difference arises when the men are asked to describe the ways in which they are supported by staff. The Milanese talk about needing help when they feel anxious or unwell, while the London men see help more in terms of the completion of tasks.

15. With regard to hobbies and pastimes, some of the London men talk about domestic tasks, while the men in Milan list activities which might be thought of more conventionally as leisure. It might be that staff in the London project use the Active Support model (e.g. Emerson *et al* 1994) as developed throughout residential services in Britain to engage the tenants in tasks (an hypothesis which would need extensive evidence to support). Household chores perhaps provide straightforward structures for enabling staff and service users to look at the 'progress' made - the tasks usually have a beginning and an end. Their appropriateness in this context is debatable, however, as it could be argued that leisure time is important and should be spent engaging in recreational activity. Of course, there is also the possibility that the men interviewed *enjoy* participating in domestic tasks, and would therefore choose to do them in their free time. How much of this is enjoyment of the activity in itself, and how much the enjoyment of the security experienced when completing a familiar task, is open to question.

16. Holidays tend to be a group activity for the men in Milan, whereas there seems to be a strong emphasis on individual holidays for the London project. Going on outings as a group used to be common in many learning disability services, and the London tenants have photographs of themselves and other people at the institution taken at various holiday destinations. Here perhaps is more evidence of implementation of the normalisation approach, this time in terms of both individualisation and integration - although two of the 'individual' holidays mentioned by the London tenants were organised by disability charities. It would appear that the service is content for the tenants to be on holiday with other disabled people, as long as those people are not known to them.

To summarise even more broadly for the two groups of men (see Table (viii).

Table (viii): Overview of main differences in style and focus of response between the two groups of service users in London and Milan

LONDON	MILAN
1. Choice-making is evident in most areas of life	1. Choice-making is limited
2. Staff help with completing tasks e.g. "they tell me when I do well"	2. Staff help when tenants are 'anxious'
3. Tenants spoke as individuals i.e." I..."	3. Tenants spoke as a group i.e. "we..."
4. All tenants collect benefits	4. Tenants are paid wages as other workers
5. Little or no contact with neighbours	5. Contact with neighbours

Speaking to support staff in London and Milan

(i) Background and training

This is a key area in which the two services have very different approaches; the responses given seem to accurately reflect the positions outlined in the respective operational policies.

London: Of the five people interviewed, the time spent in service with the local authority by the members of staff ranged from 9 months and 25 years. The other three people had been employed by the service for 4 years, 5 years and 7 years respectively. During this time they had all worked in the hostel with various groups of service users with learning disabilities including some or all of the five men living in the new project, except for the member of staff who had been employed by the local authority for 9 months at the time of interview.

Qualifications among those interviewed vary: one person has a degree in psychology, which included some practical experience with people with learning disabilities. This was the person's first experience of the concept of normalisation. A second interviewee has a qualification in social work (CQSW). The other three members of staff interviewed have no relevant qualifications or formal pre-work training.

Milan: All of the workers interviewed have worked at the project since it first opened in January 1991. Some of the staff (3 people) had known the service users when they were living in the Institution - in one case, the acquaintance has been for over 20 years. This person happens to be one of the 'domestic' staff, who lives alongside the men permanently at the project. People applied for their jobs for one of two reasons:

- they had met and supported the service users while in the institution, and wanted to continue working with them after the move into the *communità allogio* (3 people);

- they wanted to pursue career interests in the field of learning disability - what is referred to by the interviewees as a career in educational and social development (3 people).

All of the Milanese staff interviewed have professional qualifications, and there is a two-tier system within the project: those employed as 'domestic staff' (2 people) have completed nursing training with specialisms in language and rehabilitation. Those employed as *'educatori'* or support staff have completed the professional 3 year training course, with a specialism in pedagogy and psychology (3 people). All of those staff interviewed reported that no service users were involved in their recruitment.

(ii) Being a support worker: How time is spent at work

While the nature of the tasks themselves differed - the Milanese staff talk more about the importance of encouraging the development of relationships with others compared to the London focus on domestic tasks and a 'normal' life - it is also interesting to note that the London staff are as a team more inconsistent in their responses compared to the Milanese team.

London: Responses varied to questions asking staff about their role. All of the staff talked about how they are required to juggle their time between supporting the residents and completing administrative tasks in the 'sleep-in' room. The support is described as 'fulfilling their personal and social needs' and 'to see that they live life as normal, and to the full'. One member of staff answered the question by breaking his work into tasks; these included:

...talking to people, helping them with cooking, laundry etc., going out socially with them, making sure that they get to their dates/appointments. Time is also spent thinking about the clients (sic.) with their longer-term needs in mind.

The perceived main tasks for support workers in the London service are summarised in Table (ix).

Table (ix): Perceived main tasks required - responses given during interviews with residential learning disability support staff in London

PERCEIVED MAIN TASKS: SUPPORT WORKER
Administrative duties.
Supporting service users in leisure activities.
Supporting service users in performing household chores (e.g. cooking, cleaning, laundry).
Thinking about service users' long term needs.
Supporting users in fulfilling their personal and social needs.
Dealing with 'Departmental issues'.
To see that service users 'live life as normal as possible' (i.e. more independent).

Milan: When asked to list the main duties entailed in being a support worker, two definite clusters of responses were given according to role. These are summarised in Table (x).

Table (x): Perceived main tasks required according to support role - Responses given during interviews with residential learning disability support staff in Milan

	JOB TITLE	
	EDUCATORI	DOMESTIC
PERCEIVED MAIN TASKS	Encouraging socialisation. Enabling independence. Encouraging the development of relationships (with staff, peers and others). Encouraging autonomy at home and at work.	Housework and domestic chores - usually without input from service users. Meeting service users' 'primary needs' (providing emotional support, cooking, providing a 'safe place').

When asked how much time was spent during a shift with the service users, all respondents said 'as much time as possible'. As all of the men living in the project work full time, this in reality means that residential staff support them in the evenings, at weekends and during leisure time or holidays. Six of the staff interviewed stated that mealtimes are the most important contact time, as this is when the service users are encouraged to talk about their day and what has been happening.

All of the staff interviewed said that they regard the service users in a similar way to friends, and get on well with them most of the time. The house manager is referred to by some of the service users as 'Daddy'.[27]

Making decisions

Again, this is an area in which no consensus arose with the London team. The situations quoted in both services are similar, with the exception of the mention of care plans in the London service. This, along with care plans not being mentioned by the Milanese staff supports the evidence from the analysis of planning services in the two authorities (see chapter 5.)

London: The responses given are summarised in Table (xi), but it should be noted that each person answered differently.

Table (xi): Involvement and non-involvement of service users in decision-making as reported by support workers in the residential service, London

Service Users are involved	Service Users are *not* involved
In care plans.	'Staffing issues'.
In 'everyday life'.	General administration e.g. house
Social events.	repairs.
Redecorating the house.	Staff recruitment.
'Most decisions about their lives'.	
Listening to music/watching TV/ deciding what to eat/going out.	

Milan: Occasions when service users are involved in decision-making appear to be clearly defined, with all respondents agreeing on the issues concerned: these are summarised in Table (xii).

---

[27] This is interesting to note when one remembers that the men living in the project have either been orphaned or unable to trace their natural parents.

Table (xii): Involvement and non-involvement of service users in decision-making as reported by support workers in the residential service, Milan

Service Users are involved	Service Users are *not* involved
Deciding what to watch on television (a rota). Deciding what to eat (group decision). Choosing where to go on holiday (group decision). "General everyday things around the house" (e.g. where to hang a picture).	The nature of workers' shifts. Money management. Administration of medication. When to go to bed if they are working the next day.

(iv) Communicating with service users

Difficulties in communication are tackled differently in each service. The London team feels that it is their role to be creative in the use of strategies they adopt. The Milanese agree that communicating with service users is not usually a problem, but if it is, the strategy is to help the person make contact with another person with learning disabilities to share the issue. This is in the context of communicating within relationships, rather than within the nature of the communication itself.

London: All of the staff describe the way they communicate with residents as taking time and ensuring that the meaning has been understood. The team do not seem to feel that there are any problems around communicating with the people they support. Consequently, there is no mention of any input from other professionals or any form of assessment being conducted. One member of staff states that it is important to communicate 'in the normal way', suggesting that 'sometimes you have to tackle it with a different approach'. This difference is not expanded upon.

Milan: Staff do not find that there are communication difficulties between themselves and the residents, or amongst the residents themselves. When relationship difficulties arise, the most common strategy is to identify another person with learning disabilities who has similar interests to the person experiencing difficulty.

(v) House meetings

These appear to occur more regularly in the Milan service. The Milanese staff also talk about the importance of more informal discussion between service users and service providers.

London: These are held, but all of the respondents reported that their occurrence is irregular. This has meant that the residents have not had the opportunities for developing the necessary skills for meaningful participation in such meetings.

Milan: These are held weekly and always chaired by the house manager. All participants (workers and service users) are entitled to speak, and both home and work issues are discussed. Any problems that are brought to the meeting tend to concern everybody; more personal issues - referred to by the staff here as of a 'psychological' or 'emotional' nature - are managed separately.

As well as house meetings, more informal discussions are held more frequently. The forum that seems to be the one most valued by the staff is that of the evening meal, when staff report that they encourage as much dialogue as possible. As well as discussing issues that have arisen during that day, decisions are made that typically include what to watch on the television that evening or specifics around the next day's events.

(vi) Supporting service users in making requests

The Milanese staff seem clearer on how to deal with this, and are more consistent as a team in their responses compared to the London support staff.

London: Again, staff responses differed when questioned about supporting requests. Some feel that people are supported individually, usually via a complex combination of negotiation and making the service users aware of the resources available (or not) to help them do as they wish. Another replied that the users are supported in their requests "to the best of our [the staff's] abilities". Two of the respondents said that they simply ask the residents what they want to do, and then try to meet their wishes as far as possible.

Milan: All of the staff interviewed stated that when one of the service users asks for something or for something to be changed, it is the role of the staff to do two things:

- check that any action taken would be compatible with the wishes of the other service users,
- check that any changes are compatible with the aims of the project.

(vii) Involving service users in planning how to spend their time

The Milanese staff again appear clearer on the function and nature of planning and value its role as part of their daily working life.

London: The residents are involved on both an individual and group basis, and it is felt that they are 'given the space and choice to give their own opinions'. No formal or organised system was referred to by any of the staff during interview.

Milan: All of those interviewed felt that this is a key strategy for effective support work, as it:

- Can give people self-confidence.
- Helps them to acquire responsibility for their actions.
- Enables time for 1:1 interaction and discussion, when the consequences of actions can be explained.

(viii) Links with the local community

Despite the references within the 'ordinary living' approach to the importance of links with the local community and its interpretation in the operational policy for the London service, it appears that there is no team strategy or agreed evidence that this is working in practice. The Milanese staff are a little clearer on the efforts that have been made in this area, and also have some idea of its degree of efficacy.

London: Staff talked from their own perspectives about how they perceive that the service users are involved or have been involved with neighbours. While one talked about the residents being 'acknowledged in the streets', the others said that contact with neighbours is either 'minimal' or 'non-existent, as far as [the member of staff is] aware'.

Milan: Staff report that some distrust and prejudice from local residents was sensed at first, but no informal or formal protest was made. This is felt to be due to the preparation work carried out by the Social Services Department, who introduced the scheme to the neighbourhood before the service users moved in. This was in the form of open meetings, although there was some 1:1 contact with individuals.

The current situation reported by staff is that neighbours are invited to parties held by the service users, and 'pass the time of day'. It is generally felt that neighbours are not deeply involved in the service users' lives, but appear to respect them.

(ix) On being a support worker

While both teams are clear about the importance of relationships as part of their work, the London team are more focused on relationships with other members of staff, compared to the Milanese value of the relationships between staff and service users.

London: Most of the staff interviewed talk about their place in a 'supportive team', which they value and feel is necessary in order to function effectively. One respondent believes that the project is more 'homely' compared to others. Negatives about the job include working alone for long periods, not having enough staff and the lack of financial resources generally. One member of staff simply said that the job can be 'wearing'.

Milan: The worker who lives in sees the best part of the job as the 'familial setting' that has been created; others feel that the nature of the continually developing relationships between service users and staff is particularly positive.

The negatives expressed about the job included personal factors, such as living too far away (1 person), feeling unvalued (1 person) or sensing sporadic team disharmony (1 person).

The other 3 people interviewed were unable to think of aspects of their work that they didn't like.

(x) Perceptions of the support worker's role

Consistency is once again an important difference between the two sets of responses. In addition, the Milanese staff see themselves as friends, while the London staff were less able to agree on one role - although 'friend' was not mentioned.

London: Responses to questions asking the staff about how they perceived their role were diverse. They included:

...as a support worker who is on hand whenever needed;

....someone to help people fulfil their lives..."; "..helping them to help themselves...helping them to make relationships with friends and families, not just paid workers.

Milan: All of the *educatori* considered their role to be that of a 'friend' to the service users, while the domestic support worker who lives at the project sees her role as being a 'mother figure'.

(xi) How is quality of life enhanced?

The diversity of responses among the London team contrasts with the clear indications offered by the Milanese.

London: Quality of life was defined by members of the team in a variety of ways. One person said that it should be about letting the service users 'take the initiative', and that seeing to the needs of five people is 'as big a job as you want to make it'. Others referred to the importance of people learning new things and 'organising their time appropriately', or ensuring 'progress in any new task or project'. Helping people to 'achieve their lives to the full' was also mentioned.

Milan: All of the staff responded that their contribution to the process of enhancing the quality of life of service users includes:

- meeting small and everyday needs (domestic staff),
- giving personal respect above everything (all respondents),
- supporting service users in the social world,
- seeing any difficulties encountered as part of everyday life.

Table (xiii): Summary of main differences between the roles and experience of support worker as reported by the two groups of residential staff in London and Milan

LONDON	MILAN
1. Inconsistencies in training and background	1. Professionally qualified
2. Encourage independence & individual development	2. Encourage group living and decision-making
3. Integration is paramount	3. Peer relationships essential
4. 'Enabler'; 'Advocate'	4. 'Friend'; 'mother-figure'
5. Independence & autonomy	5. Supporting service users in the social world

7 Participant Observation: Daily Life in the Two Projects

Interview data form one part of a picture which is made more complete by taking samples of daily life from the projects taking part in the study, using participant observation. The findings can then be placed alongside the results obtained from interviewing participants to provide a clearer sense of how service principles translate into real experience for the service users in each project.

The samples taken here are first set in the context of specific environments. The procedures adopted are then detailed, and the findings presented, followed by discussion looking at how the findings relate to service principles.

Setting the scene

Aim

The central objective behind the participant observation conducted in each project was to gain some sense of everyday life, particularly with attention to how the men living in each project interact with each other and with staff. Accurate collection of such data is difficult, and thus certain parameters had to be set, consisting of the following:

(i) Data collection did not happen immediately: in the case of the Milan project, it was not until the third visit that the men had begun to feel comfortable to the extent that the inhibiting effect of an observer's presence was considered minimal. For the London project, the observer had to select appropriate times so as not to draw attention to the act of recording interaction - usually parts of the day when the men were engaging in their usual routines such as getting up or at mealtimes.

(ii) Interaction has been divided into the following categories to simplify analysis and help focus on how the data can be linked with the responses given at interview and the information gleaned from operational policies.

Interaction between the tenants and members of staff

Staff → Tenant

A: Staff to tenant interaction that takes the form of a *direct* imperative (e.g. 'Please sit down, Clive').

B: Staff to tenant interaction that can be described as an *indirect* imperative - a suggestion or recommendation for the tenant to do something (e.g. 'It might be a good idea to put your washing on').

C: Staff to tenant interaction which consists of general conversation, with no focus on particular tasks or instructions (e.g. 'Was John at the day centre today?').

D: Staff to tenant interaction which forms a response to a question or comment initiated by the tenant (e.g. 'Yes, I'm working the late shift tomorrow').

Tenant → Staff

E: Tenant to staff interaction where the tenant is requesting help or assistance (e.g. 'Can you tie up my shoes?').

F: Tenant to staff interaction containing general conversation (e.g. 'I'm going to watch T.V. tonight).

G: Tenant to staff interaction which forms a response to a request or comment initiated by a member of staff (e.g. 'Yes, I would like to go out tonight).

Interaction between tenants

H: Initiation of interaction between tenants (e.g. 'What's for dinner ?').

I: Response to the initiation of interaction by another tenant (e.g. 'I don't know').

Interaction between members of staff

J: Interaction that could be said to be related to work (e.g. 'Do you want to help Clive with his bath tonight or shall I do it?').

K: Interaction between members of staff which is unrelated to work (e.g. 'Did you see that great film on T.V. last night?').

(iii) The context of the interaction being recorded was noted to provide more meaning to the data. This was particularly important for avoiding assumptions being made about interaction which appears heavily skewed, and also helps explain why in the Milan project it was deemed necessary to separate the period 'before dinner' from 'after dinner' - as the interaction observed differed to such a high degree.

The Findings: London

Three time slots were selected according to the activities taking place in the project:

> Time 1 - Weekday morning: 7.30am - 9.00am
> Time 2 - Weekday afternoon/evening: 3.30pm - 9.00pm
> Time 3 - Weekday afternoon/evening: 3.30pm - 9.00pm

Data was collected twice for each time slot, giving a total of six samples of material.

Context of the samples

Weekday mornings:

The flat is very busy in the mornings, with the second member of staff arriving at 7.30am to join the person who had been 'sleeping-in'. One of the men is an early riser, and is usually up and dressed by this time. The first task for the staff is to wake the others, unless they have a 'training day' or day at home, which is intended for working through programmes and attending to household and personal tasks.

Once people are up, some support is needed to aid getting washed and dressed - for some this consists of verbal prompts, for others some physical assistance with fastening clothing or shaving. Breakfast is a joint effort - the tenants are able to help themselves, but again are prompted and assisted by staff. The minibus arrives around 8.45am to take some of the tenants to the day centre. Peter and Alan, who use sheltered employment schemes and an alternative day centre respectively, walk or use public transport. By 9.15, only those spending the day at home remain - usually only one of the tenants at a time.

This general description applies to the sample presented here; there were no other significant events that might have influenced interaction that could be easily perceived.

Recording took place in the kitchen and the adjoining lounge: this notes the ways in which the household interacts together, but does not include one-to-one interaction taking place in tenants' bedrooms while being assisted with personal care or tidying room. Aside from the practical difficulties involved in collecting such data, it was considered inappropriate to intrude in this way.

Weekday afternoons and evenings:

Observation began as the tenants returned home from their various activities at around 3.30pm. A minibus brings those people who have spent the day at the day centre, while Peter and Alan return home by foot or by bus. Initially there are drinks and snacks prepared with the support of staff, and some catching up on what has been happening throughout the day. The tenants then go into their rooms or into the lounge to watch television. Staff plan the preparation of dinner, discussing amongst themselves who will take the lead and which of the tenants, if any, will be involved. The tenants are sometimes consulted when deciding the content of the meal. Cooking is carried out in the main by a member of staff - sometimes one of the tenants will go out with the other member of staff to buy additional ingredients.

When the food is ready, the tenants are summoned from their rooms and in the main, people eat together at the kitchen table. The kitchen space is small, and on occasion a member of staff will eat in the lounge particularly if there are three people working on shift. During the meal there can be some conversation, but it seems to be generally a quiet affair, with staff initiating most if not all of the conversation. Once the tenants have finished their food, they place their plates and cutlery in the sink, and return to their rooms or go to the lounge. Staff will sometimes ask for help with cleaning the dishes, after which there might be discussion about how to spend the evening - who will be going out with whom, where and for how long. This discussion usually involves considering whose 'turn' it might be to go out, as staffing levels do not always allow all of the tenants to go out when they would like; the policy of avoiding the 'group outing' also means that staff seem reluctant to go out with more than two tenants at any one time, and try to avoid accompanying more than one tenant whenever possible.

The tenants left at home during the evening watch television, either in their rooms or in the lounge. David tends to use the lounge, while the others all use their own rooms. Staff will also encourage the men to take baths and perhaps do their laundry, depending on how much is to be done. If the tenants go out in the evenings, they usually return at or before 9.00pm, as this is when the member of staff who is not sleeping-in will go off duty.

The findings

The three samples have been combined and the average percentages of total interaction are represented by category in Table (xiv).

Table (xiv): Average percentage of total interaction by category over three samples of observation of daily life in the London project

CATEGORY	AVERAGE PERCENTAGE OF TOTAL INTERACTION
A	7.7
B	8.5
C	16.2
D	3.4
E	1.0
F	15.0
G	16.5
H	1.6
I	0.7
J	11.9
K	11.8
TOTAL NUMBER OF INTERACTIONS	97.3

Immediate categories of interest in the table have been highlighted. Categories A and B, indicating direct imperatives and indirect imperatives from staff to tenants respectively, together constitute 16.2% of the total interaction, suggesting that just under one fifth of the time staff were instructing, teaching or engaging the tenants in particular tasks. The scores for categories H and I suggest that interaction between tenants is minimal - only a combined 2.3% of the sample involved direct peer communication. This is supported by the observation that on the occasions when tenants needed to speak to each other - examples include asking to borrow shampoo and Clive asking whether Peter wanted to go to the pub with him - they spoke through a member of staff. In other words, that member of staff acted as facilitator, even using phrases such as, 'Peter, Clive was wondering whether you might like to go down the pub with him tonight - what do you think?'

The highest scores in the table are for interaction described as general conversation initiated by tenants and directed at staff (15% of the total interaction: Category F); staff initiating conversation directed at tenants (16.2%: Category C) and tenants replying to that general conversation (16.5%: Category G). It is interesting to note that staff responses to general conversation initiated by tenants (15%: Category F) constitutes a comparatively low overall score (3.4%: Category D), implying that staff were not always responding to tenants in this context.

Examples of the most frequently occurring interaction:

(Clive): "Ken [member of staff]......"
(Ken): "Yes, Clive?"
C: "Who's sleeping-in tonight?"
K: "It's Tracy [other member of staff on shift]...but you know that already, don't you? You know the rota better than I do!"
C: "[laughs] When are you on again?"
K: "[laughs] In the morning......stop winding me up!"

This is representative of conversation initiated by residents which focused on issues about the administration of the house - who would be working, what time things would be happening, the plans for the evening. Another example is how staff initiated interaction with tenants. This shows interaction initiated by staff and directed at tenants was often asking about things they had been doing at work or at the day centre, or asked them about things they would like to do:

Tracey [staff]: "Did you have a good day, Peter?"
Peter: "Yeah"
T: "What did you do? Anything good?"
P: "Yeah"
T: "What kinds of things?"
P: "Painting. Did painting. Had dinner"
T: "What did you paint? Can you remember?"
P: "No"
T: "No? Can't remember? What else did you do?"
P: "Don't know"

Indirect imperatives are also interesting to consider:

Don [staff]:   "Hey, Alan, d'you fancy a bath?"
Alan: "Oh!.....I had a bath last night!"
D: "I know, but it's a good idea to have a bath every night. What d'you reckon?"
A: "No.....don't want one, thanks Don"
D: "Well, I think you might need to, Alan - you don't want to smell, do you?"

A:	"It's all right, I'll have one tomorrow"
D:	"Look mate, I don't want to nag, but I think it would be a good idea...it won't take long...I'll give you a hand. And then you can come out again and it'll be time for 'Eastenders' [one of Alan's favourite television programmes]"
A:	[Grimaces]
D:	"Go on...the longer you take to get in there, the longer it will take to get out again....I'll go and run it, shall I?" [Goes to bathroom and begins to get the bath ready for Alan]

One has the sense that while Dan is not *instructing* Alan to have a bath, he wasn't going to end the conversation until he had managed to persuade Alan that he needed to have a bath. This strategy, or something similar, can be observed in many of the interactions taking place between staff and tenants, be it getting out of bed, going to bed, washing up, getting dressed or tidying a bedroom.

Here is an example of staff initiating interaction - on this occasion, planning activity for the evening - and how interaction between tenants arises via staff encouragement rather than happening spontaneously:

Tracy (staff):	"So - what's happening tonight, then?" (Pause) "Does anyone want to go out?"
Clive:	"Yes!"
Tracy:	"Where d'you fancy - got any ideas?"
C:	"Pub"
T:	"OK"
Alan:	"Can I go?"
T:	"Well......hold on a minute, you did go out last night, didn't you? Clive hasn't been out for a couple of days"
Don (staff):	"Yeah, and you really ought to have a bath tonight, don't you think?"
A:	"Oh!......but I ......"
T:	"Come on, Alan. Clive, d'you want to see if Peter wants to go?" [Clive nods]
T:	"Go and knock on his door then - ask him if he wants to come" [A few minutes later]
C:	"Can we go in the car?"

T:	"You'd better ask David"[1]
C:	"[Going into the living room to speak to David] Can we use the car, David?"
D:	[Nods]
C:	"[Returning to the kitchen] he said yes"
T:	"OK then, shall we go? Is Peter coming?"
C:	"Don't know"

The findings: Milan

Four samples were taken:

> Time 1 - Weekday evening: 6.00pm - 7.30pm (Before dinner)
> Time 2 - Weekday evening: 6.00pm - 7.30pm (Before dinner)
> Time 3 - Weekday evening: 7.30pm - 9.30pm (After dinner)
> Time 4 - Weekday evening: 7.30pm - 9.30pm (After dinner).

Context of the samples

Weekday evenings

Initial visits to the project in Milan quickly revealed that for the observer, there needs to be a differentiation made between the time spent before dinner and the time spent during and after dinner, as the nature of interaction between tenants and members of staff appears to be completely different.

During the week all seven of the men go to work. They return home around 6.00pm, with the exception of Dario who has further to travel. Assunta is in the kitchen cooking at this time, usually with one or two of the tenants with her, either assisting (cutting vegetables, for example) or just chatting about their day. As the men arrive home they each greet the staff and each other, going into the bedrooms to do so. This precedes a shower and change of clothes, all without any prompting from staff, suggesting a well-established routine. Activity in the house is now split into two: work and conversation in the kitchen with Assunta, conversation between the tenants in the bedrooms and sometimes in the lounge. After a signal from the other member of staff on duty, the other tenants set the table, which is large

---

[1] Under the 'motability scheme', two of the tenants have surrendered the mobility component of their disability benefits in order to buy a car between them. While 'belonging' to these two men, it is used by all of the tenants - although staff encourage the other three men to ask permission before they use it with staff.

enough to seat everybody - including at the time of observation, two extra guests. The ease with which the tenants and member of staff accommodate these extra people suggests that such an event is commonplace.

The tenants sit at the table, and Assunta serves the food. The atmosphere then becomes noisier, as conversation seems to split into two: the staff talk amongst themselves, sometimes with Dario who appears to enjoy being at that end of the table. At the other end, the men interact with each other. Snippets of conversation included 'Have you got a cigarette?', 'What shall we watch on T.V. tonight?', 'How are you?'

The two groups of conversation also become one at intervals, and then return to two groups once more throughout the meal. One is reminded immediately of a large family eating together. One visit, which wasn't recorded in detail, included accompanying everybody to the local pizzeria, which judging by the reception that the men received from the restaurant staff, is a regular activity. The patterns of interaction seen there in terms of groupings was very similar to that observed back at the flat.

After dinner, the tenants clear the table and help with clearing up, again automatically as if their roles within the completion of these tasks has been clearly established. Once everything is finished, everyone sits in the lounge to watch television, although there seems to be as much conversation as concentration on the screen.

The findings

These are summarised in Table (xv). The figures are average percentages by category of the total interaction observed.

Immediate categories of interest have been highlighted in Table (xv). None of the interaction between staff and tenants was perceived to contain direct imperatives (Category A). The percentage of indirect imperatives increased during dinner, from 2.8% to 6.4% of the total interaction. Of greater significance, perhaps, is the extent to which the tenants were interacting with each other. Combining categories H and I produces a percentage of 26.1% which increased to 39.5% during and after dinner. This suggests that approximately one third of all the interaction observed during the experimental period took place between service users. General conversation initiated by staff and directed towards tenants (Category C) also increased during and after dinner, from 1.6% to 7.2%.

Table (xv): Average percentage of total interaction by category over four samples of observation of daily life in the Milan project

CATEGORY OF INTERACTION	AVERAGE PERCENTAGE OF TOTAL INTERACTION (Before dinner)	AVERAGE PERCENTAGE TOTAL INTERACTION (During/After dinner)
A	0	0
B	2.8	6.4
C	1.6	7.2
D	29.0	0.4
E	1.7	0
F	36.0	6.8
G	3.2	10.0
H	14.9	21.7
I	11.2	17.8
J	0	7.0
K	0	15.3
TOTAL NUMBER OF INTERACTIONS	97.5	131

Quoting examples of interaction here reveals different types of interaction.

Take a group of the tenants talking while setting the table:

Dario: **"We'll use this table cloth"**
Paulo: **"It's not big enough, look - let's ask Assunta first"**
Roberto: **"That's all right, look - we're sitting at this end anyway [as opposed to the two guests who had been invited to stay for dinner], it doesn't matter that there's not enough of it" [Assunta enters - the men arrange the cloth as she suggests]**

This sample of interaction took place during dinner, perhaps the noisiest part of the day observed in the house. The tenants have just sat down - all at one end of the table - and are about to begin eating:

Dario: **"What's are we eating?"**

Stefano:	"What are we eating?" (teasing Dario)
Paulo:	"You saw it - pork, I made it, did it.
	[The other tenants are talking about their journeys home from work, which had been late]
D:	"Mammona! Mammona!"[2]
P:	"[laughs] Mammona! I'm having a drink - [to Stefano] pass me the water?"
S:	"[passes water jug to Paulo] Is football on tonight? [punches the air and starts singing a football chant]"
P:	"[also punches the air, in similar way to Stefano] Don't know [Assunta enters the dining room with a large plate of food for distribution]"
S:	"[to Assunta] Not salad"
A:	"Yes, yes, I know - here you go [dishes out food]"
S:	"Thanks"

A fair proportion of interaction between the tenants consists of gentle teasing:

Stefano:	"I'm hungry"
Paulo:	"[mimics Stefano in a whiny voice] I'm hungry!"
Stefano:	"Shut up"
	[Paulo pulls a face at Stefano, who then mimics him]
Paulo:	"What's on TV?"
Stefano:	"I want to watch football"
Paulo:	"Yes - football, football!"

Observing interaction: Comparing the findings

Any comparison between these sets of data is done with caution; the descriptions of the two settings reveal that there are differences between the ways in which the two groups spend their time, as well as use their living space. The difficulties in gathering the information also needs to be registered: often the complexities encountered when trying to observe the interactions of nine people in the case of the Milan project and seven in the London project meant that important considerations could have been overlooked. However, the sampling times were deliberately chosen to focus on the most interesting parts of the day in each project, as well as the most convenient and perhaps routinized. This explains why the sampling was

---

[2] This is the word the tenants - and one in particular - use for Assunta, the member of staff who lives at the project. It is derived from the Italian work 'mama', the informal word for 'mother'. The tenant who uses this word the most also draws pictures of 'mammona', and leaves one on the table for her every day before going to work.

different in each case, and enables the findings to be seen with some confidence as being representative of daily life for the service users.

1. *Interaction between service users*

This is the most striking difference between the samples, with a far greater percentage of peer interaction observed in the Milan project. This interaction was also spontaneous and exclusive of support from staff - this again differs from the London project where any interaction between service users tended to require the facilitation of a member of staff. The opportunities for interaction between tenants are perhaps increased with the sharing of bedrooms, as well as perhaps the group approach to integration that has been adopted by the Milanese Social Services. Having one's own space without the input which would help to increase socialisation - as well as an emphasis on increasing interaction with non-disabled people - would not offer as many opportunities or indeed encourage peer interaction between tenants. One is also led to consider whether for those men who attend the same day centre, they would want to spend time talking about their day with the same people with whom they have spent that day. Even in the case of Peter and Alan, who use other day services, the settings and other people present are known to all of the tenants, either through direct experience or by word of mouth. A substantial proportion of the conversation heard between the Milanese service users did consist of anecdotes from their workplace, all of which are completely different.

The London house seems to be designed in such a way as to prevent communal activity between *all* of the men, and more than two would find difficulty in finding plentiful space in any one room at one time. The living room does not have chairs for the tenants and staff to sit together, neither does the kitchen have the space for potentially seven adults to sit comfortably eating together. This makes mealtimes very different in London compared to Milan, for not only are there occasions when the London group are not eating together, those who do so are in a confined space - hardly conducive to relaxed conversation, which is supported by the observation data showing little if any inter-tenant interaction over dinner this time. This could therefore, be influenced by other factors apart from culture.

One senses that this atmosphere of forced physical proximity is present throughout the house: the men appear to be 'under scrutiny', in that there are no spaces for them to be with each other or be alone apart from their own rooms - which are of modest proportions. Unlike the hostel where they used to live, there are no spaces where the tenants can enjoy the support of staff without them being in direct contact; the lack of a garden, which was often used by one of the tenants at times when he seemed to feel a little 'crowded out' at the hostel, has possibly forced a change in the way that the men relate to each other. This begs a question: would the tenants have agreed to live with each other in the new house if they had fully understood that doing so would mean living in such close proximity with little opportunity to wander around the larger expanses of the hostel and its grounds?

2. *Interaction between staff and service users*

The London project provided evidence for levels of conversation initiated by staff and directed towards tenants which were higher than those recorded in the Milan project. This was perhaps influenced most significantly by the situation during mealtimes, where the Milanese tenants spend time talking amongst themselves as well as with staff. Conversation during mealtimes for the London project was usually initiated and facilitated by staff. There is also evidence that staff were responding to interaction initiated by tenants more in the Milan project (29% before dinner) compared to the score in the London project (3.4%). One possible explanation which arises from combining these data is that the interaction taking place between tenants in their rooms before dinner enables staff to respond fairly easily to requests or conversation initiated by other tenants and directed at staff. In contrast, the role of facilitator for interaction between tenants which staff find themselves fulfilling in the London project perhaps leaves them less able to respond to all tenant-generated conversation.

Case study: Summary of main themes

Taking the interview and observation data together, it would appear that the two groups of service users taking part in the study have very different ways of life. A degree of this difference needs to be attributed to cultural factors, for British and Italian societies are divergent in ways far too complex for discussion here. What needs to be addressed, being the purpose of this comparison, is the extent to which the differences found in the data can be traced to the principles of care underpinning the respective services.

The central differences in the data seem to centre around the following themes:

- independence (London) vs. inter-dependence (Milan): integration and living as individuals (London) vs. integration and living as a group (Milan),

- staff acting as enablers/guides (London) vs. staff providing 'a loving atmosphere' (Milan),

- learning socially valued behaviour (London) vs. understanding the implications of one's disability (Milan),

- staff with varying backgrounds and levels of experience and qualifications providing services as set out by a local operational policy which follow a generally accepted set of principles (London) vs. services provided by consistently trained staff following service principles set out in a local operational policy which is informed by Regional and National legislation.

These issues will be revisited in the full discussion (see Chapter 10). First it is important to pick up on the last point concerning staff training: having examined service policy and sampled the outcomes in each service, time will now be spent looking at the approach to training taken in each case, to assess the role played by human resources and how normalisation influences their development.

A broad overview of the approach to training staff for learning disability services will be followed by an account of the training strategy developed by the Milanese local authority.

8 Training Staff in Britain: Approaches to Developing the Professional in Learning Disability Services

Introduction

It is a difficult task to describe the overall nature of staff training in Britain, mainly because of the great variation, both between and within services. One of the serious effects of this is a lack of consensus in terms of the purpose and aims of support and the most effective training strategies for developing important skills.

The situation has been clearly described by Mansell & Porterfield (1986:1):

> The variety of services, from different agencies organised in incompatible ways, presents a confusing and complex picture. This, together with different professional roles and attitudes can create serious difficulties in service planning, design and delivery...

The explanation for this confusion is likely to be complex. However, it can be said that the absence of clear conventions or legislation providing either a philosophical framework or widespread value base mean that the effectiveness and quality of any training that *does* take place depends on the experience, approach and theoretical standpoint of the individual trainer.

The only assumption that is reasonably safe to make is that the majority if not all of staff development courses operating in Britain are based upon the principles of normalisation (e.g. Wolfensberger 1972) and ordinary living (e.g. O'Brien 1985).

The issue here however, is the extent to which training in Britain aims to develop *professionalism* in the field of support work (particularly residential support work) in a uniform, organised way, and this chapter attempts to review some of the main issues.

181

Identifying a clear need for training

Deinstitutionalisation has brought with it a series of demands on the providing agencies, not just in terms of the need for establishing staff teams with appropriate practical abilities in social care, but equally the realisation that creating an ideologically-driven consensus of approach is crucial. Brown & Alcoe (1987:21) observe:

> If true integration into community life is its aim, the development of 'community care' for people with disabilities demands much more emphasis on values-based training for the staff who will plan, manage and deliver the service. All too often, training is centred on the acquisition of technical and practical skills without the necessary philosophical context to ensure their just and appropriate application.

In a similar vein, McGill & Bliss (1993) suggest that the service developments arising from community care legislation created a need for training personnel in daily practice. The authors suggest that by moving from "segregated" to "integrated" facilities, service users are required to learn how to use local amenities *without* the support and/or security of the institution. In turn, support workers then need to be able to support service users in doing this without themselves having the safety that is deemed to come with being part of a larger organisation. The implication is then that deinstitutionalisation in Britain has forced the development of greater independence in both service users and staff members alike - and that such a shift in the approach to social care requires a significant shift in the thinking which underpins services.

Striving for a professional approach: Established training frameworks

The size and complexity of the task might have been recognised by academics, but how have those with the responsibility for providing training responded to such demands?

Initially, strong advocates of normalisation developed specific training workshops, such as PASS (Wolfensberger & Glenn 1975) and PASSING (Wolfensberger & Thomas 1983), which were held in Britain through CMHERA (Campaign and Mental Handicap Education and Research Programme). These 5 day events were based on complex evaluation systems, assessing the extent to which environments had adopted the principles of normalisation. However, attendance at these workshops is not compulsory for learning disability support staff; indeed, it is very unlikely that a random sample of support staff taken today would include anyone who had completed such a course. Even if the PASS approach has influenced a significant number of people, the values underpinning the approach rarely permeate an entire service system in a uniform manner.

Carpenter *et al* (1991) considered an integrated approach to care provision as a response to the NHS Community Care Act (1990), concentrating mainly on the nature of appropriate training and organisational development. The *Caring for People Joint Training Project* aimed to identify the necessary training needs for the implementation of 'Caring for People' (1989), which advocates a joint approach to service delivery by health and social services, and the voluntary and independent sectors.

The research team summarise the variety of national strategies that have been initiated:

There have been a number of national initiatives to bring workers together to explore issues of joint concern in the provision of community care services. Bodies such as CCETSW, the ENB and particularly the NHSTD have run multi-agency training programmes, many of them focusing on the issue of joint working. There have also been local initiatives, often incorporating, or initiated by, the voluntary sector, which have addressed issues of working together to provide health and social care. More recently the framework of the NVQ has provided opportunities for workers from different agencies to develop common skills and competencies.

Nursing training and the NVQ, probably the two most influential frameworks underpinning the delivery of professional training in Britain, have their problems and warrant some attention here. While considering nurse training, Brown & Wood (1991) comment that

> ...contradictory trends at work in the nature of vocational and nursing training and a resultant tension between employer led training initiatives and the move to more college based training envisaged under Project 2000......Funding of nurses specifically for the Mental Handicap option is difficult as students will study a common core for 18 months before committing themselves to RMNH.

The same authors have a similarly pessimistic view of the NVQ, suggesting that while potentially it has been an important development for both purchasing and providing agencies, the competencies which have been outlined by RDDC and Health Care Auxiliary projects have omitted important aspects of work with people with learning disabilities in community settings. More positively, the NVQ does hold the attraction of allowing for alternative routes to higher level qualifications and hence some kind of career progression for candidates. Staff can develop competencies which secure entry into managerial posts, therefore by-passing more traditional qualifying routes. Furthermore, if the NVQ framework is developed flexibly, it allows for the targeting of specific skills more effectively than current nursing qualifying training.

However, the competencies that have been established within the NVQ framework have been derived from more traditional residential services, and being generic, draw heavily on care practices for older adults. The values underpinning such practices are likely to be inappropriate and irrelevant to the lives of many people with learning disabilities.

Despite these difficulties, and noting here that the very introduction of NVQ has been difficult, the framework is still very much around.

A multidisciplinary, national qualification?

There are, then, programmes in place to encourage the development of a professional workforce in social care, but as yet, none of the schemes mentioned here have been acknowledged to the extent of forming prerequisites for the selection process across all social care services.

The Milanese model, as detailed in Chapter 9, is based on interpretations of both national and regional legislation, and focuses on the conclusion that deinstitutionalisation requires a consistently trained team of personnel whose core competencies would be recognised and required by all social care provision affected by that legislation. In contrast, there has been a different response to the suggestion of national training initiatives in Britain. Jones (1990) suggests that:

> ...there was overall support for a national training and development framework but not for a prescriptive, bureaucratic centrally-driven machine which would impede local flexibility and self determination. There was a significant demand that a national framework made a clear and explicit statement about values and philosophy. In this context, the central concept of a needs-led service which is based on real consumer involvement was seen to be crucial.

Indeed, the British national framework does make explicit statements about values and philosophy, mostly in terms of the importance of integration and accessibility. What is less clear are the strategies for implementing service principles, and the pathways to the attainment of such values.

Services are in the position of being able to recruit direct support staff who are usually well-voiced in O'Brien's Five Service Accomplishments, but are sometimes much less clear about how the principles can be put into practice. There may well be justified criticism of normalisation as reviewed earlier (see Chapter 1); what is perhaps of more immediate concern is the confusion over what constitutes professionalism in providing social care and the role that recognised training needs to play. With just the interview process and references as evidence, service managers are in need of far more guidance if they are to recruit staff of a consistently high calibre. Mansell & Porterfield (1986) comment that:

> Training cannot be the solution to every problem in a human service; a great deal of care still has to be exercised in selection and recruitment to find staff with the vision and commitment and skill needed to serve people well.

The introduction of a multi-disciplinary, national qualification might go some way in alleviating this pressure.

Training as ongoing development

Whatever one's view about the role of a national qualification, it cannot be a panacea to all that is troublesome in service provision. The ongoing nature of training needs to be acknowledged as a necessity rather than reward for enthusiastic staff.

Induction, however intensive and thorough, is equally inadequate as a stand-alone strategy, due to its failure to account for the developing individual. Carpenter *et al* observe:

> Training will therefore, have to address a wide range of needs amongst a wide range of experiences and skills, professional backgrounds and 'status' in the service hierarchy. This will require ongoing training throughout a worker's career; an initial 'blitz' at the beginning is no longer sufficient to support a complex and evolving service, especially as uni-disciplinary training will not

equip tomorrow's community care staff to respond to the challenges.

This is supported by (Kingsley & Smith, 1989:16):

...training should provide continuing developmental support and so play an important role in the evolution of the service, as experience provides lessons and examples from which to learn.

Evaluating training for staff working with people with learning disabilities: Using the research literature

The main body of evaluative studies of staff training linked with working for decreasing levels of challenging behaviour as a primary objective. Once this is acknowledged, the nature of the research literature in this area is easier to comprehend.

Research studies which argue for a need to develop staff vary in their foci. McGill & Bliss (1993) provide a selection including work by Emerson et al (1992), which looks at the low rates of "appropriate" interaction between staff and service users; the claim that when interactions do occur they can fail to encourage appropriate behaviour (Felce, Saxby et al 1987); a suggestion that not enough staff time is spent training (sic) service users (Hile & Walbran 1991), or in providing "purposeful activities" (Mansell, Felce et al 1982). Furthermore, the approach taken by McGill & Bliss (1993) - and seemingly the majority of the staff training and/or challenging behaviour literature - defines a trained staff team as one which enables the provision of services which "protect [the service user's] community placement and enhance [the service user's] community participation" p306. See also Emerson et al 1994, p210).

Concern over the widespread failure of services to meet these goals in terms of staff training have led to the development of two university-based courses, which aim to establish core competencies in this area.

1. The Tizard Centre, University of Kent: Diploma in the Applied Psychology of Learning Disability (Challenging Behaviour)

This part time, two year course is aimed at staff with direct responsibilities for the provision of community based services. Students are usually residential team managers, day service staff or peripatetic community support staff, working in Health Authorities, Social Services and voluntary organisations. Typical credentials of participants include qualifications in nursing or social work; other students might be working directly with service users in various settings.

Teaching

This is workshop based: students attend the university for a total of 50 days over the two year period. There are no practical placements, but the requirement is that people complete practical assignments within their own organisations, thus applying developing skills to their everyday work.

Course content

The main principle of the Diploma is that challenging behaviour needs to be seen within a functional framework, providing for the person with learning disabilities a means of controlling his/her environment. The aim, therefore, is that students are assisted in acquiring the necessary skills for supporting service users with challenging behaviours in developing alternative ways of communicating.

The ultimate goal is that students implement "progressive programming" (La Vigna et al 1989), described by McGill & Bliss (1993) as having two main components: the management of challenging behaviour, and the development of programmes which use an analysis of the service user's behaviour - the intention being to decrease the occurrence of that behaviour. The complexity of this task is such that the course also looks at the nature of managerial and professional support, as well as the ethical issues of service provision.

Assessment

i.)   There are four aspects to assessment on the diploma:

ii.) Students are asked to make a video which demonstrates their ability to "engage" service users in appropriate activity.

iii.) A report is written, which describes the methods adopted by the student in training another member of staff in the engagement of service users.

iv.)   A report which talks about the ways in which their current service orchestrates the engagement of services users, in terms of environment and service design.

v.)   An essay on the importance of engagement with relation to challenging behaviour.

2.   *The University of Manchester Diploma*

The Diploma - full title "Behavioural Approaches for Professionals working with Individuals who have Learning Disabilities (Kiernan & Bliss 1992) - is a full time, post-qualifying course of 37 weeks duration and validated by the English National Board for Nursing, Midwifery and Health Visiting (E.N.B) and the Central Council for the Education and Training of Social Workers (C.C.E.T.S.W.). Students receive the certificate ENB 705, while the University of Manchester has recognised the course as a Diploma since 1992. Based at the Hester Adrian Research Centre, the Diploma has the support of Burnley, Pendle and Rossendale Health Authority and the East Lancashire College of Nursing. Students tend to be from the whole range of learning disability residential and other support services.

Teaching

The course consists of 5 modules - one covering academic aspects of behavioural theory and practice; three comprised mainly of practical work placements; one final module which centres around a case study identified in the last of the preceding practical placements.

    Although behaviourism is the focus of the course, it is not taught in complete theoretical isolation. Other orientations, such as psychoanalysis, gestalt and existentialism are presented to enable students to draw parallels between their own experiences and those of people with learning disabilities. The behavioural approach can then be explored in terms of its weaknesses, as well as its strengths.

    The courses above share a common evolution, having originated as part of the recognition that the success of community care is deemed to be contingent upon the development in staff teams of effective skills for the management of challenging behaviour. Emerson & McGill (1989) suggest that although the two courses take the behavioural orientation as their theoretical framework, both also appear to acknowledge the need for an understanding of the organisation of service provision as well as the values inherent in adopted models of care.

The future of staff training: Where next?

While the course described above are a significant step towards acknowledging the need for qualified, professional and competent people to work in services, such an approach has its limitations.

Firstly, impact. The intake of students each year may have positive effect at a local level, but the extent and longevity of such an impact is difficult to establish. Many of the behavioural approaches studied during the courses require both the support from management and a consistent team approach. This is asking much from students who may well graduate from the course with more skills than the person who will be supporting them, thus finding themselves in the role of trainer once back in the workplace. Furthermore, this training role could well encompass the entire team, if s/he wants to ensure the consistent implementation of a programme, and this in turn might create issues of role conflict within particular organisations.

Secondly, there is the issue of staff retention. Students returning to the workplace with a diploma will be highly sought after, as many challenging needs services struggle to provide appropriate support with largely unqualified staff. Given the reasons outlined above, it is understandable that students leave the original service, seeking either a service able to provide a culture conducive to that described during their studies, and/or one which recognises the student's skills with remuneration. Staff retention has long been a problem in learning disability services (particularly those for people who challenge and/or those with profound and multiple disabilities) and partial training could lead to a failure to retain trained individuals.

Thirdly, on-going support for students is often lacking for the reasons outlined above, leading not only to feelings of isolation, but also a situation where the student's personal development needs cannot be addressed.

(1) *The role of the multidisciplinary team*

There are potential solutions to these problems. Introducing a national qualification could well be one of them, but this is unlikely given the stance adopted by government over the last 20 years, and the general lack of interdisciplinary co-operation. This last point has interested some writers. Brown (1996:106) comments:

> Understanding the situation of the team does not require a complex
> organisational model. One metaphor ...is of services being like the

leaky radiator in an old car which is welded out of two even older, leakier radiators, namely Health and Social Services.

She continues:

Parents, informal carers and the voluntary sector stop the contents falling out of the bottom, overlapping welds cause friction and there are gaping holes in its fabric. Into this leaking vessel the prodigal mechanic simply pours in a 'multidisciplinary team' and hopes, in the face of all the evidence to the contrary, that holes will be stopped and corrosion halted. (p106)

So is training multidisciplinary teams the answer to the training dilemma? Brown suggests that they could at least provide an important piece of the jigsaw with a role consisting of three main activities: building up a comprehensive picture of local services, monitoring all requests for services whether met or unmet to indicate where the gaps fall and identifying any area of 'overkill'. Not a total solution, but a key component of the overall picture nonetheless.

(2) *Taking a strategic approach*

If training is to remain local, it is important to be realistic about the task ahead. Avoiding a single solution but advising on a strategic approach is possible in such circumstances.

The essential challenges for implementing a training strategy have been outlined by Carpenter *et al* (1992):

- identifying common values, knowledge and skills across professions and work settings and creating a shared philosophy,
- ensuring that a strategy for training is developed, based in the shared values and goals of the agencies involved,
- integrating training and staff development into the planning and management of services and defining clearly how they relate to the local purchaser/provider arrangements,
- determining local arrangements for the delivery of services, and ensuring that training grows out of these arrangements,
- building bridges between agencies in terms of understanding work roles, statutory requirements of each agency, organisational practices and models of service provision,

- promoting equal opportunities and anti-discriminatory practice throughout all training events,
- integrating the process of quality assurance into all training activities,
- maximising the impact of NVQ, thus enabling both workers and employers to meet national standards of competence and promote for individuals a planned continuum of professional development,
- recognising that good joint training provides a model for joint working and helps the latter to work more effectively.

The term 'whole environment training' has been coined (e.g. Mansell & Porterfield, 1986), which covers:

a. the aims and philosophy of the service
b. the biographies of the individuals being supported by the service
c. the personal skills needed in staff to help develop and broaden user competence
d. organisational and administrative tasks

This model tends to underpin the system-wide consultancy model adopted by organisations such as the Tizard Centre at the University of Kent.

Localised training then has to be well structured and organised if it is to be successful. According to Kingsley & Smith (1989:16) there are at least two main 'streams of activity' in an ideal strategy:

1. one directed towards communicating the organisation's goals, policies and values and encouraging a wider ownership and understanding of them
2. one focused on developing the practical capacities of staff in the organisation to achieve those goals

This is certainly an important foundation from which to achieve real progress.

Conclusion

Identifying common approaches and perspectives to training in British services for people with learning disabilities is no easy task, and the issues and observations here are not comprehensive. Instead, they give a flavour and some insight into the complexities faced by service providers trying to meet the needs of people with learning disabilities living in the community. The environment is summarised vividly by Mansell (1991):

> People leading the development of services are often likely to be doing this against a background in which there is no clear policy mandate for community-based services as opposed to institutional solutions; where existing services and service agencies can be expected to respond to change with a degree of 'dynamic conservatism'; and in which simplistic ideas about services abound....

Given this confusing picture, it is no great surprise that opinions differ as to the nature and future of training support staff. Further illumination of the dilemma is attempted in the next chapter, by describing the regional qualification that has been established in Lombardia.

9 The Training of *Educatori* (Support Staff) in Milan

The Official Bulletin of the Lombardian Regional Government (Serial 19, 10.5.89), a document authorised by the President of that Government, sets out in great detail the process and nature of training for staff who wish to become support workers with people with learning disabilities. It is stressed at this point that the workers in question are direct care workers, working in both residential and day care settings, and are not the equivalent of the British Social Worker or Care Manager.

The following outline of Lombardian training provides an overview of this document, and precedes a discussion of key differences between the Milanese and British training strategies. The latter differ in the sense that professional training is not a legal requirement for those working with people with learning disabilities. Normalisation indeed recommends that an 'ordinary life' is perhaps best supported by 'ordinary' people, and this approach, combined with the absence of a comprehensive legislative framework for staff training in the field of learning disability, provides an important contrast to the Italian model.

The legislative framework in Lombardia

The Official Bulletin of the Lombardian Regional Government (Serial 19, 10.5.89) was produced in response to the National Republican Law 95/80 which refers explicitly to deinstitutionalisation. The Official Bulletin outlines the need for professionalism in the Region, particularly in articles 18 and 46 - and takes a didactic stance, calling for a socio-educational approach. Although the Republican Law required formal action, moves towards the professionalisation of support work had been discussed in a Regional Article published on 27.7.77, updated in 1980.

The Ministry of the Interior commissioned a study to examine and define the professional profile and entry requirements for support workers. The results, produced in a decree from the Ministry of health (10.2.84, Article #1, Decreto Pubblico di Repubblica #761) suggested that support workers were at that time employed without any formal, adequate training. This realisation, along with the belief that successful and effective deinstitutionalisation required a professional body of staff, moved the Regional Government to establish a formal training course for support workers in association with the University of Milan. Although this intended to regulate the status of personnel, it was recognised that existing staff, particularly those working in large institutions which were due for closure, had many valuable skills and had built up effective relationships with service users. These people were therefore assimilated into the course, even if they were unable to meet university requirements, on the condition that their service managers recommended their ability to complete an academic course. This provision was gradually phased out, with current training requiring all prospective support staff to be able to meet university entry requirements. Article #2 of the Health Ministry's decree (1984) specifically calls upon Regional Governments to adapt and create the infrastructure to enable the implementation of the Republican Law.

Co-ordination of the resettlement task became the responsibility of the Regional Government Secretary, who realised that support workers would be needed in a variety of settings - in small group homes, day settings, providing support to families, in respite care and other aspects of social services. To ensure an adequate supply of staff, a total of four training schools were established in Lombardia, each operating the state regulated three year course: the Regional School for Social Workers for the Comune di Milano, Via Daverio; the Regional School of Social I.A.L./C.I.S.L. di Brescia, Via Castellani, 7; Regional School of Social workers E.S.A.E. di Milano, Piazza Castello, 3; Regional School for Social Workers, la Nostra Famiglia, di Bosisio Parini.

Recommendations of the 1982 Commission

In addition to recognising a need for creating a professional body of support staff, the 1982 Commission described the diverse nature of the required provision.

Three main decisions were outlined:

- The Commission defined the professional profile and entry requirements for the *'educatori'* training course, as well as the methods of examination and programme of studies.

- Courses originally intended for support workers have been modified and upgraded - hence students graduate as *'educatori professionale'* (professional support workers) as opposed to *'educatori speciale'* (support workers trained in specific areas e.g. learning disability).[1]

- Regional bodies have been given the mandate to create schemes for the professional training of support workers, with administrative support from the National Government.

The professional support worker: Definition and function

'Educatori Speciale' are defined by the Official Bulletin Serial 19 (1989) as support workers who have received specific theoretical and practical training in what are termed 'educational projects'.[2] These projects aim to promote an 'equilibrium of personality', which is said to be aided by the integration of marginalised service users.

This primary objective is addressed by working closely with service users, their families, relevant institutions, health, social and education services and within the service user's personal environment and situational context. Support workers are also expected to supplement their work with research and case study documentation.

Educatori professionale are employed to work with a variety of groups in society - training specialisms are available as part of the three year course to enable graduates to meet the needs of specific groups of service users. As well as people with learning disabilities, the groups include children and adolescents, people with physical disabilities, those with mental health problems and young offenders.

Explicit functions of *'Educatori Professionale'*

The Official Bulletin (1989) states:

---

[1] Courses for *'educatori speciale'* are optional, whereas all new support workers now employed by the Comune di Milano are required to have completed the training for *'educatori professionale'*

[2] *"L'educatore professionale è l'operatore che, in barse ad una specifica preparazione di carattere teorico-practico, svolge la propria attività mediante la formulazione e la realizzazione do progetti educativi, volti a promuovere lo sviluppo equilibrato della personalità, il recupero e il reinserimento sociale do soggetti portatori di menomazioni psicofisiche a rischio e in situazioni di emarginazione sociale".* [A professional support worker is one who has undergone specific training in theoretical and practical aspects of educational projects, which have the aim of developing and promoting an equilibrium of personality, integrating people who are marginalised from society for any number of reasons.]

La familglia tende a formire conoscenze scientifiche, acquisizione di esperienze, metodologie e techniche, che determinino capacità critiche di intervento e la conseguente assunzione di una specifica professionalità educativa. (p1864)

[Support workers are expected to] raise awareness of the scientific approach, acquiring the methodological and technical experience that determines the critical capacity for intervention, leading to the formation of ability for making professional judgements that will enhance the quality of life of service users.

The understanding is that an *intervento* or intervention, becomes valid when its design meets specific aims which staff learn during their training:

- the service user's circumstances need to be understood objectively, particularly their history and development,

- support staff must have a clear knowledge and evaluation of the resources available, and ways of utilising them,

- any interventions undertaken must have the capacity for empirical assessment: support workers need to act on the results of such assessments, either continuing or modifying the original assessment,

- graduates of the course will have a theoretical grounding in appropriate human disciplines, specifically psycho-pedagogy, social anthropology, economic law and health studies,

- the *educatori* training provides a system which enables support workers to make informed judgements regarding action which needs to be taken to ensure that vulnerable people are provided with the support they need to participate in society,

- *educatori* receive practical and technical instruction; this helps to reinforce their theoretical understanding by applying knowledge to real life case studies.

Entry requirements and course content

Applicants are admitted to the course once they have completed a secondary education and passed their university entrance examination.[3] Potential students are required to undergo a psychological assessment to see if they are appropriately disposed to the demands of the course. Completion and graduation as *'educatori'* takes a minimum of three years, but students are able to complete the final examination within six years.

Course content

Continuous assessment operates throughout the three years, with students needing to attain specified standards in order to complete the course:[4]

Year 1

The disciplines covered are: general psychology; educational pedagogy and experimental pedagogy; general sociology; cultural anthropology; social medicine and health education; technical methods of educative intervention and socio-psychological rehabilitation; constitutional law; administrative and legislative aspects of personal social services; paediatric neuro-psychiatry and mental health. Students spend between 50 and 70 hours on each discipline throughout the year.

Year 2

The middle year looks at the sociology of the family, the sociology of education and the sociology of deviance (all taken together as part of one discipline); neurology: sensory and motor functions; psychiatry; social pedagogy; developmental psychology; special psychology; methods and techniques for intervention in education and psycho-social rehabilitation; family law and juvenile law. Between 40 and 60 hours are spent on each of these areas during the second year.

---

[3] This examination is comparable in standard to the English 'A' Level.
[4] The Italian university system, while requiring the applicant to have passed the entrance examination, has a reputation for being rather indiscriminatory in allowing students to access further education. The training for *educatori* is somewhat different, in that not only do applicants have to meet specified criteria as assessed by psychological testing to be accepted for the training at all, they are asked to leave the course if they fail the assignments and other assessments during the three years.

Year 3

The final year looks at the following disciplines: social politics; special pedagogy; the psycho-sociology of organisations; methods and techniques for intervention in education and psycho-social rehabilitation; development, evaluation and organisation of educative intervention and psycho-social rehabilitation; penal law. Again, between 40 and 60 hours are spent on each of the disciplines throughout the year.

As well as this time allocated to the exploration of theoretical material, students are required to spend considerable blocks of time in methodological training (150 hours during each of the three years) and fieldwork - 150 hours during the first year, 300 hours during the second and a total of 400 hours of fieldwork to be completed during the final year.

Fieldwork aims to help students learn from practical experience, enabling them to both apply theoretical material explored during lectures, seminars and their own reading, as well as providing opportunities for identifying their own abilities and capacities in the role of support worker. The *comune* usually provides students with lists of appropriate and acceptable contacts in institutions and public and private projects where effective fieldwork can take place. During the second and third years of the course, both the theoretical input and the fieldwork concentrates on the client group that the student has identified for a specialism - e.g. people with learning disabilities or mental health problems, young offenders or people with physical disabilities.

Empathy in the workplace

One of the most important aspects of the three year course, and indeed the experience of working with particular groups of people in the community on its completion, is that of understanding the need for empathy. The framework of the training is based upon the assertion that effective support work is built around the understanding which develops by empathising with both the individual and his/her situational experience, as well as the experience generally of being part of a marginalised group in society.

Role play is frequently used as one tool for assisting students in this task, with trainers suggesting that at least being aware of some of the interpersonal dynamics can make an important contribution to the overall sensitivity and acumen of the *educatori*. The intention is that by using methods to stimulate the students perception of self, as well as the perception of service users in society, s/he will be 'emancipated' from the prejudices and presumptions accompanying 'majority' status. By personally exploring the role of the marginalised and disadvantaged in this way, it is thought that students can at least be aware that their socialisation as part of one of society's 'advantaged' groups instils prejudices and assumptions which will affect the nature of support offered and the students' overall attitude towards the work.[5]

Aspects of staff training: The role of legislation and ideology in approaches to staff development in Lombardia and Britain

The role of legislation

At first sight, the motives behind developing the skills of support staff working with people with learning disabilities in Lombardia and Britain are similar in that service providers in the two countries are concerned with the impact of deinstitutionalisation and how living in the community affects the daily lives of service users. Both the Italian and the British professionals responsible for the task of resettling people from large institutions have also been directed and arguably supported by legislation, but in quite different ways. In Lombardia, the interpretation of the legislative watershed National Law 833, which called for the closure of institutions and devolution of power and responsibility for the task to local government, resulted in the establishment of a professional staff training course, with very specific objectives and great clarity in terms of theoretical and practical orientation. In Britain, the Community Care Act of 1990 similarly demanded the resettlement of people with learning disabilities into local communities, but did not provide a suitable legislative framework for enabling service providers to establish a body of professional, direct workers. This is perhaps one of the most fundamental differences between learning disability services in the two countries, and its implications will be discussed at a later stage.

The absence of a uniform, legislative framework for staff recruitment and staff development in Britain appears to have resulted in the situation described above, whereby the professional courses that have been created and accredited were largely a response to difficult and

---

[5] *"Gli stages formativi prevedono la realizzazione di giornate intensive di formazione degli allievi attraverso attività che favoriscono la presa di coscienza delle dinamiche intrapsichiche e interpersonali, utilizzando lo strumento dei gruppi autocentrati ed eterocentrati su termi connessi all'emancipazione ed alla acquisizione di un roulo professionale."*
Bollettino Ufficiale della Regione Lombardia 1989,pp1866
[Training also consists of role play, as it is believed that workers need to acquire a profound understanding of how it feels to be disabled, for example. There is a need to understand and be aware of intrapersonal and interpersonal dynamics, an awareness which liberates the student from the prejudices and presumptions of being part of a majority].

unmanageable situations, perhaps even crises in some instances. While the existence of such courses is to be commended, they do have problems which could be seen to be a direct consequence of the failure of British Government to realise the practical and ethical implications that have arisen from the Community Care Act (1990) as well as from recommendations preceding its publication (e.g. the White Paper "Caring for People" , 1989). One such problem is the difficulty in finding appropriate supervisors to work with students: effective support for the student involves identifying a supervisor who has more skills than the student in the relevant area - in this case, the management of challenging behaviour (McGill & Bliss 1989).

A second consequence of the inability of training courses in Britain to rely on Government legislation is its effect on the application of skills acquired on courses in services. Successful implementation of, in this case, the behavioural approach to challenging behaviour, relies on support from colleagues and essentially from management. Such support will be patchy if not non-existent, unless all members of a team have either completed a similar course or are at least familiar with its principles. Although great efforts are made to address this problem by both courses detailed here, the fact remains that services are very much left to develop their own ways of working.

The impact of ideology

(a) Creating consistency

Given this background, it is important to consider the respective ideologies underpinning services in the two countries. It is essential to focus on consistency here: many contemporary learning disability services in Britain place consistency at the core of working with people who need support in understanding their environment and social world. Certainly, the aim of training courses in Britain to generate a consistency of approach must surely be beneficial; what is not being addressed at the moment is the effect of employing staff team members from a variety of backgrounds, with areas of expertise which can range from appropriate to tenuous. While the mix of people in a team can contribute positively to the resource, it is suggested here that there needs to be a certain consensus towards learning disability and the nature of supporting vulnerable people . This claim for a shared framework for interpreting, understanding and facilitating is supported by many (e.g.Clements 1992; Donellan et al 1988; Zarkowska & Clements 1988). In contrast, the Lombardian model helps to create its own consistency by stipulating the entry requirements for the training course, by detailing the content and orientation and by making this training mandatory for all direct workers.

(b)(i) Theoretical orientation: The value of the multidisciplinary view

While having the force of legislation can be extremely useful, its effect could be like that of a straitjacket, preventing service providers from exploring and experimenting with the concept of support and feeling restricted by legal requirements which do not allow for progress and development. In the case of Lombardia, it has to be said that the detail of the training course, as well as the legislation which calls for its implementation, can be intimidating to the outsider, more used perhaps to a looser set of parameters. The potential rigidity posed by the Lombardian courts is offset by the multidisciplinary, holistic nature of the approach towards disability. Services rely on the input from a list of professionals and therefore on a variety of perspectives. The one unifying principle, however, is that staff need to realise their personal position in society as being advantaged, and thereby develop skills of empathy in order to understand the individual needs of service users.

The multidisciplinary approach is linked in many ways with the Lombardian view of the category "disability"; learning disability is part of a unified model of general disability, and people with learning disabilities are not in a sense treated as a *separate* category of people needing support. The Social Services Department has a disability office which aims to meet the needs of all disabled people, and only after assessment are service users supported in accessing specific learning disability resources.

(b) (ii) Theoretical orientation: Exploring the familial environment

The two British courses outlined in Chapter 9 both use behavioural intervention as their main orientation, although the University of Manchester does place this within the context of other approaches. While this could just be a result of the deficits in legislation and a reaction to difficulties in behaviour faced by those working in community placements as alluded to earlier - it is perhaps also indicative of wider, societal views towards disability. By thinking about the *individual* with learning disabilities, as normalisation and therefore the British courses tend to, staff are encouraged to place community participation and integration at the centre of their support work. This ignores to some extent the emotional and psychological aspects of living a life that is far from "ordinary"; there seems to be a great concern with developing a person's skills, discouraging unacceptable, age-inappropriate behaviours while in many ways neglecting the person's right to affection and security within a personal, safe environment. The emphasis on independence and individuality can at times overlook the need for dependence and a feeling of belonging, which it is argued here, is part of the human condition for people of all levels of ability. During the course operating in Milan, students explore the role of the family in providing comfort and security, the view being that from this position - and possibly only from this position - a person who finds his/her environment difficult to understand can begin to acquire the skills necessary for leading a more independent lifestyle (Cassaro 1995). This view is held with *any* service user, whatever his or her level of disability.

(c) Training as an isolated concept

Commentators on the type of staff training courses run in England highlight the need for graduates of those courses to re-enter the workplace with support from organisational and management structures (e.g.Page et al 1982), and the problem of finding like-minded and supportive colleagues has been raised (McGill & Bliss 1992). The situation appears to be that the development of a body of recognised, professional direct support staff - low key though this may be at present - is occurring in quite isolating circumstances. Not only are there difficulties for the trainees to implement their skills in the workplace, but they are expected to encourage the integration of people with learning disabilities into a society of non-disabled people for whom, in the main, there has been no notable experience of living with people who once lived in institutional care. The credibility of the impressive work on stigma and self-esteem in relation to learning disability (e.g. Szivos 1993) suggests that if integration is to be a positive, valuable experience for *all* concerned, then all parties involved need support. "Teaching" service users and training support staff is not enough.

In Lombardia, projects have been established for some years which attempt to tackle this issue in a number of ways. Firstly, local neighbourhoods are informed by service providers well in advance before service users move into the area; this attempts to dispel many fears about the people coming to live in the community, and encouraging greater levels of understanding. Secondly, work is conducted in the wider community: schools are visited by projects which employ service users to educate young people about learning disability, while local television networks inform the viewing audience about events and developments around disability in their area, as well as advertising for volunteers to provide informal support to people with learning disabilities.

The Lombardian view, then, is that training staff needs to be consistent and holistic The contrast with the British approach is marked, and while it is acknowledged here that this discussion does not consider what are possibly extremely effective methods of training currently operating within individual services, it is fair to say that the two courses outlined are representative of current programmes which aim to establish a professional workforce. Possible reasons for the differences between the two approaches to learning disability will be explored in the discussion of the research findings presented in this study.

10 Normalisation for the Millennium: Towards Better Implementation in Learning Disability Services

The importance of assessing the impact of specific approaches to social care, particularly those which claim to ameliorate previous models, was observed by Townsend (1962):

> Social reforms are only as good as the individuals who put them
> into practice or as the means they are given to put them into practice.

This comment is apt when looking at the impact that normalisation has had on learning disability services under the guise of deinstitutionalisation, a policy lacking in clear practice guidelines resulting in variable interpretation and implementation of its main principles.

The study reported here has tried to provide evidence in support of Townsend's argument, using the differences observed between learning disability services in London and Milan. The findings which establish these differences can be discussed in a variety of ways; the rationale adopted here is that it is normalisation in the form of O'Brien's Five Service Accomplishments (e.g. 1985) which is under scrutiny, and therefore its main principles provide a convenient framework for discussion.

The evidence that has been gathered during this study will now be used to illustrate three central elements in an attempt to understand how the normalisation approach is implemented, and the effects that this implementation has on the lives of the people with learning disabilities who participated. The identified elements are:

a) The assumption that the Five Service Accomplishments as set out by O'Brien (e.g. 1980) can act as benchmarks by which providers measure the effectiveness of their services. This will be addressed using the data collected from the services in London, helping to establish the extent to which normalisation in its more tenable form is being implemented in reality for the service users and staff who participated.

b) Having explored the evidence for the presence of normalisation in everyday life and in service structures, the approach's main tenet - encouraging independence - can be placed alongside the central tenet of the Milanese approach, interdependence. This contrast forms the heart of the discussion, and helps to underline the main character of normalisation while encouraging examination of its implications.

c) With the implications of normalisation detailed for these London services, the Milanese approach provides material underpinning some suggestions for the future of ordinary living for people with learning disabilities. Comparing the two designs for living is one way of interpreting Jones' (1985) 'lessons from abroad'. While not advocating a complete revolution in terms of supported living, evidence has been provided here to suggest a need for looking at alternative provision when addressing the threat of hegemony and its appropriateness.

Living with a learning disability in London: How do services interpret normalisation?

The Five Service Accomplishments (O'Brien, *op cit*) provide a convenient framework for service providers and researchers alike, as they enable both groups to understand an *approach* to support for people with learning disabilities.

Using the description from Emerson (1992), the Five Accomplishments are:

- ensuring that service users are *present* in the community,
- ensuring that service users are supported in *making choices* about their lives,
- developing the *competence* of service users,
- enhancing the *respect* afforded to service users,
- ensuring that service users *participate* in the life of the community.

They will be examined individually using evidence from the data.

Presence in the community

Evidence for this is not striking. While the London tenants talk about feeling 'all right' about getting around by themselves, most of their conversation in this area was about settings far away from the local community - perhaps day trips organised by staff. Relationships with neighbours are not strong (indeed are non-existent for some of the tenants), while no mention was made, by staff or tenants, of regular venues or activities which tenants attend, apart from service-related settings such as day centres or sheltered work projects. It appears that the reference in the operational policy to the 'proximity of this house to other housing and public amenities' is the only clear way in which the service users are present in their community.

Making choices in everyday life

Choice making by the tenants is easier to identify in the data. They are choosing their clothing, what to eat and when and where to go out. More important decisions - perhaps the shape of their personal futures - are not addressed, and it is unclear how staff help tenants to be involved in more life-changing decision making.

Developing competence

This is clearly observed, and one is struck by the ease with which the service implements and interprets this concept. The individual planning process is also task-oriented, and breaks down strength and needs into activities which service users can try, with their supporters, in order to develop skills in certain area. Self-help skills are a particularly common focus, reinforcing the drive towards independence. Interestingly, when interviewed about their hobbies, the London tenants talked about domestic tasks - which could be interpreted as an indication of their perception that life at home is as full of task-focused activity as life at the day centre or work place.

Affording respect to people with learning disabilities

If respect is defined in terms of privacy, the London tenants have plenty. Locks on the door, personal living space, an individual approach which intends to identify individual needs - all of these can be observed. However, if respect is taken to be more about accepting a person's diversity and differences of ability, the evidence is not quite so clear. The gravity of the implications from the list of 'rights and responsibilities' found in the operational policy certainly respect the tenants in the sense that they are treated as any other human being - but it would appear that the extent to which such responsibilities have genuine meaning for the group is not considered. Expectations placed upon people with no detailed account of assessed levels of comprehension of the implications of those expectations could be interpreted as showing little sign of respect for the person's disability.

Taken to its logical conclusion, having a uni-dimensional approach to supported living for a group of people with such diverse needs as the learning disability population, does warrant clarification if it is to avoid the risk of being insulting to its users. The danger of hiding people's needs is very real in such a context. Theoretically, the same approach to supported living is taken with people described as profoundly and multiply disabled and others who use public transport unassisted. It is difficult to ratify the claim that services are concerned with providing individualised support when the ideology supporting all learning disability services is so palpably skewed towards the more able sector of the population in question.

Participating in the life of the community

The same evidence discussed for exploring presence in the community can be applied here. Equally, people who are still reliant on State benefit cannot be said to be fully integrated with their local community, while the decision not to be proactive in making links with local residents in any organised way is likely to have contributed towards the present situation. Unsurprisingly, there is no reference in the operational policy to *how* tenants could be supported in participating - even though it is stated that levels of their participation will be monitored. The precise way in which this monitoring is to be conducted is also unclear.

It would appear, therefore, that while certain aspects of the normalisation approach can be observed in the data collected, it cannot be said that the approach is being implemented in an entirely consistent and cohesive way. The implications of this are manifold. Not only are staff expected to work in a way that is not clearly defined, resulting in them needing to interpret ordinary living according to their own life experiences and abilities, it means that people with learning disabilities are being given inconsistent messages as part of the support they receive. Particularly in the case of people with high levels of dependency and limited understanding of their immediate environments, this could lead to confusion as to what constitutes the elements of an effective and appropriate service. Both staff and service users are therefore being exposed to the dangers which accompany an approach which relies on the integrity, personality and abilities of the manager of the service in question.

Running through each of the Service Accomplishments, and indeed throughout normalisation itself, is the theme of independence. People with learning disabilities are encouraged to lead more independent lives, implying that dependency - perhaps in any form - is not desirable. Indeed, inter-dependency is felt to be inappropriate if it involves solely people with learning disabilities, as the effective integration of people with learning disabilities requires them to form relationships primarily with non-disabled others (Wolfensberger & Thomas 1983). This observation provides the basis for discussing the central difference between the services in London and Milan.

Independence versus interdependence: The role of relationships with others in learning disability services

Independence is discussed by Dally (1992:109) as forming an important basis upon which the normalisation approach is built:

> ....there is an emphasis placed on privacy, independence, the separation of public and private domains, an acceptance of accompanying notions of gender division and women's subordination and the preaching of a creed of sturdy self-reliance...An ideology that advocates self-reliance, traditional gendered roles and private solutions to issues of social responsibility may be inimical to the capacity of individuals for development.

The operational policy for the London service studied here has clearly been influenced by this approach:

> Tenants have the right to independence, choice and to take responsibility for their actions.....Tenants have the right to be supported in caring for themselves as far as they are able.

In contrast, the Milanese services, while agreeing that independence can be beneficial to those able to 'cope' with its pressures, do not use it as a starting point from which to develop services. Conversely, interdependence is felt to be an important beginning from which people with learning disabilities can gradually gain the confidence required to take their place in the social world.

The interdependent design for living

Evidence for this strategy is seen throughout the services which participated in this study. The residential service adopts interdependence in two key ways, one physical the other psychological. The layout of the building is intentionally geared towards the support of interdependent living; not only do the men share bedrooms, but the rest of the apartment comprises of living space which has much potential for shared activity. The dining area, with its large table - big enough to seat tenants and staff on duty together, with space for at least three guests - sees much sharing of time and space, be it for eating, watching television or chatting. The kitchen is also a large room: it has a large table which also enables tenants and staff to cook together under the supervision of Assunta.

The tenants are living together for specific purposes laid out in the project's operational policy:

> the programme provides the experience of family life, the reciprocal collaboration of living in the house, participation in the local community and opportunities for using local recreational and leisure facilities.

Group living is seen as a crucial prerequisite for developing the skills needed to integrate with the local community. Peer support is felt to be the key, and is valued rather than seen as anathema. The group lived together in the institution before they moved to the apartment, and this history is valued rather than assumed detrimental. Indeed, the Milanese approach is described as being 'socio-educative', the implication being that education and learning in general is developed within a social context, and that the most appropriate people for providing and receiving the support needed when learning and developing are one's peers. In this case, the peers are the other tenants. While each of the men has full time employment, the function of their work is not primarily to integrate with other non-disabled people. Rather, work brings with it financial reward, and it is this which service providers believe to be the key to self-esteem - financial independence, freedom from State benefit.

Interdependence in Milan also spreads outside the project, and indeed outside the service itself. Relationships with neighbours seem positive, as does interaction with local restaurateurs and bar staff. However, these links and relationships rely on the security derived from the nub of peer support available within the project. The men are still integrating with the non-disabled community, as advocated by the British service - but they are integrating *as a group* rather than as seven individuals. In a sense, the Milanese service have achieved integration with the community by default: while not placing it as a chief aim, preferring that the men support each other in the first instance, they have managed to attain the principle targets set by the British service as indications of effective local integration. While this was probably helped by the pre-move work completed by the authorities in terms of informing and explaining to the neighbourhood the intentions of the project - a strategy absent in the British approach - it could also be attributed to the emphasis placed on group integration and support before individual integration.

Substituting the family

For the Milanese, interdependence is also about familial relationships. This is perhaps the most obvious area where cultural factors and history need to be considered. The family - which is often extended in nature - has an important role in Italian society, and its influence cannot be underestimated. It has a complex history which cannot be detailed here, but seems to be typical of south Mediterranean cultures (Yanigasako 1991). This would mean that profound kinship ties relating to the historic culture of ownership of land and property has led to the idiosyncratic family culture observed in Italy today (Yanigasako 1991), although generalisations need to be made with caution - particularly with the ever-widening regional differences observed in modern Italian society.

For people with disabilities, the support they need is usually provided by their family, with the State pledging most of its funding for support to be provided in individuals' congenital home environments. Since the deinstitutionalisation programme, supported with legislation from both Regional and National governments, it tends to be the case that residential services, administered by the State often with help from religious organisations, are for those without family to support them. This is so for the seven men who participated in this study. Such is the importance bestowed upon the family in terms of support and well-being, that this residential service has set out to attempt recreating family life for the tenants as far as possible. This is evident in the operational policy, which talks of the need to provide a 'loving presence' for the tenants.

In practice, one can observe a certain 'familial' atmosphere, albeit a stereotypical one as seen through the eyes of a British observer. The project manager, male, is referred to as 'Daddy' by one of the tenants, while one of the female staff appears to assume a role of cooking and cleaning. There is a high rate of inter-tenant interaction, as well as opportunities for the whole household to sit together at mealtimes to solve difficulties and make decisions. The view taken here is not to completely condone what could be interpreted as a sexist model of home life, but to argue that cultural factors need to be considered carefully. While it would not be appropriate to suggest that all female staff should assume such roles in learning disability residential services, it would also be unfair to condemn this aspect of the model altogether. The matter of choice informed by personal and cultural experience and socialisation for women faced with this situation must surely be raised at this point.

The importance of the family and its relevance for British services

While British people with learning disabilities are certainly encouraged to maintain their familial relationships, staff are not given any useful guidance on how best to support service users in doing this. Individual planning services, such as the one studied here, involve parents and other relatives if they so wish, but their role does have the sense of being somewhat peripheral. The Milanese model places the familial context at the very heart of the individual planning process, believing it to be the key to providing the most effective support in ways which are most respectful to the service user.

Again, cultural differences need to be acknowledged. The family in Britain has a very different role and is valued in many different ways. The term 'family values' has strong political connotations, often associated with political alignment which is right of centre. The extended family in Britain tends to be very different from that found in Lombardia, and it would probably be an exception for adults to live with their parents well into their twenties - a more common experience in Northern Italy (Yanigasako 1991). It is to be expected, therefore, that service provision within this cultural landscape would have a different outlook on the importance of family ties in the lives of people with learning disabilities. However, some resonance with his approach can be found in the British literature. Townsend (1964:437) has commented, somewhat disparagingly, on how services perceive the role of the family:

> Social workers tend to overlook the complex events which give rise to individual crises and in particular they overlook the strengths of family relationships.

Although this was written over thirty years ago, it does have some bearing on services at the end of the 20th century. Perhaps one contributor towards the failure of residential care in Britain meeting its objectives is through its unwillingness to recognise or address the relationships that people with learning disabilities have with their families and/or significant others - with or without disabilities themselves.

Normalisation for the Millennium: Towards better implementation in learning disability services

This study has suggested that by using a comparative research method, the ways in which normalisation truly affects the lives of individuals can be revealed. At the same time, the difficulties faced by service providers when implementing the main principles of normalisation are realised when it is established that clear guidelines are often lacking.

It has not been the intention here to suggest in any simplistic way that the Milanese approach to supported living is 'better', nor that the normalisation approach should be dispensed with altogether. Rather it is more the aim that the difficulties encountered need to be shared, as well as the extent of its unchallenged influence debated more widely. This final area of discussion outlines a possible strategy for the future, which has at its centre a focus on better implementation of normalisation's more tenable elements. The strategy has been derived from evidence gathered in this study.

The three main elements of the strategy 'Towards better implementation of normalisation' are

1. A careful re-thinking and systemic approach towards the training of support staff.
2. An holistic framework for individual planning for people with learning disabilities.
3. Establishing the need to review and debate the intention and function of residential care.

(1) The future of staff training

This is one area where it would seem that 'lessons from abroad' can be applied. The Milanese system provides an holistic professional training, the content of which may or may not be transferable to other nations - mainly as the values underpinning the training are likely to be culture-specific. The important point here is that the task of deinstitutionalisation and subsequent support for people in the community was felt to be so great, that it required a commitment to shared values by all concerned. This realisation did not seem to occur in Britain to the same extent - or if it did, it led to a very different approach to completing the task. Explanations for why Britain chose not to adopt a national approach to training staff are difficult to establish, but are likely to include the costs that such a strategy must incur, the influence of normalisation and its call for 'ordinary' people to provide role models - or just a different cultural view of what is needed in terms of support by people with learning disabilities.

Sainsbury (1989:132) provides an important summary with recommendations which are pertinent here:

> Furthermore, professional prestige tends to be associated, both for reasons of history (the failure of residential work to attract trained staff until recently), and skill (the range of diagnostic and treatment skills, particularly those based on methods derived from psychology and psychiatry) with work with children and families. Until the professional hierarchy is reversed, and the knowledge acquired through field social work is seen as an essential preparation for work in residential care, a setting in which people are at their most vulnerable....field social workers with post experience training...would seem to be the most appropriate personnel from whom to make appointments for the post of registration officer.....such courses could become the basis for the professionalisation of residential care work and the enhancement of its prestige.

It must also be acknowledged that the *Comune di Milano* was operating within Regional and National legislation. Consistency in the Milanese approach can be traced back to the origins of the call for care to be provided and supported in the community.

It may not be possible for Britain to legislate for staff training. As well as the likelihood of inadequate available funds, it is possible that such a step might not be achievable during the present political climate of individualism (Dalley 1992), or might just be going against Britain's political grain. However, it does seem possible that consistency throughout services could be achieved, which would require multi-agency teams to be working in the same ways as direct support teams and vice versa. Barriers encouraging rivalry and conflict between professions would need to be removed. The normalisation approach leaves much to the individual to interpret, and so if consistency is to be achieved, services would all need to be working to policies which not only set out its aims and objectives, but include *how* to achieve them.

In the absence of legislation setting out the values and requirements of a service, there might also be the need for debate which values the opinions of all those involved in learning disability services, including support workers as well as professionals, and paying special attention to the involvement of service users, their families and carers.

Setting up a working party

While establishing a professional qualification in support work through national legislation might not be the objective for all interested parties, there does seem to be agreement that services would benefit significantly from the development of recognised core competencies. Service providers are clearly at the stage of supporting the notion of establishing core competencies in specific areas of provision, for example personal and intimate care (Carnaby 1997; Carnaby 1998). It seems a straightforward step from this acknowledgement to agreeing that general competence in support work needs to be both recognised and established. One way of addressing this would be via a working party comprised of a variety of stakeholders (including service users, parents and carers), whose brief would be to propose a series of professional standards. Time would need to be spent in trying to understand why the NVQ has thus far failed in delivering its promises, allowing lessons learned to be incorporated into the development of any new approach.

(2) An holistic approach to individual planning

Developing the role of support staff to enable them to work consistently together and with others would lead towards an environment of shared values. This is crucial to the development of appropriate services which are primarily user need-led, as energy which would otherwise be channelled into disputes between personnel and their views about what is and isn't appropriate can be directed towards people with learning disabilities themselves.

Services use individual planning to implement their main principles, and the two services studied here have very different ways of doing this. What is striking about the Milanese service is that the input of support staff to the individual planning process is valued in the same way as contributions from psychologists, psychiatrists and other members of the multi-disciplinary team. This could be due to a specific way that such teams operate, but is likely to be influenced by the fact that support staff are consistently trained to professional levels, and are perceived more as equals in this sense. Their responsibility in the planning process is to provide data about the person from their perspective, as do the other team members. The responsibility for the success or failure of the individual programme is shared by the entire team, as implementation and evaluation of the plan is a joint process.

This is different from the British situation, where keyworkers are not only trained differently - if at all; the responsibility they carry for implementation of the individual plan seems to be theirs entirely. Therefore it would seem that the value placed upon support staff in terms of status (illustrated by inadequacy or absence of training) is inversely proportional to the burden they shoulder during the individual planning process. This seems not only unfair but self-defeating on the part of the service, as providers are placing perhaps the most important role, in terms of developing quality support, with the least valued personnel.

The second point to consider here is the *nature* of the individual planning process in Britain. While it may be important to explore and identify a person's strengths and needs, comparison with the Milanese system reveals a whole area of life that is usually ignored. Relationships with the family and their situation may or may not be part of a service user's individual plan - for the Milanese, these factors are central. There does seem to be an emphasis on the British individual plans being a positive experience, with the person at the centre deciding what he or she would like to do and how to do it. This might seem a very useful approach, if staff are equipped with the skills to enable this to be adopted with all users whatever their level of disability. The evidence presented here suggests this is not the case.

This is not to say that self-advocacy is not important. The Milanese approach does not include service users in their planning meetings, which perhaps jars on the professional conscience of the British provider. It does seem appropriate that service users be present at their own planning meetings, or else be involved in some way in making their wishes known. The way that Milanese service users formally influence decision making, it at all, is not clear. However, the history and role of relationships with others, particularly family and loved ones, surely needs to form part of the input which helps providers get to know service users better and have more of a sense of what they need in all areas of life. Individual planning in Britain therefore could become more holistic in the way it establishes the needs of service users, while working harder to involve service users of all levels of disability

The transition from a 'meetings only' approach to meaningful involvement.

'Involving service users' is a phrase found in many operational policies, and is increasingly used as a marker of quality. The individual planning system is generally viewed as the most obvious means by which services can measure their levels of user involvement, and as the study here suggests, the findings are not always positive. 'Allowing' service users to sit in on meetings which might have little meaning to some is not enough, and it is surely time that we took a more creative approach which starts with the individual.

As it is recognised that 'paper' approaches to individual planning are largely there to enable services to monitor and audit their resources, support staff need encouragement to venture away from the traditional meetings-based model. A project is underway at the Tizard Centre, University of Kent, which involved the development of a 'Formats' approach to individual planning. A working group comprised of local service managers and researchers in learning disability wanted to enable support staff to look at involving service users by starting with the ways in which each individual with learning disabilities communicates. With input from a speech and language therapist (also part of the working group) three formats for involving individuals have been developed:

1. Format One: A traditional format for people with learning disabilities who speak for themselves and have an understanding of the planning process and planning meetings. If necessary, extra support could be offered in the form of sessions to practice speaking in front of others and making decisions.

2. Format Two: A modified version of format one, for people who need moderate levels of support with communication. The person might not attend the meeting for its duration, but any participation would involve the adoption of the individual's personal methods of communication. Obvious examples might be the use of video, photographs and objects of reference, as well as signs and symbols such as Makaton.

3. Format Three: This approach would be for people with high support needs who would not understand much of the content of planning meetings. Their involvement would be in terms of 'influencing' the planning process, working closely with staff and having input by reacting to activities and experiences offered to them. Clear records of these reactions would be valued as much as participation in any meeting, and shared with other people in the individual's life as appropriate.

The format to be used with any individual would be selected according to careful decisions made as a result of communication assessments. Furthermore, the three formats above are not prescriptive or comprehensive, acting only as a guide to ensure that any approach taken starts from the service user's perspective.

This project is in its developmental stages, but like any other system which claims to have user involvement as its objective, it will need to be introduced throughout the service system to ensure that its values are adopted by all professionals and supporters, as well as direct staff. A service culture which encourages the sharing of responsibility for successful planning will also lead to support staff feeling less threatened when the project is evaluated and recommendations for improvements are made.

(3) Debating designs for living

The most difficult area of this discussion about supported living and yet probably the most important, is the debate around the very nature and purpose of the residential model itself. Recent research in Britain does not appear to allow itself the space to question assumptions about how people who need long term support in their home environments should live, and alongside the vagaries of normalisation, it is no wonder that services might not always be providing services which reflect some of the values set out in their operational policies.

Townsend (1962:435) summed up the tangle that became residential care, and much of his observation about services for older people has resonance for current residential learning disability services:

> These disadvantages may of course be minimised by introducing liberal policies but it is extremely doubtful whether they can be overcome entirely. They spring from the very nature of communal Homes. Individuals from diverse localities and backgrounds are brought together under one roof and are expected to share most of the events of daily life. Staff are employed and a common routine is established. The resulting 'community' is in many ways an artificial one because it does not consist of people of both sexes and all ages, who are linked by a network of family, occupational and neighbourhood ties and whose relationships are reinforced by the reciprocation of services.

There is, therefore, no role model on society which can guide providers in what is appropriate. In British society, it is rare for a group of adults to be living together, particularly if they share no previous history or relationship - or if they have nothing in common apart from their disability. Indeed, the only people who do find themselves living in this type of environment tend to be those with a disability; those people *without* a disability or some other disadvantage, be it economic, social or political, would probably have the choice of an alternative arrangement.

There is no sense of *how* people need to be living together in this context, and this is compounded by the fact that the adults in question are supported in this home environment by paid staff. People finding themselves in this situation surely cannot be described as living an 'ordinary life'. Again, this is supported by Sainsbury (1989), who emphasises the individualisation found in residential care which mirrors that found in society:

Furthermore, the overall social policy objective of ensuring a 'normal home life' for everyone, by emphasising the superiority and goal, of life and care in private households for those who are dependent is based on the assumption that such households are 'integrated' into the 'community'. As such, it is a policy which denies the possibility of the creation of a sense of community within an institutional setting, or, when faced with such a community, regards it as a regrettable aberration, because it subsumes individual autonomy. .....It is a point of view which underscores the highly individualised styles of living prevalent in our society, while paying lip service to notions of community or defining community as no more than the aggregate of highly autonomous individualised views.

The second area of debate here concerns the ability of residential services to adhere to the principles of normalisation. The evidence presented here suggests that, in the service which took part in the study at least, there are gaps between principles and practice. There is reason to believe that, as normalisation is an approach rather than a model, this experience is similar to many other residential services throughout the country.

Normalisation in practice also reveals an important contradiction. One of the approach's main objectives is for people with learning disabilities to be spending time with non-disabled others, as this encourages integration and encourages them to acquire valued behaviour and hence valued status in society. What seems to be overlooked is that by definition, people with learning disabilities living in a group home are residing with other people with learning disabilities, and would often be spending time with them during the day. Integration is also argued as being vital for the personal development of people with learning disabilities - and yet it seems that it is assumed that by physically being in the community, integration has been achieved. The question of how people can be fully integrated if they are 'working' but still dependent on the State for financial support is not addressed.

Important evidence from the research literature has also provided grounds for questioning the very nature of the residential service environment. People with learning disabilities have very specific needs in terms of understanding their own environment, which have been summarised by Griffith (1994:9):

Whatever the cause of a cognitive impairment, it means that the individual will experience some degree of difficulty with:

■ making sense of the world

■ feeling secure and safe in the world
■ predicting and understanding cause and effect
■ conceptualising and generalising
■ symbols and symbolic representation

The degree of difficulty will differ, not only because of different degrees of impairment, but because individuals have different personalities, life experiences and opportunities for learning.

In her work on stigma and self esteem in people with learning disabilities, Szivos (e.g. 1990; 1992; 1993), has argued that people need to feel the security which results from spending time with peers - or with people with whom they feel comfortable, usually the same group. This approach has been adopted in Milan where interdependence is not only thought to be positive, but essential to self esteem and hence an acceptable quality of life. Assuming that interdependence is *detrimental* to the well-being and general development of people with learning disabilities (a view inherent in the normalisation approach) could be considered a little naïve, if not arrogant, particularly as it is a decision which often does not involve the consent of service users themselves.

In summary, the third component of this proposed strategy for moving 'towards better implementation' of normalisation is the importance of debate. The issues listed above are likely to have some resonance for British service users, and warrant attention, not just from resource managers, commissioners and academics, but by everybody interested and investing in the lives of people with learning disabilities. Important decisions affecting the everyday lives of people using services are often made without widespread consultation; when consultation *does* happen, it can be in a form which alienates many people or demands timescales for comments which are unreasonable. The excuse of 'there just isn't time' has worn thin. We need to make time. Initial decisions about the philosophy underpinning a support service take place during an important period in that service's history, and it is usually straightforward to justify time, money and effort in these early stages. Of equal importance is the energy, time and sensitivity allocated to constant review and evaluation of the service once it is established. This process needs to involve *everyone*, helping to create a culture of awareness as well as equity.

The missing element? 'Dependable love' and its place in support service culture

The strategy outlined above in many ways builds upon characteristics already evident in British learning disability services. By adopting a comparative approach to understanding normalisation the weaker elements are highlighted, leading to proposals which centre around its implementation.

However, there is an aspect of 'ordinary living' which the majority of support models in Britain appear to have neglected altogether. The origins of this 'missing element' can be found amongst the rhetoric about supporting people in the community, particularly debate as to the meaning of 'dependence' and 'independence'.

Bowlby and Townsend revisited

Bowlby (eg 1952), in his work on attachment and maternal deprivation, talked about the need in human beings for dependence on others, a concept which Townsend (1962:336) supported and used in his critiques of institutional care. The relationships found between family members was felt to be crucial for enjoying an acceptable quality of life:

> Within an organic unit of three generations, largely preserving its identity and independence on the basis of the recognition of biological attachment, the individual achieves a large measure of self-fulfilment, and can satisfy many psychological and social needs, first as a child and later as adolescent, husband or wife, parent and grandparent. The family unit may not be the only unit which can serve these complex functions but it is the one which does so for the vast majority of the world's population, and moreover, it seems to be particularly difficult to replace.

This appears to be exactly what the Milanese service is striving to do. Townsend goes on to talk about the need in everybody to have reciprocal loving relationships:

> One suspects that if this is understood in the wider sense of the need to give as well as receive affection and to perform reciprocal services within family, or quasi-family group, the same need may exist for all individuals of all ages.

This need, postulated thirty years ago, has not even reached the debating table in terms of designing residential services for people with learning disabilities in Britain. Yet in Milan, this precise strategy and mindset seems to have been adopted.

Disturbingly, it seems that those in society who might generally be perceived as being more 'dependent' than others are required to work harder at their ability to be 'independent'. Residential environments are particularly emotive settings for putting this into practice. It appears that in no sense do British learning disability services account for the need for people to receive and indeed give dependable love. While all human beings surely require this to enjoy an acceptable quality of life, it is something denied a group of people who, because of their disability and socialisation, are possibly in need of dependable love to an even greater extent - giving them the affirmation needed to help increase their understanding of the world. Paid staff are perhaps not best placed to fulfil this role, and attempting to do so could well lead to a catalogue of disasters both professionally and emotionally.

The end of this millennium has witnessed significant progress in our view of people with learning disabilities, and the central role played by normalisation in this evolution cannot be disputed. Nevertheless, there is no room for complacency, as the case study reported here reveals. More lateral and systematic thinking around what constitutes an 'ordinary life' is required. However residential care in Britain is described, it does not appear to be 'normal' or ordinary - or indeed a design for living that would be acceptable to the rest of society.

References

ACTS OF PARLIAMENT:
   Mental Deficiency Act (1913), HMSO, London.
   Mental Health Act (1959), HMSO, London.
   N.H.S. and Community Care Act (1990), HMSO, London.
Adams, D. (1941), 'Correlates of satisfaction among the elderly', *Gerontologist*, vol. 11, pp. 64-71.
Adaptive Behaviour Scale (1974), Revision in O.K. Bros (ed), All Wales Strategy for the Development of Services for Mentally Handicapped People. Welsh Office: Cardiff.
Andrews, F.M., McKennell A.C. (1980), 'Measures of self-reported well-being: Their affective, cognitive and other components', *Social Indicators Research*, vol. 8, pp. 127-155.
Andrews, F.M. & Withey, S.B. (1976), *Social Indicators of well-being: Americans' perception of life quality*. Plenum Press, New York.
Andrews, F.M. (1974), 'Social indicators of perceived life quality', *Social Indicators Research*, vol. 1, pp. 279-99.
Atkinson, D. (1988), 'Research interviews with people with mental handicaps', *Mental Handicap Research*, vol. 1:1, pp. 75-90.
Audit Commission (1989), 'Developing community care for adults with a mental handicap', HMSO, London.
Audit Commission (1989), 'Making a Reality of Community Care', HMSO, London.
Baldwin, S. and Hattersley, J. (1991), *Mental handicap: Social science perspectives.* Tavistock/Routledge, London.
Bank-Mikkelsen, N.E. (1969), 'A metropolitan area in Denmark: Copenhagen', in R.B. Kugel and W.P. Wolfensberger (eds), *Changing patterns of residential services for the mentally retarded*, President's Committee on Mental Retardation, Washington D.C.
Barclay Report (1982), 'Social workers: Their role and tasks (Report of a working party under the chairmanship of Mr P.M. Barclay)'. Bedford Square Press, London.
Barton, L. and Tomlinson, S. (1984), 'The politics of integration in England', in L. Barton and S. Tomlinson (eds), *Special education and social interests*, Croom Helm, London.
Barzini, L. (1964), *The Italians,* Penguin, London.

Basaglia, F. (ed), (1968), *L'istituzione negata*, Einaudi, Torino.

Basaglia, F. (1973), *Che cos'è la psichiatra*, Einaudi, Torino.

Baxter, C., Poonia, K., Ward, L. and Nadirshaw, Z. (1990*), Double discrimination: Issues and services for people with learning difficulties from black and ethnic minority communities*, King's Fund Centre, London.

Bercovici, S. (1981), 'Qualitative methods and cultural perspectives in the study of deinstututionalisation', in R.Bruininks, C. Meyers, B. Sigford and K. Lakin (eds), Deinstitutionalisation and community adjustment of mentally retarded people, Monograph No.4, American Association of Mental Deficiency, Washington D.C.

Blumer, H. (1967), 'Society as symbolic interaction', in J. Manis and B. Meltzer (eds), *Symbolic Interaction*, Allyn & Bacon, Boston.

Blunden, R., Evans, G. and Humphreys, S. (1987), 'Planning with individuals: An outline guide', Cardiff Mental Handicap in Wales: Applied Research Unit.

Bogdan, R. and Kugelmass, J. (1984), 'Case studies of mainstreaming: A symbolic interactionist approach to specific schooling', in L. Barton and S. Tomlinson (eds), *Special education and social interests,* Croom Helm, London.

Bogdan, R. and Taylor, S.J. (1975), *Introduction to qualitative research methods*, Wiley & Sons Ltd, New York.

Boggs, E.M. (1986), 'Ethics in the middle of life', in Docecki, P. R. and Zaner, R. M. (Eds), *Ethics of dealing with persons with severe handicaps: Toward a research agenda.* Paul H.Brookes, Baltimore, M.D.

Bolletino Ufficiale della Regione Lombardia (1989), Serie Ordinaria N.19-10 maggio.

Booth, T., Simons, K. and Booth, W. (1990), *Outward bound: Relocation and community care for people with learning difficulties,* Open University Press.

Bortner, M. (1978), 'A.A.M.D. Adaptive Behaviour Scale 1974 Revision', in Buros O.K. (ed) *The eighth mental measurements yearbook.* Highland Park, N.J.: The Gryphon Press.

Bowlby, J. (1980), *Attachment and loss,* Vol. 3, Basic Books, New York.

Bowles, W. (1988), 'Quality of life: Models, maths and mystery', Unpublished manuscript, Macquairie.

Briton, J. (1979), 'Normalisation: What of and what for?', *Australian Journal of Mental Retardation,* vol. 5, pp. 224-9.

Bronfenbrenner, U. (1977), 'The Ecology of Human Development', *American Psychologist*, July, pp. 513-531.

Brost, M. and Johnson, T. (1982), *'Getting to know you: One approach to service assessment and planning for individuals with disabilities'*, Wisconsin Coalition for Advocacy, distributed in Britain by CHIMERA.

Brown, H. and Alcoe, J. (1987), 'Ideas and actions', *Social Work Education,* vol.. 6:3, pp. 21-22.

Brown, H. and Smith, H. (eds) (1992), *Normalisation: A reader for the nineties.* Routledge, London.

Brown, H. and Wood, J. (1991), 'Training for Community Mental Handicap Teams', in S. Brown and G. Wistow (eds), *The roles and tasks of community mental handicap teams,* Avebury Studies of Care in the Community, Avebury, Aldershot.

Brown, P. (1985), *The transfer of care: psychiatric deinstitutionalisation and its aftermath.* Routledge and Kegan Paul, London.

Brown, R.I., Bayer, M. and MacFarlane, C. (1988), 'Quality of life amongst handicapped adults', in R.I. Brown (ed), *Quality of life for handicapped people,* Croom Helm, London.

Brown, R.I., Bayer, M., & MacFarlane, C. (1989), *Rehabilitation programmes: Performance and quality of life of adults with developmental handicaps,* Lugus Productions, Toronto.

Bruyn, S.T. (1966), *The human perspective in sociology: The methodology of participant observation,* Eaglewood Cliffs, N.J., Prentice Hall.

Bulmer, M. (1987), *The social basis of community care,* Unwin Hyman, London.

Burbach, H.J. (1981), 'The labelling process: A sociological analysis', in J.M. Kauffman and D.P. Hallahan (eds), *Handbook of special education,* Eaglewood Cliffs N.J., Prentice Hall.

Butler, E.W. and Bjaanes, A.T. (1978), 'Activities and the use of time by retarded persons in community care facilities', in G.P. Satchett (ed), *Observing Behaviour,* Vol.1, University Park Press, London.

Campaign for Mentally Handicapped People (1984), *'Hope for the future?', CMH's evidence to the Social Services Committee on Community Care,* CMH, London.

Canosa, R. (1979), *Storia del manicomio in Italia dell'Unità a oggi,* Milano, Feltrinelli

Carnaby, S. (1997), *'Issues in Personal Care',* Workshop at the 1st Tizard Learning Disability Summer School, Tizard Centre, University of Kent at Canterbury.

Carnaby, S. (1998), *'Supporting People with Personal and Intimate Care: Questions and Issues',* Workshop at the Conference 'Planning for People: Services for People with Profound and Multiple Learning Disabilities, ORT House, London.

Carpener, J., Onyett, S., Smith, H. and Williams, J. (1992), *'Caring for People Joint Training Project',* Centre for the Applied Psychology of Social Care, University of Kent at Canterbury: Canterbury, Kent.

Cassaro, S. (1995), (Director of Social Services, Comune di Milano), *La Inabilità e L'Handicap nel Comune di Milano,* Paper presented at the London School of Economics.

Castellani, P.J. (1987), *'The political economy of developmental disabilities'*, Paul H. Brookes, London and Baltimore.

Cicourel, A.V. (1964), *Method and measurement in sociology,* Free Press, New York.

Clarke, A.D.B. and Tizard, B. (1983*),* *'Child development and social policy: The life and work of Jack Tizard'.* British Psychological Society, Leicester.

Clarke, A.D.B. and Clarke, A.M. (1991), 'Research on mental handicap: Past, present and future', in Segal S.S. and Varma V.P. (eds), *Prospects for people with learning difficulties,* London, David Fulton.

Clarke, A.D.B. and Clarke, A.M.(eds), (1976) *'Early experience: Myth and evidence',* Open Books, London.

Clarke, A.D.B. and Hermelin, B.F. (1955), *The abilities and trainability of imbeciles, Lancet,* vol. 2, pp. 337-9.

Clarke, A.D.B., Clarke, A.M. and Reiman, S. (1958), 'Cognitive and social changes in the feebleminded - Three further studies', *British Journal of Psychology,* vol. 49, pp. 144-57.

Clarke, M. and Clarke, A.M. (eds), (1958), ' *Mental deficiency: The changing outlook',* Methuen, London.

Clarke, M. (1982), 'Where is the community that cares?', *British Journal of Social Work,* Vol.12, pp. 453-69.

Coleman, J.M. (1983), 'Handicapped labels and instructional segregation: Influences on children's self concepts versus the perceptions of others', *Learning Disability Quarterly,* vol. 6, pp. 1:3-11.

Collins, J. (1992), *When the eagles fly: A report on resettlement of people with learning difficulties from long-stay institutions,* Values Into Action.

Comte, A. cited in Lenzer, G. (1975), *Auguste Comte and positivism: The essential writings.* New York, Harper Torchbooks.

Cottle, T. (1972), *'The Abandoners',* Little Brown, Boston.

Cottrell, N.B. and Epley, S.W. (1977), 'Affiliation, social comparison and socially mediated stress reduction', in J.M. Suls and R.L. Miller (eds*) Social comparison processes,* John Wiley and Sons, London.

Crocker, T. (1989), 'Assessing consumer satisfaction with mental handicap services: a comparison between different approaches', *British Journal of Mental Subnormality,* vol. 35, pp. 94-100.

Dalkey, N.C., Lewis, R. and Snyder, D. (1972), 'Measurement and analysis of the quality of life', in N.C. Dalkey, D.L. Rourke, R.Lewis and D. Snyder (eds*), Studies on the quality of life,* Lexington Books, Lexington, MA.

Dally, G. (1992), 'Social welfare ideologies and normalisation: links and conflicts', in H. Brown and H.Smith (eds), *Normalisation: A reader for the nineties,* Routledge, London.

Darwin, C. (1859), *The Origin of Species,* John Murray, London.

Davies, L.M. (1988), 'Community Care - the Costs and Quality', *Health Services Management Research*, vol. 1:3, pp. 145-55.

Davies, N.J. (1975), *Sociological constructions of deviance,* Dubuque, Iowa, Brown, de Kock, U., Felce, D., Saxby, H. and Thomas, M. (1987), 'Staff turnover in a small home service: a study of facilities for adults with severe and profound mental handicaps', *Mental Handicap,* vol. 15, pp. 97-101.

De Peri, F. (1984), 'Il medico e il folle: Istituzione psichiatra, sapere scientifico e pensiero medico fra otto e novecento', in F. Della Peruta (ed), *Storia d'Italia, Annali 7, Malatti e medicina,* Torino, Einaudi.

Declaration on the rights of the mentally retarded person (1971), Geneva, United Nations.

Department of Health (1993), *'Services for people with learning disabilities and challenging behaviour or mental health needs: Report of a project group',* (Chairman Professor J.L. Mansell), London, HMSO.

DHSS (1989), *'Needs and responses: Services for adults with mental handicap who are mentally ill, who have behaviour problems or who offend',* HSMO, London.

DHSS (1971), *'Mental Handicap: Progress, problems and priorities',* HMSO, London.

DHSS (1980*), 'Better services for the mentally handicapped',* HMSO, London.

Disability Service Publicity Leaflet (1994), The Life Planning Team, Greenwich Health Authority.

Donnellan, A.M., LaVigna, G.W., Negri-Shoultz, N. and Fassbender, L.L. (1988), *Progress without punishment,* Teachers' College Press, New York.

Donnelly, M. (1992), *The politics of mental health in Italy,* Routledge, London.

Dossa, P.A. (1989), 'Quality of life: Individualism or holism?', A critical review of the literature, *International Journal of Rehabilitation Research,* vol. 12, pp. 121-36.

Douglas, J. (1970), *Understanding everyday life: Toward the reconstruction of sociological knowledge,* Aldine, Chicago.

Drugge, C. (1990), *Using the opinion of people with mental retardation to measure quality of services,* Vasteras, County Council Vastmanland, Social Welfare for People with Mental Retardation, Sweden.

Drummond, M. (1981), *Studies in economic appraisal in health care,* Oxford University Press, Oxford.

Durkheim, E. (1938), *The rules of sociological method,* Free Press, New York.

Edgerton, R., Bollinger, M. and Hess, B. (1984), 'The cloak of competence after two decades', *American Journal of Mental Deficiency,* vol. 80, pp. 345-51.

Edgerton, R.B. (1975), 'Issues relating to the quality of life among retarded persons', in M.J. Begab and S.A. Richardson (eds), *The mentally retarded and society: A social science perspective,* University Park Press, Baltimore.

Ellis, K. (1993), *Squaring the circle: User and carer participation in needs assessment,* Joseph Rowntree Foundation, York.

Emerson, E. and McGill, P. (1989), 'Normalisation and applied behaviour analysis: Rapprochement or intellectual imperialism?', *Behavioural Psychotherapy,* vol. 17, pp. 309-13.

Emerson, E. (1992), 'What is normalisation?', in H. Brown and H. Smith (eds), *Normalisation: A reader for the nineties,* Routledge, London.

Emerson, E., Beasley, F., Offord, G. and Mansell, J. (1992), 'An evaluation of hospital-based specialised staffed housing for people with seriously challenging behaviours', *Journal of Intellectual Disability Research,* vol. 36, pp. 291-307.

Emerson, E., Felce, D., McGill, P. and Mansell, J. (1994), 'The nature of the challenge', in Emerson, E., McGill, P. and Mansell, J. (eds), *Severe learning disabilities and challenging behaviour: Designing effective services,* Chapman and Hall, London.

Emerson, E.B. (1985), 'Evaluating the impact of deinstitutionalisation on the lives of mentally retarded people', *American Journal of Mental Deficiency,* vol. 90, pp. 277-88.

Felce, D., Saxby, H., de Kock, U., Repp, A., Ager, A. and Blunden, R. (1987), 'To what behaviours do attending adults respond?: A replication', *American Journal of Mental Deficiency,* vol. 91, 5, pp. 496-504.

Ferraro, E. (1995), (Residential Service Manager*),* Interview given as part of research study, Comune di Milano.

Festinger, L. (1954), 'A theory of social comparison processes', *Human Relations,* vol. 7, pp. 117-40.

Fischoff, B., Slovic, P. and Lichtenstein, S. (1980), 'Knowing what you want: measuring labile variables', in T.S. Wallstein (Ed), *Cognitive processes in choice and decision behaviour,* Hillsdale, N.J. Erlbaum.

Flanagan, J.C. (1982), 'Measurement of quality of life: Current state of the art', *Archives of Physical Medicine and Rehabilitation,* vol. 63, pp. 56-59.

Flynn, M. (1986), 'Adults who are mentally handicapped as consumers: Issues and guidelines for interviewing', *Journal of Mental Deficiency Research,* vol. 30, pp. 369-77.

Finkelstein, V. (1980), *Attitudes and disabled people: Issues for discussion,* World Rehabilitation Fund Inc., New York.

Foxx, R.M., Bittle, R.G., Bechtel, D.R. and Livesay, J.R. (1986), 'Behavioural treatment of the sexually deviant behaviour of mentally retarded individuals', in N.R. Ellis and N.W. Bray (eds), *International review of research in mental retardation*, vol. 14, pp. 291-317, Academic Press, London.

Fryer, A.E., Chalmers, A., Connor, J.M., Fraser, I., Povey, S., Yates A.D. and Obborne, J.P. (1987), 'Evidence that the gene for tuberous sclerosis is on chromosome 9', *Lancet*, i, pp. 659-61.

Fulcher, G. (1989), *Disabling policies? A comparative approach to education policy and disability*, The Falmer Press, London.

Galton, F. (1869), *Hereditary genius*, Macmillan, London.

Garfinkel, H. (1967), *Studies in ethnomethodology*, Prentice-Hall, New Jersey.

Gibbons, F.X. (1985), 'Stigma perception: Social comparisons among mentally retarded persons', *American Journal of Mental Deficiency, Vol. 90, No. 1* , pp. 98-106.

Ginsberg, N. (1992), *Divisions of welfare: A critical introduction to comparative social policy*. Sage, London.

Goddard, H.H. (1912), *The Kallikak family*, Macmillan, New York..

Goffman, E. (1970), *Stigma: Notes on the management of spoiled identity*, Penguin, London.

Goode, D. A. (1988), *Quality of life for persons with disabilities: A review and synthesis of the literature*, New York, Mental Retardation Institute, Westchester County Medical Center.

Goode, D.A. (1991), *'Quality of life research: A change agent for people with disabilities'*, Paper presented to the 1991 American Association on Mental Retardation National Meeting Round Table Program, Washington DC.

Greasley, P. (1995), 'Individual planning with adults who have learning difficulties: Key issues - key sources', *Disability & Society*, Vol. 10, No. 3, pp. 353-63.

Gresham, F.M. (1982), 'Misguided mainstreaming: the case for social skills training with handicapped children', *Exceptional children*, vol. 48, No. 5, pp. 422-33.

Griffith, M. (1994), *Transition to adulthood: The role of education for young people with severe learning difficulties*, David Fulton, London.

Griffiths, R. (1988), 'Community care: Agenda for action'. HMSO, London.

Grunewald, K. (1972), 'The guiding environment: The dynamics of residential living', in V. Shuman (ed), (1972), *Action for the retarded*, World Federation of Mental Health & H.S.M.H.C., London.

Gunzberg, H. (1970), 'The hospital as a normalising training environment', *Journal of Mental Subnormality*, vol. 16, pp. 71-83.

Halpern, A.S., Nave, G., Close, D.W. and Nelson, D.J. (1986), *An empirical analysis of the dimensions of community adjustments for adults with mental retardation,* Paul H. Brookes, Baltimore MD.

Halsey, A.H. (1974), 'Government against poverty in school and community', in D. Wedderburn (ed), *Poverty, inequality and class structure,* Cambridge, Cambridge University Press, pp. 123-39.

Harris, J. (1987), 'Qualifying the value of life', *Journal of Medical Ethics,* vol. 13, pp. 117-23.

Hawkins G.D. and Cooper, D. H. (1990), 'Adaptive behaviour measures in mental retardation research: Subject description in AJMD and AJMR articles (1979-1987)', *American Journal on Mental Retardation,* Vol. 94, No. 6, pp. 654-60.

Haycraft, J. (1985), *Italian labyrinth,* Penguin, London.

Headey, B., Holmstrom, E. and Wearing, A. (1984), 'The impact of life events and changes in domain satisfaction on well-being', *Social Indicators Research,* vol. 15, pp. 203-27.

Heal, L.W. and Sigelman, C. (1990), 'Methodological issues in measuring the quality of life of individuals with mental retardation', in R.L. Shalock (ed), *Quality of life: perspectives and issues,* American Association on Mental Retardation, Washington D.C.

Heidenheimer, A., Heclo, H. and Adams, C. (1990), *Comparative public policy: The politics of social choice in America, Europe and Japan,* 3rd Edn., St. Martin's Press, New York.

Hemming, H., Lavender, T. and Pill, R. (1981), 'Quality of life of mentally retarded adults transferred from large institutions to new small units', *American Journal of Mental Deficiency,* Vol. 86, 2, pp. 157-69.

Higgins, J. (1986), 'Comparative social policy', *Quarterly Journal of Social Affairs,* vol. 2:3.

Hile, M.G. and Walbran, B.B. (1991), 'Observing staff-resident interactions: What staff do, what residents receive', *Mental Retardation,* vol. 29, pp. 35-41.

Hilliard, L.T. and Kirman, B.H. (1957), *'Mental Deficiency',* House of Commons, London.

Hughes, J. (1980), *The Philosophy of Social Research,* Longman, Harlow and New York.

Hurst, A. (1984), 'Adolescence and physical impairment: An interactionist view', in L. Barton and S. Tomlinson (eds), *Special education and social interest,* Croom Helm, London.

Jackson, R.N. (1988), 'Perils of 'pseudo-normalisation', *Mental Handicap,* Vol.16, December.

Jay Committee (1979), *'Report of the committee of enquiry into mental handicap nursing and care',* HMSO, London.

Jenkinson, C.J. (1993), Who shall decide? The relevance of theory and research to decision-making by people with an intellectual disability, *Disability, Handicap and Society*, Vol. 8, No. 4, pp. 361-75.

Jones, C. (1985*), Patterns of social policy: An introduction to comparative analysis*. Tavistock, London and New York.

Kennedy, C.H., Horner, R.H. and Newton, J.S. (1990), The social networks and activity of adults with severe disabilities: a correlational analysis, *Journal of the Association for Persons with Severe Handicaps*, Vol. 15, No.2, pp. 86-90

Keyworker's role In Life Plans (1992), Life Plan team, Greenwich Health Authority, London.

Kiernan, C. and Bliss, V. (1992), *Preparing professionals who work with people with learning disabilities and challenging behaviour*, Paper for the BISM/RMH conference, Across Discipline: Innovations in training for those working with people with learning difficulties, January.

Kiernan, C. (1985), Behaviour modification, in A.M. Clarke, A.D.B., Clarke and J.M. Berg (eds), *Mental deficiency: The changing outlook*, (4th Edition), Methuen, London.

King, R.D., Raynes, N.V. and Tizard, J. (1971), *Patterns of residential care: Sociological studies in institutions for handicapped children*. Routledge and Kegan Paul, London.

King's Fund (1984), *An ordinary working life*. King's Fund Centre, London.

King's Fund Centre (1980), *An Ordinary Life: Comprehensive locally-based residential services for mentally handicapped people*. King's Fund Centre, London.

Kinglsey, S. and Smith, H. (1989), Training for a new service, in V. Fransen (ed), *Mental health services in the United States and England: Struggling for Change,* The Robert Wood Johnson Foundation, Princeton, NJ.

Klonoff, P., Snow, W. and Costa, L. (1986), Quality of life in patients 2 to 4 Years after closed head injury, *Neurosurgery,* vol. 19, pp. 735-43.

Knapp., M., Cambridge, P., Thomason, C., Beecham, J., Allen, J. and Darton, R. (1990), *Care in the community: Lessons from a demonstration programme*, University of Kent at Canterbury, PSSRU, Canterbury, Kent.

Knoll, J.A. (1990), Defining quality in residential services, in V.J. Bradley and H.A. Bersani (eds), *Quality assurance for individuals with developmental disabilities: It's everybody's business*. Paul H. Brookes, Baltimore MD.

Landesman, S. and Butterfield, E.C. (1987), Normalisation and deinstitutionalisation of mentally retarded individuals - Controversy and facts, *American Psychologist,* vol. 42, pp. 809-16.

Langdon-Down, J. (1866), Lecture at London Hospital, cited in L. Kanner (1964), *A history of the care and study of the mentally retarded,* C.C. Thomas, Illinois.

LaVigna, G.W., Willis, T.J. and Donellan, A.M. (1989), The role of positive programming in behavioural treatment, in E. Cipani (ed), The treatment of severe behaviour disorders. *American Association on Mental Retardation*, pp. 59-83.

Lehman, A.F. (1983), The well-being of chronic mental patients, *Archives of General Psychiatry*, vol. 40, pp. 369-73.

Lemert, E. (1967), *Human deviance, social problems and social control.* Prentice-Hall, New Jersey.

Levine, H.G. (1985), Situational anxiety and everyday life experiences of mildly retarded adults, *American Journal of Mental Deficiency*, vol. 90, pp. 27-33.

Loomes, G. and MacKenzie, L. (1989), The use of QALY's in health care decision making, *Social Science and Medicine*, vol. 28, pp. 299-308.

Luckasson, R. (1990), A lawyer's perspective on quality of life, in R.L. Schalock (ed), *Quality of Life: Perspectives and Issues.* American Association on Mental Retardation, Washington DC.

Macy, T. (1984), A resource manual on transitional adjustment of mentally retarded persons, in D. Braddock and T. Heller (eds), *The Closure of State Mental Retardation Institutions*, National Association of State Mental Retardation Directors and the Institute for the Study of Developmental Disabilities, Alexandria, VA and Chicago, IL.

Mansell, J. (1991), Developing Staff, in D. Towell and V. Beardshaw (eds), *Enabling Community Integration*, King's Fund College, London.

Mansell, J., Felce, D., de Kock, U. and Jenkins, J. (1982), Increasing purposeful activity of severely and profoundly mentally handicapped adults, *Behaviour Research and Therapy,* vol. 20, pp. 593-604.

Mansell, J. and Porterfield, J. (1996), *Staffing and staff training for a residential service,* Talking Points: CMH, 4.

Mazzini, C. (1995), *(Clinical Psychologist and Day Centre Director for people with learning disabilities, CSE),* Interview given as part of research study, Comune di Milano.

McGill, P. and Bliss, E.V. (1993), Training clinical practitioners, in C.Kiernan (ed), *Research to practice?: Implications of research on the challenging behaviour of people with learning disability.* BILD, Clevedon.

McGrath, M. (1991), *Multi-disciplinary teamwork.* Aldershot, Hampshire: Gower.

Mercer, J.R. (1991), The impact of changing paradigms of disability on mental retardation in the year 2000, in Rowitz (ed), *Mental Retardation in the Year 2000*, Springer, New York.

Milbrath, L.W. (1982), A conceptualisation and research strategy for the study of ecological aspects of the quality of life, *Social Indicators Research*, vol. 10, pp. 133-57.

Mills, C. (1959), On intellectual craftmanship, in L. Gross (ed), *Symposium on sociological theory*. Row Peterson, Evanston.

Ministry of Health decree 10.2.84, *Decreto Pubblico di Repubblica* #761

Mitler, P. and Serpell, R. (1985), Services: An international perspective, in A.M. Clarke, A.D.B. Clarke and J.M. Berg (eds), *Mental deficiency: The changing outlook*, (4th Edition), Methuen, London.

Mitler, P. (1979), *People not Patients: Problems and Policies in Mental Handicap*, Methuen, London.

Mollica, R.F. (1985) (ed), The unfinished revolution in Italian psychiatry: An international perspective, *International Journal of Mental Health*, vol. 14, pp. 1-2.

Murrell, S.A. and Norris, F.H. (1983), Quality of life as the criteria for need assessment and community psychology, *Journal of Community Psychology*, vol. 11, pp. 88-97.

National Law 95/80 *[Gazzetta Ufficiale della Repubblica Italiana, Roma, 14 febbraio 1980]*.

National Law 482/68, *[Gazzetta Ufficiale della Repubblica Italiana, Roma: 30 aprile 1968]*.

Nirje, B. (1969), The normalisation principle and its human management implications, in R.B. Kugel and W. Wolfensberger (eds), *Changing patterns for the mentally retarded*, Presidential Committee on Mental Retardation, Washington DC.

Nirje, B. (1970), The normalisation principle - implications and comments, *Journal of Mental Subnormality*, vol. 16, pp. 62-70.

Nirje, B. (1980), The normalisation principle, in R.J. Flynn and K.E. Nitsch (eds), *Normalisation, social integration and community services*. University Park Press, Baltimore MD.

Nisbet, R.A. (1966), *The sociological tradition*. Basic Books, New York.

O'Brien, J. and Lovett, H. (1992), *Finding a way toward everyday lives: the contribution of person centred planning*, , Pennsylvania Office of Mental Retardation, Harrisburg PA.

O'Brien, J. (1980), The principle of normalisation: A foundation for effective services, in J.F. Gardner, L.Long, R. Nicholls and D. M. Iagulli (eds), *Program issues in developmental disabilities: A resource manual for surveyors and reviewers*. Paul H. Brookes, Baltimore.

O'Brien, J. (1981), *The principle of normalisation: A foundation for effective services*, adapted by CMH by A. Tyne, CMH/CMHERA, London.

O'Brien, J. (1987), A guide to life style planning: Using the activities catalogue to integrate services and natural support services, in B. Wilcox and G.T. Bellamy (eds), *The activities catalogue: an alternative curriculum for youth and adults with severe disabilities*, Paul H. Brookes, Baltimore MD. (pp. 175-189).

O'Brien, J. and Tyne, A. (1981), *The principle of normalisation: A foundation for effective services.* The Campaign for Mentally Handicapped People, London.

O'Connor, N. and Tizard, J. (1956), *The social problems of mental deficiency.* Pergamon, London.

Official bulletin of the Lombardian Regional government (Serial 19, 10.5.89), *[Bolletino Ufficiale della Regione Lombardia, Seria Ordinaria].*

Oliver, C. (1986), Self concept assessment: A case study, *Mental Handicap,* vol. 14, pp. 24-35.

Oliver, M. (1990), *The politics of disablement.* Macmillan.

Operational Policy (1995), *Camden Shared Housing Project - Specialist Units,* Camden, London.

Page, T.J., Iwata, B.A. and Reid, D.H. (1982), Pyramidal training: A large scale application with institutional staff, *Journal of Applied Behaviour Analysis,* vol. 15, pp. 335-51.

Parker, R. (1981), Tending and social policy, in E.M. Goldberg and S. Hatch (eds), *A new look at the personal social services.* Policy Studies Institute, London. Discussion Paper No.4, pp. 17-34.

Parmenter, T.R. (1991), Has social policy left research behind? Australia and New Zealand *Journal of Developmental Disabilities,* vol. 17, pp. 1-6.

Parmenter, T.R. (1988), An analysis of the dimensions of quality of life for people with physical disabilities, in R. Brown (ed), *Quality of life for handicapped people.* Croom Helm, London.

Parmenter, T.R. (1992), Quality of Life of People with Developmental Disabilities, *International Review of Research in Mental Retardation,* Vol. 18, pp. 247-83.

Pavlov, I.P. (1927), *Conditioned reflexes.* Oxford University Press, Oxford.

Penrose, L.S. (1938), *A Clinical and genetic study of 1280 cases of mental defect,* Special Report Series, Medical Research Council, No. 229. HMSO, London.

Penrose, L.S. (1949), *The biology of mental defect,* (2nd Edition 1954, 3rd Edition 1953, 4th Edition 1972), Sidgwick and Jackson, London.

Perrin, B. and Nirje, B. (1985), Setting the record straight: A critique of some frequent misconceptions of the normalisation principle, *Australia and New Zealand Journal of Developmental Disabilities,* vol. 11, pp. 69-74.

Powers, J. and Goode, D. (1986), *Partnerships for people: Enhancing the quality of life of persons with disabilities through incentives management,* Unpublished manuscript, The Rose F. Kennedy Center, Albert Einstein College of Medicine, Bronx, NY.

Pratt, M.W., Bumstead, D.C. and Raynes, N.V. (1976), Attendant staff speech to the institutionalised retarded: Language use as a measure of the quality of care, *Child Psychology and Psychiatry,* vol. 17, pp. 113-43.

President's Committee on Mental Retardation (1972), *Entering the era of human ecology,* Department of Health, Education and Welfare Publication No. (O.H.D.) 76-21013, Washington DC.

Ralph, A. and Usher, E. (1995), Social interactions of persons with developmental disabilities living independently in the community, *Research in developmental disabilities,* Vol. 16, No.3, pp. 149-63.

Ramon, S. (ed) (1988), *Psychiatry in transition: The British and Italian experiences.* Pluto Press, London.

Rodgers, W.L. and Converse, P.E. (1975), Measures of the perceived quality of life, *Social Indicators Research,* vol. 2, pp. 127-52.

Rose, R. (ed) (1973), Comparing public policy: An overview, *European Journal of Political Research,* vol. 1, pp. 67-94.

Ryan, J. and Thomas, F. (1980), *The politics of mental handicap,* Pelican.

Sainsbury, S. (1989), *Regulating residential care.* Avebury, Aldershot.

Sarason, S.B. (1949), *Psychological problems in mental deficiency.* Harper, New York.

Schalock, R.L., Keith, K.D. and Hoffman, K. (1990), *1990 Quality of life questionnaire: Standardisation manual,* Mid-Nebraska Mental Retardation Services, Hastings N.E.

Schneider, M. (1975), The quality of life in large American cities: Objective and subjective social indicators, *Social Indicators Research,* vol. 1, pp. 495-509.

Schreerenberger, R.C. (1983), A history of mental retardation. P.H. Brookes, Baltimore.

Seguin, E. (1846), *Traitement moral, hygiene et education des idiots, et des autres enfants.* Baillere Tindall, Barrieres.

Shuttleworth, G. (1895), *Mentally deficient children: Their treatment and training.* K. Lewis. (See Parmenter).

Sigelman, C. and Budd, E.C. (1986), Pictures as an aid in questioning mentally retarded persons, *Rehabilitation Counselling Bulletin,* vol. 29, pp. 173-181.

Sigelman, C., Schoenrock, C., Spanhel, C., Hromas, S., Winer, J., Budd, E. and Martin, P. (1980), Surveying mentally retarded persons: Responsiveness and response validity in three samples, *American Journal of Mental Deficiency,* vol. 84, pp. 479-84.

Sigelman, C., Budd, E., Winer, J., Schoenrock, C. and Martin, P. (1982), Evaluating alternative techniques of questioning mentally retarded persons, *American Journal of Mental Deficiency,* vol. 86, pp. 511-8.

Sigelman, C., Schoenrock, C., Winer, J., Spanhel, C., Hromas, S., Martin, P., Budd, E. and Bensberg, C. (1981), Issues in interviewing mentally retarded persons: an empitrical study, in R. Bruininks, C.Meyer, B. Sigford and K.Lakin (eds), *Deinstitutionalisation and community adjustment of mentally retarded people*, Monograph No.4, American Association of Mental Deficiency, Washington D.C.

Skeels, H.M. (1966), Adult status of children with contrasting early life experiences: A follow-up study, *Monographs of the Society for Research in Child Development,* vol. 31, No. 3.

Skinner, B.F. (1938), *The behaviour of organisms.* Appleton-Century-Crofts, New York.

Smith, B. (1994), An ordinary life for people with a learning disability and sensory impairment? *British Journal of Learning Disabilities,* Vol. 22.

Social Services Committee (1985), *Second report from the Social Services Committee, Community care with special reference to adult mentally ill and mentally handicapped People,* Vol. 1, HMSO, London.

Social Services Committee (1990), *Community care services for people with a mental handicap and people with a mental illness,* Eleventh Report of the Social Services Committee of the House of Commons, Session 1989-1990. HMSO, London.

Social Services Inspectorate (1989), *Inspection of day services for people with a mental handicap: Individuals, programmes and plans.* Department of Health, London.

Soder, M. (1984), The mentally retarded: Ideologies of care and surplus population, in L. Barton and S. Tomlinson (eds), *Special education and social interest.* Croom Helm, London.

St Clair, D. (1985), Chromosome 21, Down's Syndrome and Alzheimer's Disease, *Journal of Mental Deficiency Research,* vol. 31, pp. 213-4.

Stancliffe, R. (1991), *Problems with the assessment of choice based on the opinions of significant others.* (Unpublished Manuscript).

Stern, J. (1985), Biochemical aspects, in A.M. Clarke, A.D.B. Clarke and J.M. Berg (eds), *Mental deficiency: The changing outlook,* (4th Edition), Methuen, London.

Stevenson, C.L. (1944), *Ethics and language.* Yale University Press, New Haven, CT.

Strauss, A. (1987), *Qualitative Analysis for Social Scientists.* Cambridge University Press, New York.

Stryker, S. (1959), Symbolic Interaction as an approach to Family Research, *Marriage and Family Living,* vol. 21, pp. 111-9.

Sutcliffe, J. and Simons, K. (1993), *Self advocacy and people with learning difficulties: Contexts and debates.* National Institute for adult and continuing education, Leicester.

Szivos, S. (1992), The limits to integration?, in H.Brown and H. Smith (eds), *Normalisation: A reader for the Nineties.* Routledge, London.

Szivos, S.E. and Griffiths, E. (1990), Consciousness raising and social identity theory: A challenge to normalisation, *Clinical Psychology Forum*, August.

Szivos, S.E. (1989), *The self concept of people with a mental handicap.* PhD thesis, University of Exeter, Exeter.

Szivos-Bach, S.E. (1993), Social comparisons, stigma and mainstreaming: The self-esteem of young adults with a mild mental handicap, *Mental Handicap Research,* Vol. 6 No. 3.

Taylor, S. J. and Bogdan, R. (1981), A qualitative approach to the study of community adjustment, in R.H. Bruininks, C.E. Meyers, B.B. Sigford and K.C. Lakin (eds), *Deinstitutionalisation and Community Adjustment of Mentally Retarded People*, Monograph 4. AAMD, Washington DC.

Thomas, W. I. and Zaniecki, S. (1927), *The Polish Peasant in Europe and America,* (2nd edition), New York.

Thorndike, E.L. (1939), *Your city.* Harcourt, Brace and Co., New York.

Tizard, B. (1975), Varieties of residential nursery experience, in J. Tizard, I. Sinclair and R.V.G. Clarke (eds), *Varieties of residential experience.* Routledge and Kegan Paul, Boston.

Towell, D. (1985), Residential needs and services, in M. Craft, J. Bicknell and S. Hollins, (eds), *Mental handicap - a multidisciplinary approach.* Balliere Tindall, London.

Townsend, P. (1962), *The last refuge.* Routledge and Kegan Paul, London.

Turnbull, L. and Brunk, R. (1990), Quality of life and public policy, in R.L. Schalock (ed), *Quality of life: Perspectives and issues*, American Association on Mental Retardation, Washington DC.

Tyne, A. (1987), Shaping community services: The impact of an idea, in N. Malin (ed), *Reassessing community care.* Croom Helm, Beckenham. (pp. 80-96)

Wagner, G. (1988), *Residential care: A positive choice.* HMSO, London.

Wahlstrom, J. (1990), Gene map of mental retardation, *Journal of Mental Deficiency Research*, vol. 34, pp. 11-27.

Ward, L. (1992), Foreword, in H. Brown and H. Smith (eds), *Normalisation: A reader for the nineties.* Routledge, London.

Weber, M. (1947), *The theory of social and economic organisation*, (ed. T. Parsons), Oxford University Press, New York.

Weber, M. (1968), *Economy and society, 3 Vols.,* Guenther Roth and Claus Wittich (eds), Bedminster Press, New York.

Weinstock, A., Wulkan, P., Colon, C.J., Coleman, J. and Goncalves, S. (1979), Stress inoculation and inter-institutional transfer of mentally retarded individuals, *American Journal of Mental Deficiency*, vol. 83, pp. 385-90.

West, P., Illsey, R. and Kelman, H. (1984), Public preferences for the care of dependency groups, *Social Science and Medicine*, vol. 18, pp. 287-95.

Whatmore, R., Durward, L. and Rushlick, A. (1975), Measuring the quality of residential care, *Behaviour Research and Therapy*, vol. 13, pp. 227-36.

Whittaker, A., Gardner, S. and Kershaw, J. (1990), *Service evaluation by people with learning difficulties*. King's Fund Centre, London.

Wilcox, B. and Bellamy, G. T. (1987), *A comprehensive guide to the activities catalogue: An alternative curriculum for adults with severe disabilities*. Paul H. Brookes, Baltimore.

Williams, A. (1979), A note on 'trying to value life', *Journal of Public Economies*, vol. 12, pp. 257-8.

Wilmott, P. (with D. Thomas), (1984), *Community in social policy* (Discussion Paper No.9), Policy Studies Institute, London.

Wolfensberger, W. (1972), *The principle of normalisation in human services*. National Institute on Mental Retardation, Toronto.

Wolfensberger, W. (1975), *The origin and nature of our institutional models*. Human Policy Press, Syracuse.

Wolfensberger, W. (1980), The definition of normalisation: Update, problems, disagreements and misunderstandings, in R.J. Flynn and K.E. Nitsch (eds), *Normalisation, social integration and community services*. Pro-Ed, Austin TX.

Wolfensberger, W. (1983), Social role valorisation: A proposed new term for the principle of normalisation, *Mental Retardation*, vol. 21, pp. 234-9.

Wolfensberger, W. (1984), A reconstruction of normalisation as social role valorisation, *Mental Retardation*, vol. 21, No. 6, pp. 234-9.

Wolfensberger, W. and Glenn, L. (1975), *Program Analysis of Service Systems, a method for the Quantitative Evaluation of Human Services*, 2nd Edition, Vol. I Handbook, Vol. II Field Manual, National Institute on Mental Retardation 1975, reprinted 1978, Toronto.

Wolfensberger, W. and Thomas, S. (1983), *PASSING (Program Analysis of Service Systems Implementation of Normalization Goals)*, Normalization Criteria and ratings manual (2nd Edition), National Institute on Mental Retardation, Toronto.

Wright, L. and Moffat, N. (1992), An evaluation of an individual programme planning system, *British Journal of Mental Subnormality*, vol. 38, pp. 87-93.

Wyngaarden, M. (1981), Interviewing mentally retarded persons: Issues and strategies, in R. Bruininks, C. Meyer, B. Sigford and K. Lakin (eds), *Deinstitutionalisation and community adjustment of mentally retarded people*, Monograph No.4, American Association of Mental Deficiency, Washington DC.

Yanagisako, S. and Collier, J. (1987), Toward a unified analysis of gender and kinship, in J. Collier and S. Yanagisako (eds), *Gender and kinship: Essays toward a unified analysis*. Stanford University Press, Stanford.

Your Life Plan (1987), *Publicity material produced by the Life Planning team*, Greenwich Health Authority, London.

Zaner, R.M. (1986), Soundings from uncertain places: Difficult pregnancies and imperiled infants, in P.R. Dokecki and R.M. Zaner (eds), *Ethics of dealing with persons with severe handicaps*. Paul H. Brookes, Baltimore MD.

Zapf, W. (1987), German social report on living conditions and subjective well-being, 1978-1984, *Social Indicators Research*, vol. 19, pp. 25-38.

Zarkowska, E. and Clements, J. (1988), *Problem behaviour in people with severe learning disabilities: A practical guide to a constructional approach.* Chapman and Hall, London.

Zautra, A.J. and Goodhart, D. (1979), Quality of life indicators: A review of the literature, *Community Mental Health Review*, pp. 4-10.

Zautra, A.J. and Reich, J.W. (1983), Life events and perceptions of life quality: Developments in a two-factor approach, *Journal of Community Psychology*, vol. 11, pp. 121-32.

Zigler, E. and Hodapp, R.M. (1986), *Understanding mental retardation.* Cambridge University Press, Cambridge.

Index